MW01274094

JESSICA'S GRANDAD©

Robert MacGowan

Acknowledgements

Many thanks to Beverley for her patience, encouragement, assistance, computer-knowledge and proof-reading.

To Susan Camp for her interest, advice and editorial input.

To my mother, Edith Lucas, for her memoirs.

To my sister, Pamela Jean Jones, for her memories.

To all mentioned herein, for the way it was.

For Stefan

who died in suspicious circumstances

Let them remember you
and the suffering of those you left behind
Let them mourn your lost years,
but treasure those we spent together
Let them know the love for you that lives on
Let them know you

(Author, 2007)

Preface

The last, echoing notes faded into the silence of the small room as the hi-fi clicked itself onto standby, a tiny red dome shining in the gloom. Light from the computer screen highlighted silvery wisps of cigarette smoke hovering in the pungently sweet-smelling air. Distant voices could be heard from the street below but inside the little attic-room, all was quiet. Through the small skylight a few stars could be seen dotted in the grey, February sky. A black and white cat curled snugly into a corner atop a low amplifier. A young man lay on his back in front of the electric fire, with one knee bent upwards. His eyes were closed and the rise and fall of his chest was almost imperceptible. His right hand lay across his stomach whilst the left lay palm-up on the floor. He was fully clothed. The candle at the bedside flickered and died, sending thin blue spirals towards the stained ceiling. A dark-haired woman stirred in the bed and lifted her head. She peered across the room to where the man lay perfectly still and watched for a long moment before settling back beneath the covers.

The room temperature descended despite the fire as the air cleared and silence thickened. The man's breathing was almost undetectable now as his life trickled away. The cat slid from its perch, stretched its limbs and walked across to him. Tiny paws tentatively touched his chest as the animal sought a warmer sleeping position in the cooling night air. He did not move. The cat looked at him intently through round, yellow eyes, hovering, before glancing nervously sideways and backing carefully off to lie by the room's only door. The woman shifted again, rose awkwardly and retrieved a crumpled dressing-gown from the floor. Pulling it across her shoulders she walked around the bed and stepped over the man, looking down at him as she did so. She switched the fire down to one bar, glanced at the flickering computer but did not touch it, and went quietly downstairs to the bathroom.

A milk-float whirred softly down the hill as the cat escaped the room and exited through an open kitchen window. The woman returned, stepping over the prostrate man again, and climbed back into bed. Deathly silence closed once more.

The city slowly came back to life after the night's suspension. People rose to their routines. Curtains were opened, clothing pulled on, breakfasts eaten. The woman started from her sleep at the click of the letterbox, rising again and looking down at the man as she strode over him. Pausing for a moment she bent forward, searching his face intently, before descending to the hallway. The envelope was addressed to the man but she opened it on her re-ascent of the winding stairs. It was a letter from his mother containing a cheque. The woman took it to bed with her.

Other residents of the shared house began to move about. Doors creaked and banged, toilets flushed and a kettle whistled. A friend of the young man shouted up to him but received no reply. The everyday sounds of life gathered into their full cacophony as morning rays streamed through the skylight onto the floor of the attic-room.

Three hours later the woman again left the bed, brisker this time. She spoke to the man, who still lay in exactly the same position. He did not respond and she gently nudged him with her foot; again no response. She crouched close to his face. He was pale, still, and she could not see nor hear him breathing. His skin felt cold. She sat back on the bed and continued to stare at him for several seconds, then put on shoes and a coat, opened the bedroom door and screamed as she ran to a friend's house along the street. The friend rushed to the man's side and tried to revive him, but failed. His life had ebbed away during the long night.

The woman collected some cans of beer, stuffing them into both side pockets of the parka coat the young man had given her, and strolled down the hill towards the city-centre, to a public telephone.

* * *

This book is based on memories, written records, and written or verbal statements made at the time which are admissible as evidence in a court of law.

One

"In the cold of the morning,
In the burning of the day,
The thin lines stumbled forward,
The dead and dying lay.
By the unseen death that caught us,
By the bullets' raging hail,
Broken, broken, broken,
Is the pride of the Gael"

(Alan E Mackintosh – 1916)

HIS HEAD WAS BOWED between arms which reached out and upwards above him, trembling hands seeking purchase in the wet
mud that slithered through clenched fingers down to his sodden
armpits. Both feet were covered in its clinging viscosity. His heart
pounded but he breathed evenly, and methodically controlled the
waves of fear that threatened to engulf and immobilize him. His
eyes closed as he mentally transported himself far away from the
place he was, back to his home and family. In his brain all was still
and silent as he counted the seconds tick by. He sensed no movement. The deep, rhythmic rise and fall of his chest continued as a
single bead of sweat crept slowly down his cheek, and he tasted his
own salt on parched lips. Still he waited, remembering the girl who
waited for him. From the distance a familiar sound was carried to
his ears through the thin air. He tensed and his heart beat faster as
animal instinct strove to prepare him for what was to come. A shrill
whistle shattered the silence which existed only in his head, and he
looked up for the first time. Shouts called out from left and right as
he climbed up onto the rough-hewn fire-step and launched himself
over the parapet into the clear morning.

His silent world erupted into a raucous mixture of conflict-
ing sounds as he at last opened his eyes and senses to them, and
walked quickly forward. He strode as evenly as he could over the
rough ground beneath its covering of tall meadow grass. Bright flo-
ral heads danced and swayed beneath his heavy boots. Men to each

side walked with him amid the clatter of equipment, distant cries and the snort of laboured breathing. The thunderous explosions that had raged for days suddenly stopped and the rustle of footfall grew loud. An aggressive roar came from the advancing line of men in unison as they increased their speed and flying lead smacked into flesh. Blood spurted, bones shattered and men fell in waves before chattering machine-gun fire. The advance had begun.

Screams of killers and killed echoed across the flat landscape as the now-charging line of highland soldiers crashed into the first German trench and executed a rapid slaughter of those too slow to flee.

"On ye go boys" urged Duncan's sergeant in a thick Glaswegian accent, as they pointed bloody bayonets forward. Onward across open grassland they marched as the enemy gunners spread their random death. The ranks of kilted soldiers thinned but the attack moved forward unabated.

The back of Sean McNally's head, to Duncan's left, was suddenly blown off by a small piece of shrapnel which entered through the left eye-socket and as Sean fell, Duncan tripped over his torso and sprawled, dazed by the overhead shell-burst, into the grass. He lay there, mind reeling, thoughts tumbling, and wondered if Sean's mother, Agnes, still worked at the baker's shop in Claremont Road. The thunder of battle came to him from a long way off and for a moment he considered just lying where he was, calm and peaceful. Scrambling to his feet he stood swaying amid the whistling bullets. A hazy memory of Agnes giving him free scraps of bread from the shop when he was a child in rags invaded his thoughts. As the concussion cleared he steadied himself, covered in mud, slime and blood, and watched a pure white moth flutter up from the undergrowth his fall had disturbed. It spiralled in a tight ascent before flying off. Duncan looked down at his gore-stained uniform and told himself that life, normal life, carried on somewhere far away but to rejoin it he must first complete the task at hand. He picked up his rifle and followed the anguished cries of his countrymen towards enemy guns.

The now depleted battalion he caught up with tumbled into the second trench and clambered doggedly out again into open terrain, still advancing towards a third trench in the distance. Their speed was now diminishing as energy waned, smoke and dust from heavy allied shelling cleared and visibility improved despite the sweat running freely into tired and bleary eyes. The dry, rat-a-tat of machine-gun fire grew louder. The dwindling survivors staggered forward until ordered to lie down by their officers, and slumped onto the ground with bursting lungs. Death hovered close.

At 07.23 hours the 17th Highland Light Infantry, derived from the Glasgow 'Commercials' Regiment, had advanced to within forty yards of the German front line under cover of British artillery bombardment. The barrage stopped at 07.30 hours and the 'Leipzig Redoubt' was overrun by the highlanders. Their rapid advance carried straight on to take the 'Hindenburg Strasse' trench but machine-gun fire from the supporting 'Wundt Werk' entrenchment stopped the attack and pinned-down the troops with heavy casualties. The 17th Highlanders were part of 97 Brigade, which was in turn part of 32nd Division of the British Expeditionary Force. The date was 1st July 1916 and the first day of the Battle of the Somme.

Less than quarter of a mile from the point where Duncan MacGowan started his advance, another soldier left the 32nd Division trenches and accompanied the sixty thousand strong allied attack on the German defences spread along eighteen miles of front line. Jack Davison was a private attached to a Sapper battalion of the 16th Northumberland Fusiliers, made up from the Newcastle Commercials Regiment and part of 96 Brigade. Along with the 15th Lancashire Fusiliers to their immediate north, they followed a football kicked into the field as part of the initial attack on the German forces occupying much of Europe. Jack was from Jarrow, South Tyneside and would follow a football anywhere. He was not a big man but fit, a roofer by trade, and covered the slightly drier ground to the north quickly. He had intended and even practised, jinking rugby style from side to side as he advanced, to avoid the bullets he knew would come at him, but soon realized that the German machine-gunners strafed laterally and horizontally, making this survival tactic pointless and energy-inefficient. He reasoned correctly that it would also slow him down and so dispensed with the idea outright.

Climbing out of the trench Jack un-slung the Lee Enfield Mark 1 rifle from his shoulder, its bayonet already fitted, and marched swiftly with it held in front of him in both hands. But as the general advance gathered momentum he threw it back over his shoulder so his pumping arms could propel him faster. Despite the long grass, the heavy boots and equipment, Jack began to run and soon could see none of his comrades in front of him. He clearly heard the machine-guns and the whine of airborne lead as men behind him fell, and so he ran faster, as fast as the summer breeze which carried the stench of death to his nostrils. His flight from fear took on a surreal value and resembled, even became, an act of courage. In Jack's mind speed was life so onward he rushed in his personal race against death. His rifle, still shouldered, bounced around redundantly on his back and as smoke, dust and vapour-drift from the British bombardment began to lift, Jack could see the enemy gunners silhouetted behind their spurting clouds of white smoke and hear their indecipherable shouts. Realizing that the enemy were now right in front of him he did not slow or falter, but gritted his teeth and actually accelerated – his goal was in sight. Responding to the training that had been drilled into his brain and reflexes, he deftly un-shouldered the rifle again and brought its fixed bayonet to bear in the correct, forward alignment but suddenly, his flying feet lost their purchase as they entered the open space of a still-smoking shell-crater. Bullets pitter-pattered into the soft ground around him as he fell headlong into the newly churned soil. Turning slowly onto his back he could smell the sweet aroma of fresh vegetation and lay motionless with his gun still held in both hands and the rim of his helmet covering his eyes as if death had already been pronounced upon him. His crumpled backpack pushed his chest slightly upwards and tilted his head back into the helmet's webbing. His mouth opened with an expiration of breath.

The Newcastle and Lancashire regiments had advanced eastwards to the south of Thiepval village, which was occupied by German troops, and towards the 'Leipzig Salient' trench. They came under immediate heavy fire from Thiepval Fort and were pinned down in no-man's-land. Some of the troops managed to reach the German front line where it lay closest to them, north of the village, but were slaughtered by fire from the German fortifications and support trenches. The survivors from both battalions fought their way north to link with 36th Division, south of the 'Schwaben Redoubt' and north of Thiepval cemetery.

Five and a half months after the initial attack, the regrouped 32nd Division moved up to the front line again to relieve 2nd Division, in preparation for the final assault before worsening winter weather halted the entire battle. 97 Brigade relieved 112 in 'Wagon Road' and moved into already taken 'New Munich Trench' and 'Leave Avenue' to link with 51st Division. The German front line was pushed back beyond their 'Munich and 'Frankfurt' trenches, between Serre in the north and Beaucourt to the south.

At 6.10 am on Saturday 18 November 1916 the whole of the massed 32nd Division moved eastwards against consolidated German defences and driving sleet. The highland ranks, to the fore, were again decimated by machine-gun fire and although troops from the 2nd Glasgow 'Boy's Brigade' reached the German line to engage in hand-to-hand fighting, they were cut off from the main force and suffered heavy casualties. Very few withdrew successfully to the British lines and many wounded slowly froze to death in the snow before they could be rescued. Duncan was hit by shrapnel from defensive artillery fire amid clouds of chlorine gas dispersed by the enemy.

The 1916 Battle of the Somme ended the following day in virtual stalemate with only a few miles gained by the Allied Forces. They sustained an estimated 420,000 casualties including 19,000 on the first day alone.

Jack Davison was joined by others of his regiment in the shell-hole where he fell that day and there they remained, dazed and confused, sheltering from the German gunners until darkness fell. With any advance now suicidal the stranded Geordies scrambled from the crater at nightfall and retreated towards the British line, but the gloom and shelling disorientated them further and soon they were lost. After wandering for days in no-man's-land without food or water and amid the poisonous, drifting gas, the little band finally found its way back to the British trenches, to fight on for a further two years.

Jack survived the Great War and with the return of peace took his wife and six children to Canada where they settled at Saskatoon, Saskatchewan. He had run his own small roofing company on Tyneside but found that because of the extreme weather, his trade was not suited to year-round work in Canada. They had emigrated to hopefully improve the function of his gas-damaged lungs and enhance the family's quality of life, but their financial situation deteriorated and they found the restrictions imposed by the severe winters hard to cope with.

The Davisons returned to Jarrow and took up residence in the old school house in Wylam Street. The eldest daughter, Nora, secured a job as housekeeper to a family in Kendal, Westmorland and the rest of the family visited her regularly, eventually moving permanently to a house in Lound Road, on the west bank of the Lancaster to Kendal canal, overlooking the flood-prone River Kent.

The family thrived in South Lakeland and Jack's five daughters blossomed, excelling at sports and attracting many admirers. Their only brother, Jack Jnr, joined the Royal Navy and eventually settled in South Africa where he raised a family and spent his life working in the diamond mines of Natal.

Duncan MacGowan also survived the war and in the early 1920s took his family from their hometown of Bellshill, Glasgow to seek employment in the steel-yards of Middlesbrough, on Teesside. After several years the family again uprooted and headed west in search of a less industrial environment. They, as the Davisons, settled in Kendal where they also prospered and eventually rented a large Victorian house in the town's market place. Duncan's children ex-celled at academic studies but chose to leave school early and assist the family finances by starting work. The two boys, Duncan Jnr and Gordon, chose the K (Kendal) Shoes factory; the areas principal em-ployer. At the age of fourteen Gordon started boxing at a local club but at eighteen was called up to fight in another war. The year was 1941. He enlisted in the Royal Marines, served in North Africa and also became the Mediterranean-Fleet champion at Featherweight, Lightweight and Welter, trebling his army pay by competing in pro-fessional tournaments. Following cessation of armed hostilities, as opposed to those in the ring, he returned to the shoe factory though his experiences had instilled a certain restlessness in him. He met Edith Davison, Jack's second-oldest daughter, they married and had the first of their four children, Gordon Jnr, on the 11th January 1950. I followed two years and eight days later, with my sister Pamela in 1954 and younger brother John in 1958. Until 1955 we lived in a dark, decrepit three-storey house with a shared outside toilet, at the end of a narrow alley in the corner of Kendal's market place. Next door but one was the Golden Lion pub, which suited my father, and about thirty yards away was his parents' house, neither of which appealed my mother. Her most prominent memory of my brother Gordon at this time is of him coming home to collect one of her felt hats from the hall stand, unhooking the string of shiny bells from across Pamela's pram, where she had tied them in an early attempt at baby stimulation, and adorning himself with them to join a troupe of Morris dancers performing in the street. She recalls him returning with a hat-full of coins from appreciative spectators.

In my case she remembers the local policeman knocking on the door to inform her that I had daubed paint on every car in the same street, which was used as a car-park on Sundays and weekdays, and that in his opinion more control should be exercised over my activities. Clarks, the painters and decorators, had their storeroom next door but one to us and the tradesmens' entrance was often left unlocked if they went to the Lion on a Friday afternoon. Inside the storeroom stood tins containing paints of sufficiently varied hues and shades to ignite even the most non-artistic imagination, and soft brushes of every size stood invitingly in easily-reachable jars once I climbed atop a couple of pots. Perhaps our different pathways through life were mapped out for us even at that early age.

Jack Davison died from his impaired lungs whilst I was still a toddler. Duncan MacGowan followed in the same manner in 1964, the year my father took me to see him at Lancaster hospital where he was being treated. I remember sitting in the grounds with them in a little shelter. Grandad smiled at me a lot with a strange sadness in his eyes.

Two

"Onward Christian soldiers,
Each to war resigned,
With the Cross of Jesus,
Vaguely kept in mind"

(Paul Dehn – Circa 1962)

WHEN I WAS THREE my mother gathered her children and marched us to Kendal Town Hall where she demanded to see the Mayor and the official in charge of housing allocations. She was predictably told that they were both busy and politely replied that that was fine, she would wait until they were not, and made camp in the corridor outside the Mayor's parlour. Eventually his wife came along for a chat and mother made it very plain that she both wanted and deserved a home on the newly-built council estate, Hallgarth, where young families were snapping up nice new homes at the northern edge of town, close to open fields which stretched as far as the eye could see. Her argument was good and the family was given a three-bedroomed terrace on crescent-shaped Low Mead. The changes in lifestyle included a separate in-house toilet, electricity, hot water on tap and gardens to front and rear. There were hills and greenery all round, views to the surrounding fells and in those days the concept of a solid council-owned house with a secure tenancy at a fair rent, as opposed to dingy, badly maintained and overpriced private accommodation, was an attractive proposition at a time when few working people could afford to buy a home.

We could climb over the wire fence where it looped between concrete posts at the bottom of our back garden, cross a gravel path to a field where cattle grazed through the summer months, and from there conceivably walk on grassy pasture back to Scotland. One of the resident cows was whitish in colour and inevitably named 'Snowy' She was so docile that local kids took turns riding on her back around the field, usually four up at once.

My summers were spent wandering the countryside or scrambling down the banks of the River Kent looking for birds' nests, frogs, fish and anything else remotely interesting, sometimes in the company of my friend John 'Coidy' Ward, but often on my own.

On one of our joint forays to the river-bank, whilst picking our way expertly through the slick, moss-clad rocks, we came upon an angler dangling his line into the eddy pool below Aikrigg End.

"Caught owt mister?" asked Coidy with an air of knowledgeable authority inherited from his gamekeeper father, Coidy Snr.

"Just yan" the man answered, nodding at an eight-inch trout ly-ing on the bank.

"Oh aye, norra bad un" confirmed Coidy "What y'usin? Worm?"

"No, tryin' these maggots out" the angler answered, taking the lid off a small tin for us to see the writhing mass therein.

"Oh aye" repeated Coidy, poking a grimy finger round in the tin with genuine interest "Where d'ya gerrem from? Tackle-shop?"

"Aye t'new un in Stricklandgate"

As they were chatting I noticed the trout, which I had assumed was dead, flap its tail in an apparent last-gasp effort at bodily move-ment. I sidled over for a better look and watched the fish's mouth open once or twice, confirming that it was indeed, still alive. As the trout's life ebbed and Coidy's conversation flowed I wondered if it was in pain and also why I was more concerned about the fate of one fish, as opposed to a hundred maggots. Surely both are equal in God's eyes aren't they?"

"They're a lighter colour" said the fisherman "Fish can see 'em better int' murky watter"

There was no hope of rescue for the poor little larvae, surrounded as they were and doomed to a fish's belly, they would never meta-morphose into flies and make their scheduled flights so I turned back to the troubled trout.

"Ow much a' the?" queried Coidy as I hovered above the flailing fish.

"Norra lot, an' it saves 'avin to piss about diggin' worms"

"D'ya ever use fly?" Coidy asked as I swiftly picked the fish up and threw it back into the river with a resounding plop.

"That was a big un did y'see it jump?" I asked, feigning surprise as they both looked at the ring of expanding wavelets.

Coidy looked at the vacant plot of ground at my feet where once the trout had lain.

"No I don't bother wi' fly, too energetic fo' me" replied the angler.

"Aye y'can gerrin a bit of a tangle wi' 'em can't ye?" said Coidy, inching away from man and maggot before breaking into a run with me close on his heels.

"Summat fishy goin' on there" he laughed over his shoulder.

"I'm starvin' let's get fish an' chips ha ha ha ha"

Throughout the holidays I would leave home early in the morning and return when I was hungry. I fashioned and loosed scores of paper-flighted arrows from home-made bows at imaginary adversaries ranging from cowboys to the Roman legions I loved learning about at school. When I closed upon these enemies: well-armed and purple-plumed thistles, tightly-ranked stinging nettles in green tunics or white-helmeted riverbank plants that towered over me, I set about them bravely with fence-post sword and kitchen-drawer dagger until the field of battle was littered with their corpses. All fell before my flashing blade.

I had friends but was often as happy foraging around on my own and within my own imagination than playing football or cricket, which I found boring after an hour or so, whereas many boys could keep it up all day without complaint. Some poor souls were even dragged to watch more sport at weekends! As a consequence I was often left out of team games and group activities. On occasion I would try following my brother Gordon to wherever he was going but he got fed up with that and would clout me round the ear in dissuasion. Whilst trailing across Kendal Green thirty yards behind him and Chris Hayton, head down and trying to look inconspicuous after being left alone in the street when all the other kids went off on a bike ride (I never owned a bike as a child, possibly why I loved them so much as an adult) he allowed Chris to double back and punch me a few times. My brother just stood there and watched. Something started to fade that day and I never really trusted Gordon for a while after that, even though Chris punched me on the shoulder and chest and it didn't hurt very much.

Trudging wearily home from fanciful battle one lazy afternoon, my battered wooden sword dragging on the ground behind me, I came across a man and woman sitting on a low wall near Prickly Fell. They were obviously a couple but the man had a large sketch pad across his knees and a pencil in hand. As I carried my sabre past them in a more erect position, I looked down at the pad and saw that the man was drawing a picture of a house. I slowed to a stop a few feet past them and receiving no rebuke, inched a little closer the better to observe the man at work. Seen the right way up I could tell that the drawing was of an old cottage which stood by the roadside opposite. Noticing me and my interest the couple smiled and I shuffled closer until the woman beckoned and offered me a sweet from a packet. I took it, smiled my gratitude and sat down on the other side of the artist. I watched intently as his pencil flicked lightly over the paper, building up the texture of masonry, and at how little touches of shadow rendered brightly shining glass in otherwise blank windows. Clouds were created by a few smudged pencil marks blended into the background with a fingertip, and soon the picture looked complete. Then the artist, possibly noticing I was armed, flipped the page and began another drawing, this time of a person, a man who also carried a sword but one which gleamed and was obviously made of steel. I watched, fascinated as shading started dark at each side of an arm and gradually grew fainter towards the centre, where a strip of white was left to create light on a perfectly rounded muscle. And how the faster gradation of shading from very dark to white, easily distinguished a metal band around that muscle. This was much more interesting than the flat slabs of colour with black outlines that we did at school. The man plucked both drawings from the pad, rolled them into a tube and handed them to me along with another sweet. I kept, studied and copied those drawings for many years and because I had been taught the lessons on light and darkness in such a pleasant situation, sucking boiled sweets in the sunshine with the knowledge that I could up and leave at any point, I learned well and remembered them all my life. I did in fact eventually develop the principles to their maximum effect by discarding the pencil and taking my shadows into the fathomless depths of black ink.

At the age of four and a half my life had been interrupted by the need for schooling, which brought with it a whole host of new experiences, some good, some bad, many pointless. The Dean Gibson Roman Catholic School stands at the foot of Gillingate Hill. Structured from local limestone block, its east gable looks across Kendal's main street towards Abbott Hall Park at the south end of town. The building is not now used as a school but its exterior looks as it always did, and only slightly less daunting. Neither of my parents was a practising Catholic but my father's mother was and in compliance with her wishes, I was deposited there in 1956 along with two cousins and a gaggle of other disorientated kids.

My father was an atheist who failed to understand that otherwise intelligent adults could actually believe what they were told about gods and their alleged trappings. My mother however, preferred the comfort and consolations of a deity in her life but neither pressured me in any noticeable way regarding religious leanings, preferring to allow me to reach my own conclusions on the subject.

The school was run at the time by an Irish nun called Sister Conleth, and she had very different views about children making decisions on anything without being thrashed into the right choices, particularly children whose little bottoms were taking up her school's well-worn and sought-after seats. I made lots of new friends from catholic families and was taken to masses, hymn services, prayer meetings and Sunday schools; this on top of the daily dose of strict catholicism we received during school hours. I did not terminally decide however, that religion was a concept I perceived as unattractive until the age of seven. At that age my combatant genetics had assumed partial command of my behaviour, heralding a long series of schoolyard fights. After a tussle with a tall thin boy from the year above who had ridiculed my cousin for living on a council estate, Sister Conleth hit my hands with a stick until they were both bruised and bloodied. My mother confronted her but the steely-jawed nun glowered down at me from within her black hood and with lightly-concealed threat in her eyes said, in a lilting Cork accent "Oh no Mrs MacGowan we never hit de boys, Robert fell over in de playground, isn't it true dat ye did dat Robert?"

My mouth fell open, my legs turned to jelly and my head nodded.

"Der now, didn't I tellya' dat's what happened Mrs MacGowan?" she smiled at my mother "Now you say twelve 'Hail Marys' Robert fer tellin' lies and we'll hear no more about it"

Sister Conleth was in the habit of sweeping into the classroom each Monday morning with her black cape flapping in her wake, to count the children "One, two, tree…" all the way up to "…turty tree, turty four, turty five, turty six. Der now, all present and correct Mrs Wilson" she would declare, as if the poor teacher was unable to count children for herself. Sister would then ask a few random pupils which mass they had been to the previous day. Many children including myself, lied to her about their attendance to avoid further persecution, but after she deceived my mother about the split hands episode I answered that I had not been to any masses or even Sunday schools. She gave me her death-stare again and made a point of asking me first about my attendances on God, the following week. Though I was frightened of her enough to lie, I did not, and stated openly that I played football instead. Participating in sport on a Sunday was a double sin! She was obviously agitated by my refusal to give in to her iron will and failure to convert me to religious obedience, and I think she would have been happy to accept an obvious lie from me in preference to losing face. It is also true that after the first Monday morning confrontation with her, which I unexpectedly survived unscathed, I took to showing off somewhat and knew that the other children thought I was brave as well as stupid.

Next Monday the classroom door swung open and Sister Conleth glided in like an Andean condor alighting on a carcass. Her blue/grey, piercing eyes scowling out from beneath a brow contorted into deep furrows by the heavily starched white headpiece, flashed in my direction as she tucked either hand into the opposite sleeve of her habit. The black skirt-cloth swirled elegantly about her as she turned to confront the suddenly-silent class "All stand please" she instructed after nodding a curt "Good morning" to Mr Ratcliffe, who had been cut short in his long-division.

We all rose amid a clattering of desk seats and scraping of feet.

"Good morning Class Junior Two" she shouted at us.

"Good morning Sister Conleth" we chanted in response.

"Now all stand up on your seats"

We climbed up amid a few titters of restrained laughter.

"All dose who attended seven o'clock mass yesterday morning may sit down" she announced.

A few seat hinges squeaked.

"All dose who attended ten o'clock mass may sit down"

Over half the class resumed their seated positions and the rest of us shot a few sideways glances at each other.

"Did you enjoy de sermon Caroline?" she beamed at now-seated Caroline White, who had a photographic memory and could name every garment worn by the priest and every object on the altar.

"Yes Sister" she chirped back.

"And what was dee essential message it carried?"

"To thank God for all the wonderful things he has provided for us, to lead Christian lives and to remember that the Church cannot keep up its good works for the benefit of us all unless we support it in every possible way"

"Excellent" breathed the Sister "Excellent"

After a long moment her moist eyes returned as if from a dream to survey the remaining vertical children "Anyone who attended evening mass may sit down" she exhaled and most of them clambered into their seats.

She raised her eyes to mine from beneath a slightly bowed head and said, almost pleasantly "Anyone who attended Sunday school may sit down"

With a communal sigh all but five sank gratefully to a seated position on the hard oak planking. Out of the five, two said they had been ill and one said he'd been staying with his grandmother who did not live anywhere near a church or Sunday school, but he vowed to attend two masses the following weekend to make up the deficit. The Sister nodded appreciatively. The remaining two comprised myself and a close friend, Michael Gallagher, whose father was also Irish catholic.

"Hwwat excuse have you Michael for neglecting God on de Sabbath?" she demanded of him.

"I didn't neglect Him Sister" Michael replied bravely but with a hint of trepidation.

"Pardon?" she snapped.

"I read a chapter from the Bible and said ten 'Hail Marys' and ten 'Our Fathers' morning and night"

"That's hardly substitute for attending de house of God is it now?" she snorted.

"I didn't have time to go to church" he said meekly after a pause.

"Didn't have time?" she boomed "Didn't have time for God and Our Lady? What if God didn't have time for yourself when dey nailed His only son to de Cross to atone for our terrible sins?"

"Well?" she screeched after a short silence.

"I don't know Sister" Michael whispered dejectedly, looking at the worn flagstones of the floor.

"Ye don't know don't ye? Well I know alright" she hissed "You'd be condemned to de burning fires of hell after your lifetime of sin so you would"

Michael looked at her as if she was about to send him right off to hell that instant. The glaring overhead light reflected on her bulging eyeballs, the speck of saliva on her thrusting chin, and the bald part of Mr Ratcliffe's head which he kept bowed so as to disengage himself from any part in current proceedings.

Michael's mother had left her brood of four sons and a daughter with their father several years previously. Patrick (Paddy) Gallagher employed a part-time housekeeper, Mrs Halliwell and managed to keep the family together, but life was never easy for Michael, who was the youngest boy. He spent a good part of his spare time peeling potatoes, washing dishes or polishing boots and was constantly bullied by his three elder brothers. Some days he would not be seen at all or would fall asleep in class, but would never admit that his life was worse than any other kid's.

The seconds ticked by as he shuffled uncomfortably before Conleth's glare, his lower lip trembling almost imperceptibly, and I slowly turned my bowed head towards him, looking conspiratorially from the corner of my left eye as we both stood up high to be pilloried. He glanced back and we exchanged looks which said 'Fuck God and grown-ups and teachers and school, later we'll pinch a Woodbine from Paddy's pocket and smoke it in the back field'

The merest trace of a smile flickered across his freckled face.

Conleth shot a glance over her shoulder in Ratcliffe's direction and told Michael to sit down, adding that she hoped he was thoroughly ashamed of himself and that he'd better attend confession to seek forgiveness for his neglect of God at the first opportunity. She had not finished with me though. After I refused to submit to the lie that I had visited any religious meeting, she made me stand on my seat all through the lesson and told Mr Ratcliffe not to let me down until the bell sounded. She repeated the performance every Monday for six weeks until the holidays came around, but I never lied to her and never again visited a religious gathering except for weddings, funerals and the like. Not long after this, Michael, or 'Grubber' as he was nicknamed around this time by his brothers, and myself got into some scrape or other that warranted a good caning and Conleth set about the task with a will. Her smirk told me that she was saving my suffering until the end and wanted me to watch her assault on Grubber first. Fortunately for me, she broke the cane on his hand and despite making us stand while she rushed off to locate a replacement weapon, the four o'clock bell sounded and we fled. She caught up with me later in the week though and I was caned at least fortnightly for something or other.

On one occasion I accompanied Grubber to confession and told Father Hothersall I was guilty of hating a nun, and was planning to murder her with a bow and arrow. He lapsed into a coughing fit and opened the curtain to see us racing down the aisle of the church.

Three

"Then let not what I cannot have
My cheer of mind destroy;
Whilst thus I sing, I am a king,
Although a poor blind boy."

(Colley Cibber)

IN THE VERY COLD winter of 1963 my mother, a skilled seamstress, made mittens for Grubber and I from some old grey school socks. Previous darnings made them extra thick and luxurious around the fingertips. We wore them for sledging down Cannon Hill on a Lyons Maid Ice Cream sign that we borrowed from outside Nattrass's shop. Jeremy Nattrass was a friend from our class at school. We also slid around on Lake Windermere and Rather Heath when they froze over. To get there we sneaked onto the 555 Ambleside bus without paying and hid on the top deck behind the back seat. I can remember Grubber's bright ginger mop bobbing up and down with silent laughter as the ticket-man missed us time after time.

Early each November before winter closed its arctic grip on the land, a successful Bonfire Night was a major team event requiring detailed planning and dedication to duty. Preparations began in the preceding months when requests went out to all parents for any unwanted furniture, waste wood or objects of a flammable nature, and the harvest was collected to sheds and back gardens. The pyre was not built too early for fear of 'raiders' who might steal our wood for their own collection, or 'burners' who would torch it out of spite. The goal was to have the biggest bonfire in the area on the night of the 5th and having the biggest stack of wood before then meant nothing if you could not defend it against other marauding gangs. With mere weeks to go the hidden fuel was brought out of hiding to the fire site, at that time on the green to the side of the block of shops by the K11 bus stop, the one with the perspex shelter and flat roof that was easy to climb onto, but kept low so as not to attract attention too soon. Small teams then formed up to scour the countryside for fallen branches, driftwood from the riverbanks, broken fences, stained mattresses, doors with fist-holes in them and just about anything else that was stumbled upon. The mass of rubbish grew rapidly and spread across the grassy patch, watched over protectively by the collective neighbourhood children, until a week or so before the crucial date. Then the area burst into a frenzy of activity as the wood-stock was raised from the ground into a lofty wood-stack. With its erection our efforts were declared publicly and we were committed to its protection. We sat round our timber temple late into each night, nurturing and guarding it, standing periodically to re-site a stick or two to more aesthetically pleasing positions. We lit camp fires upon which we roasted stolen potatoes and the older lads smoked Woodbines and drank Marsh's pop from Nattrass's shop, or maybe Ma Buck's next door. In the evenings after chores at home were done, all sub-divisionary street teams united into one battalion and marched through the streets like a Roman legion. We trooped in age-formation, big lads to the front and us littler kids bringing up the rear, into other estates and even neighbouring villages like Burneside and Staveley. We were a raiding party, bravely entering enemy territories to destroy competing spires and take bounty from them as would victorious soldiers, and drag our prizes back to camp where the admiration of non-combatants awaited. As we marched we chanted our battle-hymn:

> *"Rai-ders, rai-ders*
> *We are the Hallgarth Rai-ders*
> *Wherever we go*
> *We let them know*
> *That we are the Hallgarth Rai-ders"*

As the eldest and toughest of our little army such as Grubber's brothers, matured and became embroiled in other of life's battle-fields, its nucleus disintegrated into several lesser and rival factions amongst whom competition was exceptionally fierce because of their close proximity to each other. The Low Mead wood-pile was positioned carefully on the corner of the scrubland at the end of the gravel track, which was the closest patch of open ground to the street and happened to be directly behind Coidy's house. Because of this he was unofficially regarded as full time guardian of the stack, and he undertook this duty seriously if not effectively.

When we suffered an 'Air Bomb' and rocket attack followed by a torching whilst Grubber was asleep inside (he was on the run from his brothers after some misdemeanour) security was stepped up. Grubs was unhurt apart from a severe singeing and some smoke-inhalation, and a lookout rota was devised. Although neither Coidy nor I was keen to give up our weekends, we were detailed to stand guard during the afternoon of Saturday the 5th until relieved of duty at 4pm. The assumption was that nothing much would happen during our watch as most kids went to the matinee picture-show, played football or helped their mothers drag the weekly big-shop from town.

We reported for duty early, conducted a quick, peripheral inspection tour of the approach area and retreated to Coidy's pigeon hut with a bottle of Cherryade, two Mars Bars and a Beano. About an hour later Coidy's Labrador, Tansy, whom we had tied to the back fence as a guard-dog, started barking and we looked out to see movement in the undergrowth. We took the dog, climbed over the wire fence and went to investigate, but were halted and repelled by a hail of stones, one of which hit me on the arm and another hit Tansy on the flank, sending her scurrying for cover with a yelp. Coidy and I hit the ground like well-drilled marines but realising we were outnumbered, slithered back to the other side of the garden fence where we knew lay plenty of ammunition in the shape of missile-size stones. Using the shed for cover we let loose with a sustained fire into no-man's-land, eliciting more than one shriek of pain. We were in a strong strategically-defensive position behind the shed and fence, knew there was not much ready ammo for the enemy out there in the bush, and thought we could hold out until reinforcements arrived at 4 o-clock. We hoped it would not be later because that was our tea time and it was often something special on Saturdays. After ten minutes of stalemate however, a detachment of attacking troops broke cover and ran at a crouch through the long grass towards the last gable of the street, from where they had unopposed access to the house frontage and via the covered walkway between Coidy's and Geoff Dawson's houses, to our unguarded rear. As they bobbed through the metre-high dock leaves we could see that it was the Garth Brow gang, including the daredevil Morris twins, Tony and Wayne.

"See that?" I asked in alarm.

"Aye, the crafty buggars" Coidy answered.

"We will be buggered if they get round behind us!"

"I know, we'll 'ave t'ead 'em off. You'ert best shot. You stay 'ere an' keep rest of 'em pinned down an' I'll see what's goin' on round t'front" said Coidy, in a voice if not accent, just slightly reminiscent of John Wayne.

He slunk off, keeping low and I gathered as many good throwing-stones, or cobbles as we referred to them, as I could, stuffing my pockets and making a ready pile at the end of the shed. Then I kept quiet, out of sight and waited, rubbing my bruised bicep and plotting revenge, thankful that I had not taken the hit on my throwing arm. Before long there was a rustling in the grass and I filled both hands before stepping out into the open, arms hanging loose like a gunslinger. Another volley winged towards me but I stepped behind the concrete clothes-line post as it passed. The raiders were up and moving forward but hesitated when I remained still, turning to look quizzically at each other. Realising I was just one of the minor Low Meaders they did not retreat nor resume cover, but walked confidently forward. Even at that age I was already a well-practised crack-shot with a cobble, and went straight into action. The first two stones did not find their targets but gauging my range with the third, it bounced off the closest raider's head sending him staggering backwards with a strangled shout. The sight of blood and a few more rapid-fire shots and they were flat in the undergrowth once more, but I realised I could not see the far side of the bonfire pile, which they scuttled towards for cover. I crouched low, missiles in hand, hobbled across Coidy's garden, through the side hedge into Dawson's and from there vaulted the back fence onto the gravel lane. I inched forward to a point from where I could see the other side of the pile but nobody was visible. I crept to my right when suddenly a head popped up from the grass, then another, looking towards the pigeon loft. I froze, then instantly fired a cobble straight at the nearest target and followed up with several more in quick succession. The raiders, assuming reinforcements had arrived on their flank from Low Mead, jumped up and fled through the ginnel near Jock McKinnon's house onto Low Garth. I ran down the entry to the street to assist in repulsing the Garth Browers' own flanking manoeuvre, in time to hear one of them shout "Arrgh, y'mad fucker Coidy"

I flattened into the walkway shadows as I realised the remaining attackers were lying behind the low, front garden wall. Looking up, beyond the canopy roof, I realised that Coidy was at the bedroom window with his air rifle and had them pinned down. Ping – a pellet bounced off the wall top causing a flurry of scuffling behind it. Click, clack as he re-loaded. Coidy was not much good with cobbles, his arms were too long, but with his father being a gamekeeper he had been around guns all his life and was a fair shot. Ping "Cum out y'yeller bastards" big John shouted from his sniper's position.

"Fuck off Coidy, we're gunna kill y'when we gerrold o' ye" came the reply.

Luckily, there were no stones lying to hand on the pavement beyond the wall but I knew that desperation would soon provoke some kind of storming attack, and we were still well outnumbered. I shouted as loud as I could "Cum on lads let's gerrem" and threw cobbles as fast I could in the direction of the would-be besiegers. Thinking I was a concerted counter-attack, they were up and off and sprinting for the corner of the street with Coidy firing away at their backsides "Yee-ha" he cried "Jus' like a turkey-shoot" (he watched a lot of westerns).

Balancing across the long parapet of Victoria Bridge above the river below was a favourite demonstration of juvenile bravery, as was quarry-jumping. Kendal's limestone quarry was cut into terraces, each about 50 feet in height and after blasting, the small stone and rubble was bulldozed off the upper parapets to quarry-floor level from where it could be cleared. This often left a wedge-shaped scree slope, broad at the base and tapering to a narrow top about ten feet below the upper terrace. Quarry-jumping involved leaping off the upper ledge and landing on the scree at just the right angle for it to allow a smooth slide, heels dug well in, down the slope to the lower ledge. Backs, knees and ankles were injured but looking down into the yawning chasm of the quarry years later, I knew it was a wonder that none of us had been killed. Quarry-jumpers were near the top of the bravery league.

I had another adventure at a different quarry, which lay beneath Whitbarrow Scar on the A590 to Grange-over-Sands, and it turned out to be quite a scary experience at the age of 11:

At school one Friday I and a friend, Paul Irving, arranged to

visit a third pal, John Ducket, who lived not far from the quarry, at
Sizergh Castle, the following day. I think John's mother was the cook
or something at the castle (which is owned by the National Trust but
occupied as it has been for hundreds of years by the Strickland family) The Duckets lived in a cottage by a pond in the grounds. Paul
lived on Kirkbarrow council estate in Kendal where I believe he en-
dured an unhappy childhood. It is said that Paul's early traumas
had a disastrous impact on his personality and caused him serious
problems as an adult.

At the castle we threw stones in the pond for a while and I was
quite happy just being out in the sunshine, listening to birds singing in tune with the lazy splash of stagnant water. John lived in the
countryside and like Coidy, was an expert on nature's secrets. He
quickly took control in his own domain and on his home turf, and
led us into the nearby wood "Know what that is?" he demanded,
pointing up into the foliage.

"It's a hen innit?" answered Paul as we squinted at something
feathered and speckled hanging from a branch.

"Don't be daft" laughed John "It's a sparrer hawk"

"A sparrer hawk" repeated Paul in a reverent whisper.

We got closer and looked up at the hawk "Is it dead?" I foolishly
asked.

"Course it's dead" confirmed John loudly "Wouldn't be hangin'
there like that if it was alive would it?"

"No, s'pose not, how'd it get to be dead?"

"Dunno, mebbe some bastard gamekeeper poisoned it for killin'
'is pheasants or summat. Can't see any blood or bullet holes or owt
in it. I just found it int' field ower there an' 'ung it up so foxes an'
that doan' eat it, 'cos if it's bin poisoned they'll get poisoned anall"

"Oh, why's it called a sparrer hawk?"

"Cos it eats sparrers. Catches 'em in mid air an' eats 'em"

"Is there a bird called a pheasant hawk?"

"Not that I've ever 'eard of" John replied after a pause, looking at
me strangely.

"Does it live in a nest?" asked Paul, scanning the leafy canopy.

"Not now it doesn't. I know where thez a Raven's nest though"

"Where?"

"Top o' Whitbarrer Scar. Wanna go?"

"Yeh" answered Paul enthusiastically.

"Yeh" said I, trying to remember what a Raven looked like.

"Come on then, I know a short cut"

We tramped through lanes and fields to the west of Levens village, heading south to where the Kent estuary dispersed its collected rubbish and factory waste into Morecambe Bay, before coming face to face with a massive, sheer edifice set quarter of a mile back from the roadside.

"Up there look, ont' rock ledge neart' top" John pointed to a dark speck on the disused quarry face, several hundred feet up towards the white clouds overhead.

"Oh aye" exclaimed Paul, squinting skywards.

"Oh aye" I agreed.

"Shu'we climb up an' see if thez any eggs?"

And off they went at a trot with me twenty yards behind after stopping to remove my shoes, which were too big and kept flying off my feet as I ran.

Head down and concentrating on catching up, a shoe tucked under each arm and both big toes poking out of holes in my socks, I mistakenly followed a different track through the rocks and boulders and as their path branched right towards the sloping ascent to the scar plateau, mine veered left towards overhanging rocks. I wasn't worried though, was confident in my climbing ability and even thought I might reach the summit before them. Upward we scrambled and gradually lost sight of each other around the curve of the Whitbarrow massif, though I could still hear them in the distance shouting encouragement to each other. I clambered along the route I was now committed to and hoped to rendezvous with them at the top, but was to be disappointed because the narrowing path took me straight onto a tiny ledge, directly under a massive slab of white limestone cantilevered out from the top of the scar. I crawled into the tiny space beneath it because there was nowhere else to go, all around was treacherously loose scree which slid in mini avalanches as soon as I touched it. The ledge was short, only a couple of feet wide and once on it, I was unable to even turn around. The slab above overhung the ledge by at least an un-negotiable six feet and beneath, the ground fell away vertically in a sheer drop. I realized that I was well and truly stuck in a dangerous predicament. I could not hear my friends now and assumed they had reached the safety of the plateau. All I could hear was the wind whistling around my rocky enclave as if trying to winkle me out of my little hermitage, and my own heartbeat, the volume of which seemed to increase in tune with my rising panic as the afternoon light began to fail.

An hour ticked agonizingly by as I crouched on the stone shelf, forcing myself to remain calm, awake and back from the precipitous edge. Far below I could see tiny vehicles, some now with headlights on, passing intermittently along the Grange road but knew for certain that their occupants could not see me. I felt exhausted and lay my head down on the cold slab. I closed my eyes and wished I was at home, snuggling in front of our new gas-fire which lit itself at the push of a button, stroking my cat, Tiger, and that I had not left my pullover at the pond.

I heard what I thought was an aeroplane in the distance but the sound changed to something resembling a car engine and, it seemed to be getting louder. My eyes clicked open and I peered down the cliff but at first could see no movement, before a pair of headlights appeared from behind a rocky outcrop travelling on an old quarry road. As I watched the lights wend their way up the rough track I realized that they must pass directly below my ledge. I braced into a kneeling position in preparation, took my white tee-shirt off, and waited. The truck, its engine louder now, finally rounded the last bend into view again and I began flapping my shirt for all I was worth. "HEEEY MISTER" I shouted as loudly as I could, but the truck kept rolling. I shouted and waved and cried as it passed right below me and I knew it would not stop. Then suddenly, it did! I shouted again and the engine stopped. My heart pounded. Yet again I shouted but nothing happened and I realized the driver might have just pulled over for a break or to light a cigarette before entering the quarry workings, further round the escarpment. But then a face appeared at the side window, looking out. I flapped and shouted until almost falling off the ledge and at last, the cab door opened and a figure emerged "HEEELP I'M STUCK" I shouted. Then to my horror, the driver climbed back aboard and drove off, his truck belching clouds of black exhaust smoke as if in desultory answer to my cries.

"You bastard" I sobbed, tears running down my face, and flopped back onto the ledge. I was now shivering violently with cold and dragged the tee-shirt back over my head, tucking it into my khaki shorts and tightening the red and blue-striped snake-belt I'd found amongst our bonfire stuff. It would soon be too dark for anyone to see me, I felt tired and weary and curled up as tightly as possible with my back to the abyss.

After a while the sound of another engine rose above the buffeting wind, higher-revving this time. I remained still until certain it was approaching before looking down for the headlights. There were none to be seen and as I peered into the gathering dusk, realized that the sound was coming from my right, in the direction the truck had taken. I stretched my neck round the rock wall at the end of the ledge to see a jeep trundling along the track. My heart lifted as I watched its lights bump up and down over rocks strewn on the path until it came to a halt directly below me. The door creaked open and a man got out, heavy boots crunching on the ground before his torchlight found me. He then set off along the edge of the road before cutting across to the rocky slope at the west side of the scree to begin his ascent. His dark shape sometimes disappeared behind boulders but I could always hear his hobnails scraping along as he climbed towards me. I listened and hoped and after about twenty minutes he popped up at the end of the ledge.

"A'm sorry mister, I got stuck" I apologized over my shoulder.

"Come on son, let's get y'down off there afore ye brek yer neck" he said calmly, holding out a massive hand which I grabbed with two small ones.

I held onto him like a limpet as he virtually dragged me off the shelf and turned immediately to the scree. His boots looked to be about a foot wide each and acted like snowshoes as he pointed them both to his left and simply walked down the slope causing a small landslide in front of us. His arm was like granite and I clutched it fiercely as we slid down the full height of the quarry face. When I lost my footing he simply dangled me in the air until I found it again, without stopping, and in no time at all we were down, panting on the gravel track where I retrieved a shoe which had come off and rolled down in front of us. He drove me to the main road and as we reached the junction I could see Paul and John trudging towards us in the headlights.

"Thanks mister" I said, clambering out of the jeep and brushing the caked dust from my clothes.

"You be careful in future lad, these quarries is dangerous places.

An' get yersels 'ome afore it gets any darker"

As he pulled back onto the quarry track John shouted to me "Bloody 'ell, we've 'ad to tramp nigh-on to Brigsteer to get back down 'ere an' ere's you ridin' round in a bloody jeep"

"Any eggs?" I asked.

"Nah"

Around this time, my last year at Dean Gibson before entering the even darker and more Dickensian world of Kendal Grammar School, a girl in my class, Mary O'Flaherty, asked me to go out with her. I'd had dealings with girls before: Victoria Hodgson; daughter of wealthy estate agent Michael, often got me to kiss her behind Mr Ratcliffe's big, free-standing blackboard but it was always a school activity. Mary was pretty with long blonde hair but when she asked me to 'go out' I thought she meant dressing up in nice clothes and going somewhere that cost money, so I said no. Her friend asked me a few more times on Mary's behalf and when I consistently and sullenly shook my head, she spat viciously that I was "Tight as a fish's arse" and I knew fishes' arses were tight! I liked Mary though and later, when we were teenagers, I did go out with her for a while.

I had another friend at this time called Ian (Jock) McKinnon and he had an elder brother named Alec who was always in some sort of trouble, even more than Jock, Grubber and I put together which constituted a considerable amount!

Jock and Alec's father was a jovial, good-natured bricklayer named Johnny, who hailed from the same area of Scotland as my paternal grandparents. His wife died when the boys and their sister Maureen were still young but Johnny, like Paddy Gallagher, struggled on alone and reared his children to adulthood.

When he was a youth, Alec was sent away to serve time at a young offenders' institute on Merseyside. Several decades later, long after his father's death, this penal establishment was demolished for re-development and amongst the rubble being transported off site, a watchful labourer noticed something shining in the dust. At the time that Alec was carted from home to commence his servitude there, he took with him a variety of small, concealable items which he hoped to sell to other inmates, thereby improving slightly the quality of his stay. One of these items was a military medal awarded to John McKinnon for conspicuous bravery in the face of the enemy, when he was a young Scottish soldier at Dunkirk. He had bought time for his comrades to avoid death or capture by attacking and nullifying an enemy machine-gun emplacement which had them pinned down and unable to withdraw. Alec, or whoever bought or stole the medal from him, subsequently lost it until rediscovered at the demolition site. It was brought home and presented to Maureen, who donated it to Johnny's old regimental headquarters to be displayed alongside their other battle honours. Until rediscovery its existence was apparently unknown generally – Johnny had not even bothered to tell anyone he had it.

Four

*"Flying high, up in the sky
The world below, passing by
On a wing-ed journey from despair
Clothes and aspirations needing repair"*

(Author – 2007)

MY FATHER WAS AWAY from home a lot of the time. He had left the shoe factory and entered the building industry. I can remember him being around at weekends when he would often throw house parties as his parents had done, which always included lots of alcohol. My mother never touched a drop though I often did. He was always in a good mood at these times and when he came back from the pub on a Saturday or Sunday afternoon, but his mood usually changed when he woke up after falling asleep in the chair by the fire. He had been impregnated with Glasgow's macho, working-class male philosophy on life and believed his sons should be brought up to be tough, hard-working and hard-drinking men.

He believed he could have been a successful boxer on the world stage if the war had not disrupted his career and maybe he could have. He did not want his sons to miss out on a similar opportunity and one of his strategies for toughening up Gordon Jnr and I was for us to glove-up and box each other, usually on a Saturday afternoon when he got back from the pub and had watched the racing results. I do not personally remember very much about these occasions, perhaps I do not want to, but Gordon and Pamela both say these 'boxing-matches' happened regularly with my father urging us both on. Gordon is two years older than me, two or three inches taller and was tough and athletic enough to be feared by his contemporaries. He remembers father instructing us to fight in the living-room at home and me coming forward at his insistence. Gordon says he knew it was wrong because he was older and bigger than I was, but that he had to keep hitting me to ward off my advance. His arms were longer than mine so I didn't often get the chance to punch him back.

My father himself did not hit either of us much though, except three or four times with his leather belt and once when I was about thirteen and he cracked a couple of my ribs with his boot. My mother tried to intervene when things got out of hand but always got shouted down by my father, though I do not think he was really physically violent towards her either, his male pride would not have allowed it.

As the final summer approached before I changed schools, one of the posh kids had a birthday coming up for which his parents were throwing a lavish party at their big house on the edge of town. He told everybody about it and used the fact that he was drawing up a guest-list as currency with which to buy friends, even if only temporarily. Anyone who did not show him enough attention and deference would be baited by the possibility of invitation, but if a person who was already invited displeased him in any way he could be struck off the golden list, having to work extra hard to re-gain entry. I never expected to receive an invitation and was surprised when my cousin did. One afternoon I was ensconced in a toilet cubicle puffing a Woodbine when I heard the boy talking to his brother, who was a year older than us and tall for his age, outside the door.

"But I've already asked him"

"Well you'll just have to un-ask him, mum won't want council-estate scruffs stealing stuff from the house and dad will have a fit"

"He won't steal anything"

"No he won't because he won't be there!" The elder brother snapped, adding the name of my cousin, John Medley.

"Snobby bastards" said Grubber in between puffs from the next cubicle.

Later, whilst standing in the dinner-queue I said something insulting to the elder brother about what I'd heard. He swung his school-bag at me and I threw him on the floor with a move I'd seen on Z Cars the night before, and for which I was reported and caned by Conleth. The younger brother approached the following morning as I was talking to John Henneberry, a posh kid who was not a snob, about some mountaineering drama he'd been involved in the previous weekend which had made the local news.

"It wasn't me who reported you Rob" the brother offered

apologetically.

I ignored him and he shuffled uncomfortably.

"Honest Rob, it wasn't me it was my stupid brother, in fact I was going to invite you to my birthday party on Saturday, Johnny's going"

I turned to face him "Is Grubber goin?" I snapped.

"Well, er no" he answered with an ill-concealed snigger.

"Well neither am I so shove yer stupid party 'cos I'm havin' one the same day anyway" I lied.

"Oh" he whimpered, backing off.

"Are you?" asked John with a big smile.

"What?"

"Having a party"

"Er, yeh course I am" I lied again to save face.

"Can I come?" he asked eagerly.

"Thought you were goin' to his?"

"Rather go to yours, probably more fun"

"Er, yeh ok then"

By lunchtime I had forgotten all about parties and on Saturday morning Coidy and I squirmed into the hen-hut on Atkinson's farm that we used as a den. He fell asleep in the warm straw so I left him amongst the eggs and feathers and went home for a jam sandwich. I actually forgot about him but he showed up at my house later, slightly perturbed at being abandoned and my mother made him a sandwich too to cheer him up. Our house might sometimes have been untidy but I could bring any waif, stray, runaway or sick animal home and my mother would do her best to help it. I was proud that people came to my mother when in need and that pride fostered in me a tendency to replicate her selfless generosity whenever I could.

Grubber was also at the house and as Coidy emerged from the front door, face covered in raspberry jam, Grubber threw a tennis ball to him. Coidy was tall like both his parents, but not well co-ordinated and the ball eluded his sticky-fingered grasp, bounced off his head and rolled onto the flat canopy roof above the front door.

"Fucksake Coidy" Grubber groaned.

"Y'threw it too high" countered Coidy.

"Well go an' gerrit, you 'eaded it up there"

"I'll gerrit" I said, scrambling up via the boundary fence post, as I had many times before when sneaking in through a bedroom window after coming home late. Plucking the ball from the murky rainwater standing on the roof because the drains were blocked, I rubbed it on my ice-blue, Varlson jeans and threw it down to Coidy, who fumbled it again. As I straightened up laughing and leaned back against the grey, pebble-dashed wall beneath my parents' bedroom window, I noticed a big car cruise slowly round the corner into the street. Cars were rare on Low Mead and I recognized it instantly as belonging to John Henneberry's father. Swinging down from the canopy like a chimp I raced into the house through the always-open front door "MAAM" I shouted.

She was in the kitchen and looked round as I entered "Mam can I have a party?"

"A party, when?"

"Now, today, right now"

"What kind of party?"

"Kinda like a birthdy party"

She looked into my eyes and seeing the desperate urgency there, picked up the hand-towel "Who's coming to this party?" she asked, watching Mr Henneberry's car through the scullery window.

"Just me, Coidy, Grubber and a friend from school" I pleaded.

"Oh well, that doesn't seem too many" she pondered.

"Pleease?"

"Alright but you'll have to play outside 'til I get things ready"

"Thanks mam" I said, racing back outside.

I re-emerged from the house just as John was walking down the path carrying a brightly-coloured package "Happy birthday, I think" he said, handing it to me.

Coidy, who did not attend Dean Gibson and so did not know John, eyed him warily. Mr Henneberry's hand flapped out of the car window as it left the kerb. Several neighbours waved back.

"Thanks" I said nervously "Me mam sez we 'avta play outside tilt' party's ready"

"What party?" asked Grubber.

"You know, my erm party, today" I said, looking intently at him.

"Oh that party, fergot fer a minute" he said with an innocent grin.

"Can I come?" asked Coidy as we ran off, zig-zagging between the fly-covered cow-pats dotted along the road between the back field and Thexton's farm, the lane to which branched off from the top of our street.

My mother did a good job and the party turned out well, without any of the bickering reported from the posh one. When John's birthday came around he invited both me and Grubber to his house and we never stole a thing, though I did knock a big plant-pot over by mistake. Although I would have liked to, I never saw John again after leaving junior school.

Thexton's farm, previously Martindale's, was a favourite playground and we often went to visit the pigs, which were as big and fierce as lions. I once leant too far over the half-door of the stable in which the sows were kept during birthing time. I was holding a carrot out to a mother sow when she reared up, grabbed my sleeve in her mouth by mistake and pulled me down onto the sodden straw. She grunted and snuffled at me in a terrifying manner but luckily located the fallen carrot before anything more vulnerable and I was back up and over that planked door like an Olympic high-jumper. I do not know whether that pig was short-sighted or maybe stupid, but she circled around like a cat before bedding down and often flopped right on top of one or other of her little piglets. It's a wonder they were never squashed to death under her massive weight but were always there when we counted them next visit, squeaking and looking up at us hopefully. I still brought carrots and stuff that my mother had thrown out, but lobbed them in from a distance like hand-grenades. I have heard that pigs are very intelligent but I do not think that particular sow was.

One day we tramped right through the farmyard towards the orchards beyond, where apple and plum trees hung heavy with fruit. There was an old car parked outside the farmhouse which had never been there before. We inspected it at length, decided it was a wreck and clambered all over it, pulling the wipers and indicator arms off to use as swords. Soon becoming bored though, we began to disperse towards the orchard gate but as we did so, one of the gang picked up a stone and hurled it at the windscreen. It cracked in a round, spider-web pattern and the rest of us scrabbled round in the mud for more stones to throw. As I stood up with a big, clarty one in hand I realised the gang was sprinting en-masse for the orchard. I turned to fling the stone before following and was knocked flat on my back in the sludge. My stone plopped harmlessly into a dank puddle and large hands grabbed the front of my pullover, hauled me up and swung me round in an arc to land with a metallic bang on the car bonnet. I looked up into the bulging, bloodshot eyes of Walter Thexton, or Thecky as we called him affectionately.

"Y'little bastard" he stammered, out of breath from either rushing or perplexity. "A'll fuckin' kill ye, y'little bastard ye"

He had a rosy, goiterous lump on the side of his neck and spit dripping off his chin. I was still wearing my maroon, custard-stained school tie and he jerked the knot tight around my neck. He continued to tighten as I began to choke, still staring up into his spluttering face.

"W, we thought it was a wreck" I squeaked in a strangled voice, my hands gripping his.

"A wreck, A'll give y'fuckin wreck y'little bastard ye"

I looked pleadingly at him as he bent over me on the car "A'm sorry Thecky, we thought it wuz a wreck, honest"

"Fuckin' wreck, I paid good money fer that fuckin' wreck at Thursder's auction y'cheeky bastard"

I sensed that he was beginning to calm just a little.

"What's yer name?" he asked, slackening his grip "A'm gunna tell t'police on ye"

The tie, still in its slipknot and now more stained than ever, stayed tight around my neck. I struggled to loosen it and gasped "Robbie, me name's Robbie"

"Robbie what y'daft fucker?"

"Robbie MacGowan, I live just over there by t'back field"

After a thoughtful pause "MacGowan, thas nut Gordon MacGowan's lad is te?"

"Yeh 'e's me dad"

"Fucksake, now look lad, Robbie" he said quietly and conspiratorially "A'll nut tell t'police on thi, they're a bunch o' bastards anyway, an' thou don't tell thi fatha 'bout this eh? What thi say, alreet?" He smiled nervously and smoothed out the crumpled collar of my shirt.

"Ok then"

"Aye, we'll not say owt, nayther on us, just keep it atween oursels eh, then there'll be nay trouble, tha knows"

"Ok Mr Thecky, sorry 'bout yer wreck, I mean yer car" I offered cheerfully, trotting hastily off to the orchard and leaving an artistic-looking mud-stain on the dented bonnet.

"Cheeky bastard" he mumbled, surveying the damage.

The street names of our estate and other places always fascinated me and though I did not have the confidence to actually ask anybody about their meaning in case I was thought stupid, I studied them and concluded that they must have been taken from what the land was like before the estate was built, probably sometime back in history. I loved learning about history. We lived on Low Mead which must have been a meadow on low-lying ground. There was a street nearby on higher ground called High Mead, obviously a high meadow. In between was Sparrowmire Lane which could have led to a mire over which flocks of sparrows swooped to catch the abundant flies in such locations. There was probably also a marauding sparrow hawk or two which swooped to catch the sparrows. The mire still exists as a large patch of boggy ground at the bottom of Atkinson's field, where our gang's hen-hut was. At the far side of the bog was Kettlewell Road, where might still lay the deep remains of an old well to which people took their containers or 'kettles' to collect drinking water, and above the road: High Sparrowmire. Branching off the lane was Low Garth and at the far side of the Estate, towards Windermere Road: High Garth; a 'garth' being an orchard or wooded enclosure. The estate as a whole was named Hallgarth, which is likely to have been an orchard belonging to a hall or large house. I am not quite sure where the hall was though there is still a big old house on the high ground above Sparrowmire Lane, on the same level as Kendal Green, where my mother worked as a cleaner when I was very young. I believe it used to be the home of Alfred Wainwright, the famous author of fell-walking books who moved from Manchester to become Kendal's Borough Treasurer. His first home in Kendal was 19 Castle Grove, the house where my sister, Pam, now lives.

At the foot of our back garden, between it and the field where Snowy the cow munched grass all day and sucked water from the metal trough in great swirling drafts, lay a rough, gravel track about ten feet wide. The track ran behind Low Mead before petering out into the large open space between it and the rear of Low Garth where we had our bonfires. At the far side of the track stood a row of rickety, pre-fabricated single garages owned by the council and leased to tenants. Across the field, at the edge of the sparrow-bog where we caught frogs and raced them up the garden path, stood another cluster of such garages. These were only about fifty yards from my aunty Doris's house where I often stayed at weekends and to where the gang came to call for me one Sunday morning.

As I pulled on the brand-new, black & white bumper boots that my mother had bought me the previous day at the Saturday market in town, I could hear Coidy outside the back door talking to my uncle Walter, who was German.

"Bloody 'ell what's that Mr Wagner?"

"Issa bat" replied uncle Walter.

"Oh aye, only a lall un though innit, mus' be just a babby"

"Ja, I sink iss pipistrelle"

"Oh aye, pissytrelle eh? A'll ask me dad, e'll know"

I finished struggling with the long white laces and looked out the kitchen window to where they were staring at a tiny black object clinging to the pebble-dashing of the out-house wall.

"What y'gunna do wi' it?" asked Coidy.

"Nossing, juss leave till find iss way home"

"Y'could purrit in a shoebox from t'factry an' 'ave it as a pet?"

"No, sink I juss leave alone so can be free"

"Oh" said Coidy, slightly disappointed.

"Come on Coidy" I said, probably to uncle Walter's relief, sauntering down the entry into the sunlight after a quick look at the little bat. I would like to have stayed longer but the gang was waiting.

"See y'later then Mr Wagner, 'ope yer pissytrelle's ok" Coidy said with the genuine concern he had for all wildlife.

"See y'later" I echoed.

The rest of the gang had drifted away by then and we followed them down the gravel decline towards the field. As we entered the cluster of garages through which the path led, two men jumped out from one of the narrow gaps between them and grabbed us. We were surprised and shouted out and the gang's tail-enders turned to look back. We were dragged into a garage and the door locked behind us.

One of the men was 'Shorty' Garnett and lived nearby but I did not know the other. There was an old iron bed in the garage with some ropes and straps lying on it. Shorty picked up a length of rope and tied my wrists together, then looped the other end of the rope over the exposed roof-truss chord and pulled it down tight. The rope bit into my wrists and pulled them up until my arms were out-stretched above my head and I was standing on the tips of the pris-tinely-white rubber toecaps of my new bumpers, then he tied the rope off to the truss. The other bloke was tying Coidy, stretched out in a star shape, face-down to the bed. When Coidy was lashed down the two men started laughing and lifted one end of the bed frame up between them, then began kicking Coidy from underneath. He squealed and shouted "Oww y'pair o' bastards"

They laughed louder and I shouted "Lerrim go y'fuckin' weirdos"

They stopped laughing, turned to me and Shorty pulled a red penknife from his pocket as Coidy's bed was dropped with a clatter onto the concrete floor.

"Now yer gunna gerrit" said Shorty, prising open his weapon.

I stared at the rusty blade as it sliced, with some perseverance, my t-shirt down the front and his mate unhooked a whip made from plaited pig-leather (probably from the pig-leather factory across the road from the Bridge Hotel) from a nail in the wall frame. Shorty still had the knife pressed against my chest as the whip cracked resoundingly in the enclosed space, sending a shower of white dust from the dry hide descending through the beam of light entering through the one small window. The knotted lash then whipped across my bare skin as I kicked out and screamed "Y'bastards"

Coidy started screeching and bouncing up and down on his rusty bed like a lunatic. Suddenly, all fell silent inside the garage as we heard distant shouts from outside. Shorty opened the door a crack and peeped out "Bloody hell" he exclaimed and disappeared through the doorway with his pal close behind.

I stretched forward to look through the open door and saw a little army of kids charging along the track towards us. The gang had gone for reinforcements, recruited some of the older lads and here they all came waving sticks and stones and a broken garden fork and whooping like a Sioux war party.

We were rescued and set free virtually intact and did not think too much more about it, but the grown-ups got to know and aunty Doris, knowing where Shorty lived, marched round to his house. I do not think she would let Walter go for fear of racist reprisals.

Shorty said some bad things and insulted her because although she was a tough Geordie, she was quite upset. Fortunately another visitor was on his way – my father. Marlise, Walter and Doris's daughter, had run round to Low Mead and caught him before he set off to the pub. Despite being told to keep away, some of the gang crept up behind Shorty's hedge but reported that they did not hear much, just Shorty whimpering and pleading for mercy and perhaps a couple of dull thuds. After that it was mostly all forgotten and nobody ever suggested calling the police, though I think rough justice caught up with Shorty's pal too not long after. I am not sure what kind of person Shorty really was, but I think probably very unhappy most of the time as I heard several years later that he had committed suicide.

I did not like school work much apart from history, drawing and writing stories. I remember having to read aloud in front of the class a tale I had made up about a galley-slave of the Romans, during which I got mixed up geographically but everyone still clapped anyway at the end of it. I also won a couple of schools' art competitions. Lots of my pictures were hung up on the classroom walls by my last primary-school teacher, Miss Dunne from Ambleside and Pam said one of them was still there two years later when she reached that class. It was a drawing of the Scottish battle against the English at Prestonpans in 1745 that Miss Dunne had told us about. I loved stories and drawing and although I was involved in weekly if not daily schoolyard scraps, I hated fighting. There was only one thing I hated more, losing, so tried very hard not to. Maybe I fought so hard because I knew how painful losing was.

The fights at home with Gordon gradually degenerated into general bullying though neither of us was aware at the time that it could be described as such, and I was certainly better off than many, Grubber Gallagher for one. My early tactic when I knew violence was imminent was to lash out in defence before hopefully bolting from brutal retribution, though usually I got caught and hammered. My favourite escape was to run into the toilet on the landing and sit on the floor with my back against the door and my feet braced against the wall opposite. I fitted perfectly at that age. Gordon would kick and batter the door trying to get at me and when I was clearing out the house after our father died in 2003, I noticed that the bottom panel of the door was still cracked from his pounding forty years earlier. Gordon Snr was none too keen on home maintenance other than painting and wallpapering, which he did quite regularly.

I undoubtedly caused a lot of the attacks myself, I was forever stealing rides on his bike or borrowing his clean shirt or jumper or something without asking, not that I would have dared ask anyway, and the vicious punishment that was initially so painful and confidence-destroying, eventually just became an accepted part of everyday life. Gordon was very good at fighting and won a School boxing competition by stopping all of his opponents in less than fifteen seconds. He was also a tough and talented rugby player. John also grew up to excel at both sports and could handle himself extremely well. On a few occasions when I was young and someone from outside the family tried to bully me, Gordon sorted them out and I also helped him a few times when he got into fights as a teenager. Both of my brothers, and sister, are decent, intelligent people with good jobs who have worked hard and enjoyed successful lives. I was without doubt the 'black sheep' of the family. Gordon and I did clash one final time in our late teens, when I had filled out a bit and learned how to punch well above my weight, and then we never discussed the subject again. He lives a quiet life in Yorkshire with his wife, Carol.

Saturday was matinee day at the Palladium cinema, or picture-house as we called it, on Sandes Avenue. Kids from all over town converged there to lose themselves in a world of make-believe played out on the silver screen. There was as much action in the stalls as on the reels of film as we cheered on Hopalong Cassidy, Zorro, Flash Gordon, and the Thunder Riders (my favourite) We shouted and threw stuff at rival gangs from other estates before galloping home with our coats tied round our necks like the capes worn by the Riders, slapping our thighs as Hoppy slapped his trusty steed to make it run faster to someone's rescue.

We paid the cheapest entrance fee which was a 'tanner' (sixpence) and then crawled under the seats to the shilling-end. This money-saving manoeuvre developed as we got older into gaining entry to evening showings, particularly those with X certificates, without paying anything at all. This became more necessary as the minimum charge was upped to a 'bob' (shilling) and there were several preferred methods. There was the frontal incursion which involved waiting as inconspicuously as possible near the main entrance until a group of people went in together, then mingling with them in the hope of slipping in unnoticed. This was a risky strategy though, requiring perfect timing and once a delinquent face became known to the fearsome concierge, Bill 'Bozo' Buckley, he never forgot it. Flanking attacks could sometimes be attempted between first and second screenings by entering via the exits located to right and left of the main entrance as the crowds came out, but urchins fighting inward against the outward flow of customers were easily noticed. By far the most successful sortie but also the most dangerous, was the rear entry: Approaching from the riverside walk between Dockray Hall and Victoria Bridge a narrow, gated footpath led to a six-feet high wall over which we climbed, avoiding the shards of broken glass set on top as a deterrent, and down the other side into a narrow lane. This in turn led to a second wall twice as high as the first but which was possible to climb using the convenient drainpipe, onto a flat roof. Across the roof and down another drain pipe to a ledge from which we hung and dropped the last yard into an open space, which narrowed into the long tunnel to the left side of the main entrance. Right in front of us was the cinema exit door from the tanner-end. Bozo kept it locked most of the time but we quickly learned that it had to be left unfastened as a fire escape during shows. We would note the time that the main feature started so we knew when the lights inside were off, then pull open the double-doors as quietly as possible whilst reaching in quickly to grab the curtains so they did not billow out with the draft we had let in. Everybody got inside, behind the curtain so that we could close the doors before peeping out to see if Bozo was about. If not we would crouch to make a hands-and-knees dash for the front row seats, straight underneath and up into an empty-looking area.

It might seem like a lot of bother just to save a shilling but the point was, that although most of the time we could probably manage to afford entry one way or the other, there was nearly always at least one of us who could not. On occasion those who could, would pay and sit near the exit door so that he who could not might easily join us. This however, left him to make the hazardous approach on his own, and in our gang, we preferred to stick together. If one of us couldn't go somewhere, none of us did. At least that was the theory

'One for all and all for one' as the Three Musketeers said in one of the films we sneaked into. There was also the fact that none of us were old enough to pay into an X, so the excitement at seeing the picture and bragging about it later was well worth the bother, which we quite enjoyed as an adventure anyway.

It was not unusual to bump into other sub-seat intruders whilst crawling around in god-knows-what on the floor, on which occasion the accepted practice was to politely acknowledge each other, territorial differences put aside for the moment, and resume hostilities once safely ensconced in a seat. On one of these occasions Bozo noticed the disturbance in his audience and trundled down the aisle, trusty torch in hand "W, w, what's goin' on theer?" he demanded in his usual stammer.

"Nowt Bill" we answered politely.

"Ave yez all got tickets?"

"Yes Bill" we assured, holding up the stubs we had collected from the floor on our crawl up.

"W, well mek sure thez nee mare noise outa yez"

"Yes Bill"

"W, w, what the fuck's that?" he exclaimed, pointing his torch at the floor beside us, just as Coidy's big curly head popped out from under the seat in front. Coidy was not a good seat-crawler – too tall and gangly.

"Any sign o' that fat cunt Bozo?" he enquired, just before Bill's meaty paw clamped the back of his collar and the rest of us made a run for it.

Another endeavour involving organised crawling was put into operation when the travelling fairground came to town for its regular, biannual fortnight on the New Road car park as it does to this day. We would note the date of arrival and therefore knew when it was due to depart. The coloured lights and piped music were always switched on at the start of the first weekend of the fortnight and departure was always on the Monday after the third weekend, weekends being the times when most money was taken. We would wait as long as possible on the final Sunday night before springing into action. Sneaking into the murky darkness to the rear of the Waltzer, we removed a rickety slatted panel which we had already loosened and crawled into the void below the thundering, unguarded machinery above. Peering through the gloom we would scoot around in a crouch, avoiding the dripping oil, litter, and rats that made their way up from the nearby riverbank to feed on discarded hot dogs, hamburgers and toffee apples that had been blown or swept underneath. Glinting amongst all the rubbish and debris was always a veritable wealth of coinage having been dropped by customers fumbling in pockets and purses, particularly whilst the Waltzer was in motion, and of course by the Friday and Saturday night drunks who fumbled whether in motion or not. The coins bounced, rolled and slid through wide gaps in the blue-painted, boarded walkways. We collected the fallen bounty and moved swiftly to the Autodrome ride at the other end of the car park, near the Provincial Insurance offices, and repeated the operation.

At weekends in high summer we often ranged further afield in our eternal quest for adventure. When we could afford the fare we sometimes caught the bus to Arnside and after clambering up and down the massive iron viaduct across the Kent estuary, went 'treading' for flukes (flatfish) in Morecambe Bay. Treading involved wading into the shallows and feeling along the sand bed with your toes to find the fish, then reaching down gently, hooking a finger into a gill and hauling them out. We took some home in plastic bags but sold most to local pubs. The tides came in very quickly and we were aware that many people had died in its rushing waters. We watched and learned about the treacherous currents and quicksands and regularly made our way right across the bay to Grange open-air swimming pool or vice-versa. I once read an article from the Westmorland Gazette of 150 years ago, about orphans collected from the streets of Liverpool and put to work in virtual slave-labour conditions at local mills of the dark, satanic type. The report stated matter-of-factly that a certain mill owner to the north of the bay, on completing a pressing order for which he needed extra labour temporarily, nonchalantly ordered them to be marched out onto the sands at ebb-tide and left there with instructions to cross the bay, in the sure knowledge that the incoming flow would dispose of the children in a cost-effective manner.

The 'bore' or river tide, flooded the estuary sands so quickly that on one occasion many years later I had to rescue my brother John's unimaginatively-named dog, Bowser. John was working away from home as usual and we were having a family day out at the seaside with his wife, Angela and kids, Jack and Eloise, who lived in Morecambe town. When the tide began to flow we headed in for tea at our regular shoreline bar but despite calling Bowser, still a leggy, un-coordinated puppy, he continued to cavort around on the flats, chasing seagulls. He happened by chance to be on a slightly raised sand-bank in the centre of the river course when the water reached him and soon he was stranded, whimpering with his black and white tail between trembling legs. We shouted, waved and whistled but the dog was confused and whirled around in circles as the tide claimed the land about him. When the kids started crying I ran down the bank and splashed across to the marooned mongrel. Scooping him up whilst he licked my face with serious gratitude, I waded out into the deepening flow just as his little island was flooded. The water was chest-height at its deepest point as I struggled against the current but reached the shore to cheers from the kids. Bowser bolted inland, shaking himself dry and as I turned to look back at whence we came, the whole river-mouth lay ten feet below surging sea-water. I watched the rushing surf crashing against the shore, dislodging vegetation, and knew that even the strongest of swimmers would struggle to survive in that raging torrent. In 2004 twenty three immigrant Chinese cockle-collectors were drowned during one tragic night in the same area.

Five

"All the rules and regulations
The punishments and degradations
Free young spirits slowly shrivelling
To the arid drone of a teacher's drivelling"

(Author 2007)

I SOMEHOW PASSED THE 11-Plus exams and reported to the local
Grammar School wearing Gordon's hand-me-down uniform and
a wary expression. During the first assembly service as I bowed
my head and pretended to pray to a god that I knew by then did
not exist, I noticed that I was wearing not only clothes that did
not fit but also shoes that did not match, though at least they were
of a similar colour, and spent the rest of the day moving around
like a cripple, trying to hide one foot behind the other. Later in
the week, re-shod and with sleeves pinned back, I and my class
attended a history lesson with a big, round, fuzzy-haired teacher
called Mr Zair. I enjoyed it and looked forward to his lessons even
though he smoked a foul-smelling pipe, but on one occasion he
was not there. His place had been taken by a much younger person,
though equally rounded and similarly dressed in the black gown
of academia. I was not dismayed however and listened intently as
the lesson began, but after a few minutes I noticed that the new
teacher kept looking at me strangely as he paced up and down the
aisle delivering his well-rehearsed oratory. Suddenly, from behind,
he grabbed the hair just in front of my left ear and twisted it violently. He then pulled upwards and I had no other option than to
rise to a standing position. Then he proceeded to haul me up and
down to sniggers from the other boys, until I seriously considered
equalizing the situation with a roundhouse right. He stopped after
a few seconds though and as I sat back down and looked up at him,
his eyes bulged at me from behind thick glasses in a maniacal grin
which would be frightening to most 11-year old boys. Afterwards,
a new friend, John Barnes from Top Thorn Farm, Whinfell said,
whilst chewing Black Twist tobacco and spitting its odorous juice

onto the classroom floor "Oo was that fuckin' weirdo?"

He was an ex pupil of the school recently graduated from university and invited back by the headmaster to gain some teaching experience. His name was David Starkey and he went on to become a celebrated historian and television personality but believe me, he was a 'fuckin' weirdo'

The school had an immediate damping-down effect on my spirit, enthusiasm and confidence. In the first Latin exam for instance, I came second, but in the second exam I placed next to last. I continually fell foul of petty, archaic rules that pushed me into a position of constant confrontation with a system which in my opinion, closely resembled organised bullying and to which therefore, I could never submit.

One drizzly morning I arrived at the grey, intimidating edifice ten minutes late because I did not have the full bus fare and had to run from two stops out with my satchel and games kit slapping against my legs. I rushed inside and up the stone steps to my form-room to deposit the bags before going to assembly, but halfway up the deserted staircase ran into a prefect called Welch, arrogantly blocking my path. I was on the left side of the steps going up so that I could use the banister rail, and he was sauntering down peeling a sweet-wrapper. He did not move so I stepped to his left to pass him but he also moved left, in front of me so that I had to struggle between the wall and his smirking face which was far too close for my liking. He made a comment about my attire as I pushed past, I replied in kind and he grabbed me by the collar. I knocked his hand away and scurried up the steps. For that he put me in detention but feeling aggrieved I did not attend and went home at the normal time. I mentioned it to my dad and he said that pupils should not be used as unpaid lackeys so that teachers can sit around on their arses even more than usual, and nor should they be given power to wield over other pupils, as they are still schoolchildren themselves and not yet mentally equipped to deal with such authority. I agreed with him wholeheartedly and when I was issued a further detention for not turning up for the first, I never turned up for that one either. Pretty soon I had amassed a whole stack of detentions which waited unheeded for my attendance, though I did show up once or twice if I felt the punishment justified or when one of my mates was detained and needed reassuring company amongst the older bad boys. The headmaster L C (Elsie) Reynolds, who more than once appeared to extract morbid pleasure from hoisting me over the back of a chair in his inner office until my feet were off the floor, and whacking my backside with a stick several times before telling me he admired the way I took it, informed me at the end of my second year that I had the worst detention record in the history of the school and his annals reached back over 300 years! Coidy and Grubber were mightily impressed when I told them the good news. They had the fortune not to be pupils of the Grammar School and I envied them immensely.

A complaint I harboured against the detention system was that detainees were not allowed to use the time, either 30 minutes or an hour, to do any of the mountains of homework we were given every day with extra at weekends. I would have found this opportunity very useful, sharing a bedroom with two others in a cramped household of six and sometimes seven when we had a lodger, but no, detentions were issued as pure punishment. I once received a detention for revising for an exam whilst in detention, and then another one for not revising enough! Gordon seemed to get his homework in on time and I truly admired his efforts, but cannot help thinking that he probably did not feel as nervous and unsettled in our home environment as I did.

Another roll-up of detentions started in Mr Morton's chemistry lab after Chris Priestley collapsed onto the floor. A group of us were larking about pre-lesson, turning the Bunsen-burners on and off and trying to create jets of flame with the matches a surprising number of students carried, but scurried to our seats as the teacher took his place behind the long bench at the front. Gas could still be smelled in the air and all of a sudden Chris, whom I liked and who was sitting next to me, fell backwards off his high stool onto the floor. We all gathered round in concern and surprise, Chris soon recovered and Mr Morton asked him what had happened. He said he did not know and must have just fainted, maybe because of the gas, but Morton dragged me to one side and demanded to know what I had done to him. I was amazed and stammered truthfully that I had not done anything, but was issued an hour's detention anyway 'just in case' and told to report to the lab that day after school. I was quite keen to learn about chemical reactions and enjoyed the experimentation aspect of the subject, so turned up for the detention because I did not want to annoy Morty, with whom I'd had no problem prior to that day. I intended to pass the hour writing out some ideas for a story I had in mind about my cat, Tiger, whom I loved dearly and who had died the previous weekend. It was not homework and only loosely connected to schoolwork at all and should therefore have been allowed, but Morty came in with a disdainful expression on his face and a newspaper in hand. He smoothed out a full page of the broadsheet on the bench beside me with an instruction to copy out the whole of the text at least three times. I looked in dismay at the page, which drivelled on forever about world finance and included not a word about chemistry, watched Morty disappear into his little rear room and broke for home.

When I first started at the school Mr Morton looked relatively normal apart from his strange, pigeon-toed walk and the fact that his trousers were always three inches short. By the time I left he was sporting a distinctly bouffant hairdo and a budding pair of breasts. Four years later when my brother John encountered the delights of chemistry, Morty was wearing full make-up, high-heels and fishnet tights, and still being left in charge of 11-year old children!

A particularly nasty piece of work lurking beneath the guise of teacher was one Mr Cordingley, who repeatedly informed us with glowing pride that he was the cousin of famous cricketer, Brian Close. Cordingley or 'Stringy' as he was known by the pupils, was charged with instructing us in the delicate art of music appreciation and he attempted this by playing classical records and exhorting us to memorise the names of long-dead composers. This was in the early 1960s at the dawn of a new era throughout the world, but I remember him stating as an unequivocal fact that The Beatles would last no longer than six months.

As I usually had to report to the school office each morning and explain my non-attendance at detention the previous night, and then be issued with an additional detention, I was often late for Cordingley's lesson which was first on the agenda. This increasingly irked the music-teacher as did the fact that ten minutes after joining his class I was bored out of my skull and leaking evidence of that boredom. But I did always attend despite his constant niggling and bickering at me for three years, and the smallness of his character which led him to report any trivial infringement of often redundant rules. He continually tried to marginalise and exclude me from group activities until one morning he finally snapped in a frenzy of lost control which required my father's intervention:

The whole school was gathered for morning assembly in the large hall where the noise and clamour was at a crescendo prior to the entrance procession of teachers and staff, apart from Cordingley who was already up on stage tinkering with his piano. I was sitting in a row of classmates halfway down the hall in the area designated for our year. Boys were still coming in, clattering about and calling to friends, all about was total chaos and Cordingley's eyes flashed around the room angrily as his presence, status and associated authority were completely ignored. I was not making any noise at all nor even moving. I was sitting calmly watching him with perhaps the hint of a smile on my face. His eyes suddenly locked onto mine whereupon he jumped to his feet like an uncoiling spring, knocking over his stool, and thundered down the wooden steps from the stage. I watched him from the corner of my eye, a strand of sandy-coloured hair bouncing up and down from the crown of his narrow head as he reached the end of the row in which I sat, and clambered past the other boys towards me. His pale eyes stared wildly from behind his horn-rimmed glasses and his buck-teeth glinted in the glaring light of the overhead bulbs. I continued to look forward but he grabbed me by the hair, which at that time was just past collar length and hung down over my forehead, and hoisted me from my seat. The noise in the room subsided as he pulled me out into the corridor and down towards the stage. He rammed me into a front row seat with the first-year boys and screamed in his high-pitched, lisping voice "That'sh your sheat from now on lad, make shure you shit there every morning"

I stared at him in amazed defiance until he retrieved his piano stool as the headmaster's procession entered. I turned back to my pals with a questioning look to which they returned uncomprehending shrugs "Mind where ye shit in future lad" they mimicked later.

The next morning Cordingley was again in assembly early as I returned to my usual seat without giving him a glance. He exploded into action immediately and repeated his performance of the day before, though this time he did not manhandle me to the front but out of the hall altogether. In the foyer I stopped and stood up from the crouch he was forcing me into by holding down my head.

Despite being much younger than my father his feeble strength offered little resistance. I was fourteen and almost as tall as he was. I jerked my head to loose my hair from his spindly fingers and he took a half step back.

"Headmashter's offish for you lad" he spluttered.

I gave him a pitying sneer and sauntered in the required direction, smoothing down my Beatle fringe as I went. Halfway down the narrow corridor beside the central staircase however, he grabbed my collar from behind and pushed me violently forward "Get a move on lad" he shouted.

I instinctively lashed out with a backward sweep of my elbow, which knocked his hand away and I hissed at him "Get your fuckin' pervert hands off me"

This time he retreated a full step, totally aghast with unmistakable fear in his staring, fishlike eyes. Saliva glistened on his pouting lower lip. I put a hand on his sunken chest and pushed him back against the wall, out of my path, as I changed direction and walked towards my form-room.

Later in the day I was summoned to the headmaster's office wherein Cordingley stood like an obedient pet, and was told by the head to apologise to him. Cordingley stuck his puny chin out but retracted it sharply when I shook my head. New headmaster, Mr Cochrane, stated that if I did not apologise unreservedly he would have no option but to suspend me from school. He meant it as a threat but it sounded like good news to me. I continued to refuse and was duly suspended. I was leaving that summer anyway and immediately started looking around for a job in the real world. I was not perturbed at all because I had older friends from Longlands, the 'Secondary Modern' school at the other end of town, who had worse records than I did but had proved themselves ideally suited to a work environment. I could hardly wait to start earning money of my own. However, Cochrane sent a letter to my parents saying that if I did not return he could not give me a reference, which would prevent me getting the job I deserved because my artwork and written English were so good, and inviting them to a meeting. He also suggested that although my general behaviour was atrocious, I might be better suited to the greater freedom and autonomy offered by university life, which he said was still not beyond my grasp. I asked why he wanted me back and father said it was simply to do with the apparent success of the school as a whole, to prove they could educate people competently as they were paid to. It all sounded like a true nightmare to me but my parents insisted that a return to school would be in my best interests.

Representation at school would normally be a job for my mother but when father heard what had happened, he said he would go instead. The school instructed us to attend on Monday morning but father changed it to the following Friday afternoon, which pleased me as it afforded a further week's holiday. The school secretary led us to the headmaster's office and knocked lightly on the door. Cochrane answered and my father entered, appearing to fill the room with his broad back and thick black hair swept straight back from his face, seemingly brushing the overhead lampshade, and was ushered to a seat in front of the head's desk. I stood behind him holding onto the back of his chair. Cordingley sat meekly in a corner behind the head and stared at my father as if in awe or fear.

"Thank you very much for coming Mr MacGowan" offered Cochrane.

Father nodded. Cordingley smiled nervously.

"Obviously you received my letter and know the reason for the meeting"

Father nodded.

"Yes, er well, we wondered what you thought of the problem we are confronted with?"

Father slowly pulled out his tobacco tin from a jacket pocket, placed it on his thigh and removed the lid. Cochrane eyed the tin as the rich aroma of Golden Virginia permeated the small room.

"As I understand the problem, you want an apology from Robert in exchange for a decent school report?" asked father.

"W, well" stuttered Cochrane "I wouldn't put it quite as simply as that but yes, we do feel an apology would be in order"

After a pause father asked "Can I enquire as to what exactly you want him to apologise for?"

"Well" answered Cochrane again as Cordingley mumbled something unintelligible "For attacking poor Mr Cordingley here"

Father poked around in his baccy tin "Is that right Mr Cordingley, Robert attacked you did he?"

"Erm, y, yesh he did"

"How exactly did he do that?"

"He, er, he hit me with hish elbow and knocked me againsht the wall"

"The attack was witnessed Mr MacGowan and I'm sure Robert won't deny it, will you Robert?" Cochrane interjected.

"No, I don't deny it" I answered.

Cochrane and Cordingley smiled smugly.

"Have you an opinion as to why he attacked you?" father persevered.

"No, I have not. I was shimply eshcorting him to the head-mashter's offish becaush he had refushed to obey inshtructionsh"

Cochrane offered a sympathetic smile as father surveyed the music-teacher with puzzlement, as he did when watching Top of the Pops on television with us.

"So you don't think his attack might have been a purely defensive action because you were actually attacking him?"

"I shertainly wash not doing anything of the kind" spluttered Cordingley.

"So you don't consider pulling a boy around by his hair to be an assault then?" father asked whilst leisurely plucking a pinch of tobacco from his tin and dropping it onto the cigarette paper he held in a trough-shape between thick, browned fingers.

Cochrane looked at Cordingley blankly as the latter removed his spectacles and proceeded to clean them vigorously with the end of his woollen tie.

"Because as you say" continued father, looking down at the cigarette forming in hands gnarled from hard work and with knuckles knocked back from boxing "Witnesses were present and although you might not attach any importance to what your pupils have to say, apart from your hand-picked prefects, I can assure you that a court of law will"

"Errm no, no, Mr MacGowan I think we've gotten off on the wrong foot here. I'm sure we can reach an amicable agreement between ourselves without recourse to the law" said Cochrane whilst his underling stared open-mouthed.

"And what sort of agreement did you have in mind Mr Cochrane?" asked father, placing the perfectly formed roll-up between his lips.

"Well, ah well, as I intimated in my letter, Robert has certain talents which should not be wasted, and we think he would have a far better chance of using those talents, those gifts if you like, if he was armed with a good reference from a highly-regarded Grammar School such as we could offer him, or indeed if he wished to develop them further at university" recited Cochane, playing his trump card.

"An' y'don't think his talents should be acknowledged if he doesn't apologise?"

"Well, yes, I agree that perhaps the apology might be dispensed with, with Mr Cordingley's agreement of course" he said, only turning to look behind him when Cordingley failed to speak. He then nodded emphatically but maintained his downward gaze.

"But we would require his return to school in the avoidance of any outside interference, and this in itself presents certain problems"

"What problems?" asked father, the spindly cigarette bobbing up and down between his lips as he fumbled in his pockets and pulled out a battered box of Swan Vestas matches.

"I'm sure you are aware Mr MacGowan, that Robert here has a rather rebellious streak and often regards rules as mere suggestions, and the fact is that we need an effective measure to kerb and funnel his energies into productive endeavour"

Father fished out a match and rolled it between fingers grown thick from manual labour "What measure?"

"Well" continued the head cautiously, glancing in Cordingley's direction "We would er, we would like your permission to thrash the boy Mr MacGowan, but only when absolutely necessary of course" he added hastily.

Father looked directly into the headmaster's eyes until they wavered. "Thrash the boy eh?" he repeated "Ummm" he mused, nodding slowly as the two well-dressed educators watched the roughly-clad labourer intently.

Cochrane turned to look encouragingly at Cordingley, who had perked up noticeably.

"Who's gonna do the thrashin?"

"Oh, well, possibly myself or more probably my colleague Mr Cordingley here"

"Even though he's already assaulted the lad?"

"Er, I assure you that any punishment would be supervised and carried out correctly"

"Mmm, supervised eh. Alright then" said father to my astonishment and dismay.

"Oh, er oh, well, that's very understanding and compliant of you Mr MacGowan" said a beaming Cochrane, sitting up straight at his desk.

"Yes, you have my permission to what was it, thrash the boy" father affirmed as my heart sank further "On condition you recognise he has the same permission"

Smiles faded "Excuse me?"

"If, while you're thrashin' the lad" father clarified, nodding in my direction "He takes it into his head to thrash one or both of you in return, then he also has my permission to do so"

I felt like kissing my dad on the top of his big bullock head but was mesmerized by the teachers' expressions, which seemed to indicate acute apoplexy.

"I, I, I'm afraid that's out of the question" recovered Cochrane.

"I agree" confirmed father, finally lighting his cigarette and inhaling deeply before standing "I think we're done here" he said, offering his nicotine-stained hand to Cochrane and exhaling a cloud of smoke in Cordingley's direction.

I did in fact return to school but never received the promised reference. "Never trust teachers and the like" advised father, watching Walter McGowan take the World Flyweight Title from Salvatore Burruni in the same year that England won the World Cup final "They spend their lives surrounded by children and don't develop any manly attributes"

My disillusionment with life, hatred of school and refusal to conform set me on a course at odds with authority in general. I became defensive, over-alert to threat and swift to apply counter-measures. My life became a mess in early teenage years, I felt confused, unfit, scruffy, and slipped easily and unnoticed into the mindset of a low achiever. Gordon and our elder cousins were relatively successful both at sport and academics and I was made to feel very inferior to them. An aunt on my father's side, Peggy, once related me to the 40s/50s musician Joe Loss, she said I must be his brother – Dead Loss. I decided not to compete on their terms and instead hung around with boys from the estate and the secondary-modern, smoking, drinking from off-licence shops, growing my hair long and wearing Cuban-heeled boots. I got a tattoo and cultivated a bad attitude. At about the same age I discovered that my father's training regime might have been successful:

I was walking home from town one Saturday afternoon clutching some colouring pencils I had saved to buy, when I passed a group of older boys I knew, lounging against a fence. I nodded in acknowledgement and was about twenty yards past when one shouted after me. It was Brendan from the same junior school who had watched me beat a giant co-pupil called Santo Labatte a few years earlier, after Santo pushed me into a schoolyard fight he thought he would win. I stopped and they all ambled up looking tough with their cigarettes and leather jackets. Brendan said to me "I told Ack I reckon you can beat him but he reckons not"

Ack was not tall but stocky and two years older. He flicked his cigarette end in my direction and started circling round me. I stood perfectly still and looked at the ground, trying not to be there mentally as grandad had shown me, and allowing a calmness to descend that dispelled fear. I knew the worst that could happen was a bit of physical pain and I was used to that. Being beaten by an older boy would not even involve much shame so I simply accepted the situation as it unfolded. He snatched the pencils, snapped them in half and threw the bits into a nearby garden to guffaws of laughter from his pals. He walked slowly round behind me and stopped. I knew what was coming next but still stood there motionless, calm, waiting. With a spring he grabbed me round the neck from behind and clamped me in a tight headlock. As he jerked my head I let myself roll around until I faced him, not wasting energy in resistance, though still clasped to his leather-clad chest. The steel zip of his jacket scraped across my face as I pushed him back a few inches, but I unfurled quickly from the crouch and unleashed a two-handed flurry of punches at his head. The blows fired off automatically without any mental input that I was aware of, and he recoiled hard against the fence with a bloody face. He did not fall down but put his hands up and started crying. Brendan said "I told you Acky, e's fuckin' lethal, I told ye"

Acky slid down the fence to a squatting position. I said "Sorry Acky" retrieved my pencils and walked home. Nobody else spoke.

Maurice Strickland was in the class above me at Dean Gibson, the same class as Paul Bagshaw who remained a friend after school days were over. I do not know whether Maurice was related to the baronial Stricklands, who owned Sizergh Castle for hundreds of years and therefore must have descended from a Norman Knight who helped conquer England in 1066, but his family was quite well-to-do and devout catholic. Maurice was a gentle soul who never got into fights, I was able to relax in his company and we became good friends. Even in his early teens he was a good rock-climber and often went off at weekends to scramble around the Lakeland crags. I went with him one Saturday afternoon in the mid 1960s and we pedalled his tandem bike all the way to Langdale, where we dismounted gratefully at the Dungeon Ghyll pub. I sat on a stone outside while he went in and got two pints of bitter – he was bigger than me and looked much older in his climbing gear. I still looked like an urchin recently whisked off the streets. We spent the whole evening there in the company of other 'crag-rats' as he called them, chatting, laughing and sometimes joining in with songs I did not know the words to but sang along with anyway. When the pub shut we walked up a stony track behind it to a cleft under a massive boulder that Maurice had discovered on an earlier visit. There we made camp, lit a fire and ate the sandwiches our mothers had made, and went to sleep behind a polythene sheet that we wedged across the crevice with small rocks. It was warm and cosy and I felt safer and more secure there than I ever did in the bedroom I shared with my brothers. I thought how wonderful it would be to live in the outdoors with no school the following day and a pub just down the lane, at least in summer. I could imagine it being very cold at Langdale during winter. Next morning, Sunday, we packed our kit and hid it under the boulder, got the tandem from behind the pub and pedalled to a little chapel not far away along the roadside. The chapel was empty and Maurice said we had missed morning mass, but he said a few prayers on his own anyway. I stayed outside and watched the scores of wild rabbits cavorting in the surrounding fields. Back at boulder-camp we retrieved our gear and clambered up and down rocky edifices until late afternoon, by which time we were tired and hungry and made our way back home.

Years later, after conquering Pike o' Stickle with friends we went for a pint and pie at the Dungeon Ghyll and afterwards, I found the boulder. Someone had stuffed a bag of rubbish in the crevice so I pulled it out and dropped it in the litter basket near the pub, right next to the stone I sat on listening to the tales of the crag-rats with

Maurice.

On another Saturday at the end of summer, Maurice and I went to see Manchester United play at Old Trafford. He was a keen United fan and had been many times before, but I had not. We saw George Best, Denis Law and others, but what I remember most of all was what happened when two black men walked by in front of us as we stood in the tightly-packed Stretford End. Everybody around us started shouting and making noises like chimpanzees and those at the front spat at the two men who, despite looking big and strong, never even turned their heads but kept looking straight forward as if they were used to such occurrences, and walked calmly past. The surge of movement created in the crowd was quite frightening as I was pressed up against a thick metal rail which crushed into my chest. I looked around the crowd after it had calmed down and everybody I could see looked like quite ordinary, grown-up people such as shopkeepers or my teachers or just people in the street, but all were shiny-eyed, loud and excitable as children at a party or gathered round one of my schoolyard fights.

I never went to another major football match after that until I watched Southampton play Sunderland at the new Stadium of Light 35 years later, and I intermittently glanced at that game from the privileged comfort of the Corporate Hospitality Suite whilst sipping complimentary lager prior to a 4-course meal.

Six

I LEFT SCHOOL AS soon as I legally could which then was at the age of fifteen, although Mr Cochrane made a last effort at persuading me to stay on for GCEs, saying I could easily become a draughtsman or even an architect if I worked really hard at maths. But I hated maths with a passion born when my father had tried to shout the principles of it into my head, wanted out, and my mother had tried to extricate me from the entanglements of that school for years, though I did not know until long after I had left. She had discussed the situation with our family GP, Dr Jackson, who opined that I was suffering what even then he described as emotional abuse. The relief of leaving forever that institution which was a restrictive and suffocating relic of a bygone age was immensely liberating, but it did not give way to a problem-free existence.

I acquired employment as an apprentice site joiner with local house-building company, Russell Brothers, because I wanted to be outdoors and a million miles from teachers and classrooms. I started work on a cold, wet March morning and immediately suffered major cultural and physical shocks. After walking three miles to work, or cycling whenever I had a bike which could make three miles, I toiled manually until 5.30pm with half an hour unpaid lunch break spent sitting on a cement bag in a tin shed, and then walked or cycled the three miles home. My first weekly wage was £3.6s.4p (approx £3.34p) and because I quickly decided I was not going to work that hard in those conditions and merely live from week to week, I saved £1 of it. The rigours and uncertainties of the building trade kicked off a saving habit that has stayed with me all my life.

Apprentices competed with each other because the joiners were paid according to how much the team produced and the faster we worked the more we earned. The fitter we were the faster we could work and the joiner gangs even offered us 'transfer fees' from one team to another once they knew we could make money for them. We received a percentage of the gang bonus which rose according to age, so a younger apprentice might be a liability but as his knowledge and speed increased, particularly in a gang of older, less mobile joiners, so did his value to them and the company as a whole. At eighteen I was earning the equivalent of a fully qualified joiner's wage with two years to go as an apprentice, and hammering nails in all day before the invention of nail-guns helped to hone and develop my already-dangerous right hand punch.

At work I was re-acquainted with Chris Crawford who was by then an apprentice bricklayer. We originally met as street kids a few years before when for amusement, we waited on street corners to jump aboard the backs of lorries as they slowed for the bend – just for the ride and the risk. We lost touch when he was sent away somewhere.

He had started boxing at a club in Windermere and asked me to go with him. I said no because I hated boxing and the not-too-distant memories it evoked, but did accompany him a few months later with the sole intention of improving my cardio-vascular capability. Physical work for ten hours a day plus the efforts of getting there and back had improved my fitness dramatically, and fitness was becoming a real passion.

The Windermere club was well organized and run by Ian Irwin, who had been a top-class amateur fighter, trained several champions from the Lakes area and went on to become National Coach of the British team in international competitions including the Olympics. He steered heavyweight, Audley Harrison, to his one notable victory. The type of fitness required for long hours of physical work as opposed to explosive competitive sport are different, and at the end of my first training session I was so exhausted that I had decided not to venture there again. Only my pride kept me on my feet. Ian was already visiting national-squad training camps, knew the modern, short-burst, maximum effort training techniques and absolutely nobody entered the ring in the renowned light-blue Windermere colours who was not 100% fit.

At the end of training I slumped onto the nearest bench, thankful that the torture was over until I watched the other lads pulling on boxing gloves from sacks thrown at them by Ian or his assistant, Archie Boardley, and realized in horror that I was expected to do likewise. Apparently it was time to spar! Why had I not escaped whilst I could instead of gasping on the bench like a tuberculosis victim? I had not thought for a moment that I would be asked to spar on my first night but my pride forced me through the motions of pulling on the big puffy sparring gloves. There was no way on earth that I could allow anyone to think that the training had been too hard for me and that I had no intention whatsoever of coming to the club again, so I sat and watched and feigned interest. As my erratic breathing stabilized I realized that Chris was pretty handy with his fists and swift on his feet, as were most of the others including championship fighters Peter Thompson, Malcolm McLeod, Bert Boardley, Graham Reid and Pat Laidler. National champion Mick Byard had retired from the club the year before. I thought more and more that boxing was not for me, I knew none of these fancy moves and combination punches and at that point was thinking about taking up darts and dominoes more seriously at the Golden Lion, some of the prizes were quite good and the social life way better. I was slowly drifting onto a different plane of thought when a shout pervaded my daydream and I realized that all eyes were upon me, including those of the very experienced Roy Laidler, standing in the middle of the floor banging his gloves together in menacing fashion. I was obviously expected to get up and fight him and smiled as if it was a joke, but Chris gave me a nudge and said "Go on, get on with it"

So I stood up with the massive sparring-gloves, known colloquially as 'pillow-cases' dangling at my sides and feeling like the heaviest, most awkward objects I had ever carried. They are oversized in an attempt to stop injuries during sparring but are never completely effective, and we never used head-guards in those days. I walked mechanically onto the floor where Roy put out a pillow-case in my direction, inviting a ceremonial touch before battle. I lifted a glove which he prodded with one of his own and whacked me in the face with the other. That first punch had a definite galvanizing effect and when Ian, acting as referee, glided behind Roy and said "Test him out" something martial stirred inside and I began to concentrate on the job at hand.

Roy was a true gentleman and a nice guy as were his brothers, Barry, Keith and Patrick. They were all respected and reasonably successful fighters but I always harboured the nagging feeling that they had been gently pushed into the sport by their father, Jack, a local bookmaker and because of that I felt an empathy with them. Roy later told me that dozens of boys came through the doors of their gym and most had no chance whatsoever of becoming anything remotely resembling boxers. Rather than wasting weeks of valuable time just to see them disappear after being clouted a few times it had become custom to sound them out early on, and avoid subsequent disappointments on both sides.

At that point Roy was certainly fitter than me, less exhausted and more knowledgeable in the noble art of pugilism. But as logical thought receded in my brain, facial expression vanished and instinct took over, I gritted my teeth. Roy pursued as I reeled from his first blow, watching the reaction in my eyes, picking his target again. I waited until he moved closer, flicking his fast jabs, then dodged one by moving my head slightly to the left and simply marched forward throwing punches with both hands as I had against Gordon a few years before. He retreated, I followed with flailing fists and after a few seconds Ian stopped us. He held onto me, waved a flustered Roy back to the bench and brought forward a tall youth with thick red hair. He shuffled up close with gloves at the ready and actually snarled at me as we were instructed to "Box"

My new opponent was at least three inches taller than me, probably two years older and knew how to fight out of a crouch in the American style. He bobbed forward powerfully but I flicked out a jab which made him cover up, moved slightly to his left and threw a right over his hunched shoulder at the ginger head behind. It was a glancing blow to the temple but he stumbled backwards and his right glove touched the floor as he flailed to keep balanced. I was aware of Ian moving towards me from the right but was after my opponent and as he stood up to his full height, dipping his chin and smiling down at me as if I was a naughty schoolboy, I whacked him full in the face with another right hand, straight through his unclenched gloves. The sardonic smile turned to surprise as he backpedalled for several yards and sat down heavily on the floor in front of Ian. I backed up but never took my eyes off him, ready to resume hostilities with a vengeance, but Ian intervened and pulled me away. I had never felt so un-tired in my life.

Ian took me to the far end of the hall and sat me down on one of the cushioned benches that lined its perimeter. The gym was actually a dance-hall at the time and had no showers or washing facilities apart from a small basin. I kept looking back towards where the big ginger lad had fallen as if he might decide to come after me, but Chris told me later that he got up, walked out and never came back. None of the other lads knew much about him because he was sullen and hardly ever spoke, but we found out that years later he was jailed for stabbing a bloke outside a pub in Lancaster.

Ian asked where I had learned to fight, laughed when I said at home and talked me into coming back again.

My first competitive bout took place at Kendal Town Hall where I fought a black youth from Wakefield called G. Ali, though I doubt that he was related to the great Muhammad. I wore the boots passed down through my cousin, Stanley Gardiner, from Walter McGowan's father and a pair of American shorts from the Exchange & Mart magazine. I was never comfortable wearing the main British brand, Lonsdale, because I knew the name came from the title of Lord Lonsdale, the Yellow Earl, who, though a staunch supporter of early boxing, was reputedly an idle gambler of his inherited wealth who never worked a day in his life.

I stopped Ali in the second round, the crowd went wild and I tasted my first sample of open respect and admiration. After a few more fights my picture started showing up in the local press and I enjoyed a touch of small-town celebrity and popularity, not least with the girls. Work was going well and I began to save money. I went out at weekends with workmates and fellow boxers and developed a busy social life. The year was 1968 and the youth of the world were having a good time, at least those with light skins were, the struggle for equality of those with darker complexions was dealt a serious blow in April of that year, when white America murdered black civil-rights campaigner and Nobel Peace Prize winner, Martin Luther King Jnr. Their struggle continues. I met many black people as a boxer and because they were boxers, automatically respected them. I have found over the years that I respect most people on first meeting them whatever their creed, colour or status. My initial respect is often lost but only on an individual basis, as a consequence of some word or action, never for a whole race of people; a reaction which could only be born of a fear that does not haunt me.

Many people thought that as a boxer I would be out of step with the hippy, free-love culture of the time but boxing burns up aggression and generally, I was a peaceable, fun-loving teenager. I did get into the odd scrape away from the gym because I was still very alert to threat or anything that resembled bullying. These situations would arise without variation because men who were bigger than me made the mistake of assuming that their size would be the deciding factor in any confrontation between us. They were often right, their size usually meant that they were slow enough to be knocked over quickly.

At the age of seventeen I went with friends to Blackpool one Bank Holiday Monday and ended up that evening in the Tower Ballroom. I'd had a few beers, was tired at the end of a long day and fell asleep in the spectator seats until closing time. The attendants came round clearing the seats and as I stood up half asleep I accidentally bumped into a big bloke who was passing by. He pushed me out of his way, towards one of his mates who in turn pushed me to a third guy. There were three of them in all, laughing as they stood in a circle shoving me from one to another. They all wore dark suits, were bigger than me and I guessed a few years older, and obviously thought I was some skinny little kid they could have fun with. I put my hands up to say stop but they laughed louder and pushed harder. The odds were three to one and they did not feel any threat because although I was a boxer, I looked more like a choirboy at that age. I knew the situation was deteriorating and tried to walk away but was repeatedly pushed back until finally, I walked directly towards the biggest of the three and as he thrust his hands out to push me back, punched him crisply on the point of his chiselled chin. He went down and his pals made a grab for me in instant reaction. I butted the next in line and he fell on top of his floored friend. The third grabbed me from behind but I turned whilst unleashing the left hook I had been practising for months on the speed ball. It missed slightly so did not deliver its full force, but the glancing blow set him off on a stumble which turned into headlong flight down the corridor. One of the ballroom attendants stared agape as I smoothed my short, mod-style haircut and straightened my white Ben Sherman shirt. He shook his head slowly, smiled and said "You'd better buggar-off quick-like son"

As the congested onlookers parted and I walked down the corridor towards the exit, a dozen policemen charged in, slammed me on the floor and carried me out in handcuffs. I was fined fifty pounds with seven pounds, ten shillings costs, which I paid weekly from a wage of six pounds.

After the case when the police had heard the full story, many came forward to shake my hand and apologise. The push-me-around guys turned out to be toughs from Macclesfield and the magistrate said there were obviously extenuating circumstances to the case. He accepted that I had been provoked beyond the point of retaliation but ruled that I had used too much force in defending myself, causing several injuries. He therefore had to make an example of me 'as Blackpool relied heavily upon tourism and the town could not afford to lose income because of street violence, especially inside its most famous landmark, the Tower itself' On the drive back into Kendal I noticed that the story had already made the newsagents' billboards.

I was sitting with a few mates on the corridor floor at a dance in Kendal Town Hall, the scene of my boxing debut, one Friday night. I was pretty bored until a girl I had seen before a couple of times came out of the cloakroom door with a female friend and walked towards us. She was wearing blue jeans and a cropped red top revealing a toned and suntanned midriff. She had long, shiny, dark hair and her Latin eyes looked away when she saw us. As she passed I said "Excuse me"

She stopped and held her hair back as she looked down at me.

"I think you're beautiful" I said.

She bent closer and said softly "Pardon"

I repeated "I think you're beautiful"

She smiled and said "I think you are too" before turning away down the corridor.

I watched her small and perfectly formed figure with a smile on my face and a flutter in my heart.

Dorothy was a virginal fifteen when we met and I had just turned seventeen. She lived with her parents and younger brother in the nearby village of Burneside and worked at the sock-making factory in town. She was a factory girl who looked like a film star.

She had two elder brothers plus one who died in a car crash the year before we met, at the age of nineteen. He, Martin, was married to my cousin Margaret but we had only met briefly once or twice.

Less than a year later Dorothy and I were the parents of Stefan, born 6th August 1970, though she and I had actually split up prior to his birth and before I even knew of the pregnancy. It was something I was generally happy about and proud of and the split would probably have been temporary, but her family complicated matters and polarized us by insisting on taking me to court for a maintenance order. I had been quite prepared to pay as much as I could towards the baby's upkeep and the court actually ordered less than I had planned, but the intrusion of family and officialdom did not help our relationship.

The maintenance payments decimated my low wage and income suddenly became a priority. I was still unbeaten as a boxer and had defeated several contenders, was training towards the ABA Championships and been told that I had the punching power to be a successful professional, but packed it all in and took on as many spare time cash jobs or 'foreigners' as they are known in the North West, as I could. I was also offered a job bouncing, still at the age of seventeen, at a college disco in the Low Wood Hotel near Ambleside, which led to other such work.

Chris had been sent away to the lock-up again and when he came out he seemed determined to make a name for himself as a street fighter, possibly trying to cash in on some bouncing money. He picked a fight with me twice when I was ill with bronchitis and lost both. The second fight got serious when he kicked me in the groin, and his cousin Bruce had to pull me away from hammering him with both fists in the alley outside the Seven Stars pub, where I left him lying on the concrete. He got over it though and we remained friends despite his leaving to set up home in Santa Barbara, California, several years later. Bruce and I were good friends for a few years but eventually lost touch as we matured from youths into men and accepted the attached responsibilities. I was with him and a few others going into the Elleray Hotel in Windermere one Saturday night when a girl ran out of the door straight into us. Right behind her came a leather-clad, long-haired biker who was at least 6'4" and pushed people aside as the girl stumbled on the pavement screaming. I stood between her and the big guy with my palms

up but he took a wild swing at me. He was so tall; I was only 5'9"
that I jumped up, grabbed his lapels with both hands and butted
him in the face. He went down and the girl got up to run off across
the road. We stepped over the fallen rocker into the hotel bar. Later,
inside the dance hall, I was surrounded by half a dozen of his pals,
one of whom identified himself as the tall guy's brother. They were
from Carnforth, just over the Lancashire border, and reckoned they
were dangerous enough to ensure I did not leave town alive. Things
were looking grim but Ian, the boxing coach, was a bouncer at the
dance and came to my rescue with two or three colleagues. The bik-
ers calmed down anyway when they found out that only one person
had hit the brother and the situation dissipated. I met them again in
the same pub a few weeks later but the tall one was not present. His
brother told me he was a decent bloke generally but tended to bully
women, and that the one he was chasing that night was actually his
current girlfriend. But then he added "Mind you, you've blinded
him in one eye"

I was stunned and felt immediate remorse "I'm sorry" I said.

"Don't worry, he'll get over it"

"I suppose he'll be looking for revenge?" I asked.

"No I don't think so, you taught him a lesson he needed to learn
that night – his size doesn't frighten everybody. And he's getting on
much better with his girlfriend"

The Lake District in summer was a busy place with visitors con-
verging from all over the country. Glaswegians came on holiday in
large numbers and Liverpudlians migrated north in droves to work
in the hotels. Kendal lies within the M6 corridor and when the motorway was being built during the late 1960s the area was akin to
the Wild West with hundreds of construction workers settling there
temporarily and whooping it up on big wages. There was an excit-
ing buzz in the air and my teenage years flew past in a hedonistic
haze outside work. I knew a lot of girls and went out quite often
with Helen Rigg, whose family owned local bakery shops. She became pregnant but told me that I was not the child's father. I often
saw the lad, Alistair, when he was growing up. He had light hair,
was slender and sometimes played with Stefan, who was stocky and
dark. I did not think much more about this at the time but the topic
did come up again later in life.

Seven

"Any man's death diminishes me,
Because I am involved in mankind;
And therefore never send to know
For whom the bell tolls,
It tolls for thee"

(John Donne – Meditation XVII)

WHEN I REACHED THE age of twenty and completed my apprentice-ship I took off to see some of the world outside the UK. I had never been abroad except to Germany with my aunty Doris, uncle Walter and Marlise when I was eleven. Uncle Walter had been a tank mechanic in the German army and was taken prisoner in France in 1944. He was sent to Bela prison camp at Milnthorpe, a few miles south of Kendal and after the allied victory in Europe, was released to work as a labourer on a local farm. He met 16-year old Doris, my mother's sister who worked there as a babysitter, and her visits became more frequent afterwards. They eventually walked out together and although initially shunned by some, the budding romance blossomed to the point where Doris told her father, Jack, he who had been lost on the Somme battlefield whilst fighting the Germans, she wanted to marry the dashing young Walter, who had been a soldier since the age of 15 when he and his brother Rudi were enlisted. Rudi marched to the battle of Stalingrad with the Waffen SS but as many thousands of others, never left that hell-on-earth. The surrounded Russians lost millions of men, women and children as they and the harshness of their winter halted Hitler's Third Reich and signalled the beginning of its end.

"A Jorman prisoner" exclaimed a stunned Jack, pipe dangling from a slack jaw when his daughter first told him of her intentions.

"Yes but I love him, I'm going to marry him and if you try to stop us we'll run away"

"Oh y'will will ye, an' where will y'run tee, Jormany?"

"Maybe, maybe not, just somewhere we can be happy together"

"Well divn't mek it Jormany hinny, thez not much left o' that place these days"

She turned to leave but Jack called her back "Alreet pet, bring 'im roond to see wer on Sunda' mornin' fer a bit chat"

Sunday arrived and Doris nervously entered the living room to confront an expectant audience comprising the whole family. Silence descended as she stood before them smoothing the front of her best weekend frock.

"Well where is 'e then pet?" asked Jack encouragingly.

"He's waiting in the hall"

"Well bring 'im in hinny, bring 'im in, we'll not bite tell 'im"

She poked her head out of the door which then opened wide and a very smart, good-looking young man entered. He marched to the centre of the room, halted with a military lift of the right knee, clicked his heels together and bowed his head sharply "Hallo, I am very pleased to meets you" he said in a distinctly teutonic accent.

"Eeee" inhaled Mary Ellen, Jack's wife, as his pipe fell to the floor.

"Bloody hell" exclaimed Winnie, one of the sisters "I thought he was gonna do the Nazi salute for a second"

The shock soon dissipated though, they married, Walter got a job at the shoe factory and was a good husband. He bought an old Jaguar car, spruced it up and sorted its mechanics with my valued assistance, and drove us all the way to his hometown, Homburg where the hats originated, for a month's holiday.

I loved staying at their home near the sparrow mire, it was a haven for me where I could escape the perils of home. Doris was very keen on popular songs of the day, playing records or the radio all day long, and this fostered a lifelong love in me for 1950s music. They eventually emigrated to South Africa and were together for over 40 years until Walter's death.

Whilst saving for the holiday in Germany I happened to visit a sports day in Abbott Hall Park. On the gravel path to one side of the grassed area was a stall which caught my eye immediately. It was surrounded by brightly coloured balloons which the stallholder was filling with gas from a big red cylinder. He then handed them to their respective purchasers who promptly released them into the air. They floated high up into the stratosphere which was dotted full with balloons of all different colours, and from those which had not yet drifted too far away I could see a white card dangling. I went over to the stall and read a sign which said 'Balloon Race' – buy a balloon, write your name and address on the card and send it up into the sky. Eventually, when the balloons lost their buoyancy they would come back down to earth with the cards still attached. The print asked whoever found a card to return it to the address of the race organizer and the owner of the balloon which floated the farthest would win a prize of £50, which was a considerable sum in those days. I spent some of my savings and soon proudly clutched the string of a big green, gas-filled, racing-balloon. I watched the sky to see which direction the wind was blowing and then walked way over to the far side of the park, right to the end nearest the main street because I could see that lots of balloons were caught up in trees or against buildings. I asked mine to go as far as it possibly could but not to worry if it did not win, just try its very best like I always did except maybe at school. Then I whispered goodbye to it and let the string slide slowly through my hand. When it got to the end I held onto it for a few seconds until I felt an upward surge before finally letting go. It headed straight up and even seemed to dodge around other balloons which were not as fast as mine. I stood in the corner of the park and watched until it became a tiny little dot way up high in the distance, and finally disappeared.

Weeks went past and I forgot about the balloon race but one day a man with a trilby hat on came to our door and asked for me. My green balloon had found its way right across the sea to the city of Cork, in Ireland where Sister Conleth came from, and won the £50! I thought that was extra lucky because if Sister Conleth had found the card with my name on, she would probably have burned it.

I often thought about that balloon afterwards and about the wind direction and the others caught in the trees, and figured that if you really wanted to do something and planned it out, and did not think too much about what other people said or other stuff that could put you off, you could do quite a lot of things that might have otherwise seemed impossible.

I set off hitch-hiking one cold, frosty January morning in 1972 with Joe McFarlane, who had shoulder length hair hanging onto a broadly striped jacket and £5 in his pocket. He was penniless before we passed Manchester but made it intact to Jersey, where we planned to stay for a few weeks. The ferry crossing from Weymouth was reported in the local newspapers as the worst in forty years. The weather was heavy, the waves big and even some of the crew were hanging over the sides vomiting. The boat was tossed around so much that two passengers' cars were damaged and the ship's docking gear put out of action. As a consequence it had to bob up and down in St Helier harbour until the machinery was repaired and we could dock. I made the crossing without being sick but the harbour delay did for me. Joe had previously been in the merchant navy and was one of the very few who disembarked in full control of his stomach. We had a few beers on board, which might have counteracted the swaying of the vessel, and when crew members did the rounds handing out long, narrow bags in which to be sick, Joe put one on his head and asked where the party was. He liked Jersey and decided to hang around the beach bars at St Brelade's Bay. I carried on alone aboard the hydrofoil to St Malo, the French port where my father's elder brother, Duncan, was taken prisoner by the Germans at the start of the 1939-45 war. From there I hiked south-east across France to Paris, then to Lyon and over the Swiss border. I had received a message from a friend, Stuart Clegg, who had acquired a kitchen job at the Hotel de Nyon on the north shore of Lac Leman (Lake Geneva). I spent a couple of weeks there but he had to wait until the end of the month for his wages, so I moved along the shore to Lausanne where I also secured a job as kitchen porter.

The Restaurante Aux Trois Bonheures was owned by a Chinese family from Hong Kong and appeared to be a junction point for many independent travellers. The manager was Danish, his girl-friend French, the Chef Swiss and I worked with Domingo who was Spanish, Portugese Michel and Ruben Dario Arana de Salamanca from Bogota, Columbia, South America. I became very good friends with Ruben, pronounced Roo-ven to rhyme with hen, over the following months. He said I had the face of a revolutionary and in the photographs he showed me, his sisters looked gorgeous. We used to visit the Spanish quarter for a few drinks on our days off work and one sunny afternoon in a terrazzo tapas bar, he showed me how to get rid of unwanted tattoos. He took a pull on his cigarette until the end was bright red then simply stubbed it out on his arm, screwing it down hard into the skin. I took a gulp of Carlsberg lager mixed with Guinness, his favourite beverage, and did the same. He laughed and said I would always remember him now and he was right, the scar will always be there. He had broken his left leg in thirteen places when he crashed his motorbike into a tree in Bogota, and limped if he had been standing all day at work. He once got caught up in a fight over a disputed bill between some Scandinavians and the Chinese staff in the downstairs bar. I pulled him away amidst a hail of flying fists during which two Danes ended up in a pool of beer on the floor. The place quieted down immediately and the Norsemen retreated to the street carrying their wounded. The boss asked if I would work in the late bar every night after that when I had finished my normal duties. All I had to do was sit around, eat or drink anything I fancied and sort any trouble out. After the bar closed Ruben, Michel, myself, some of the other blokes and most of the waitresses would usually have a little party in one of the upstairs rooms.

Ruben wanted to come to the UK with me but got sacked for throwing a knife at the chef, and I never saw or heard from him again. He was last seen by Michel heading for Sweden in a Volkswagen beetle. Shortly afterwards I returned home via Jersey and found Joe hiring out deckchairs at St Brelade's, where we hung around for a week or two. He had also acquired a job in a hotel kitchen and also fallen foul of an arrogant, bad-tempered chef whom Joe described as a 'fat, beer-swilling bastard' Part of this hatred derived from the fact that the chef had fleeced Joe at poker to the tune of a few hundred pounds, and Joe felt absolutely certain that the chef was cheating and being assisted by his kitchen lackeys. We visited the staff quarters one night whilst the kitchen was in full swing, retrieved Joe's losses plus interest and dined out in the hotel restaurant on the proceeds. Joe made a point of sending his compliments to the chef. I gave him some more cash so he could get to Birmingham and see a girl he had met whilst she was in Jersey on holiday, and I flew to Bristol to see a girl, Julia Druce, whom I had met at Newquay, Cornwall, the year before when I hitchhiked down there with Robert Galt, the brother of Janis, who later married my old mate Bruce Ellison. Joe never returned to his former life in Kendal.

Arriving back home to strikes, power-cuts and a 3-day working week, I joined Buller Gilpin and Ernie Richardson who had the joinery contract on a housing site to the south of town, where we worked 7 days a week. Conditions in the building industry were so bad at the time that 150 workers were dying needlessly each year and the national building strike had not changed that fact very much. Busloads of flying-pickets toured the country and two of them, Desi Warren and Eric (Ricky) Tomlinson were eventually jailed on dubious charges relating to an alleged conspiracy and unlawful assembly at a site in Telford, west of Wolverhampton. It was widely and sensationally reported that strike-breakers were routinely assaulted and maimed throughout the land by the strikers. There was little unionism in Kendal and definitely no militancy, and trouble might have been expected upon arrival of the pickets if the rumours were to be believed. When they did arrive however, at two large sites off the town centre, they were cheered by the erstwhile strike-breakers who gratefully trooped off to the White Hart to celebrate with them.

On his release from prison Ricky was blacklisted throughout the industry and trained as an actor, eventually becoming well-known through film and television roles. Desi died in 2004 from a complaint which began in prison.

The following year, 1973, brought the climax of the miners' strike and the ongoing tragedy of their defeat.

I was out one evening, celebrating Andrew King's last night of bachelorhood with my brother Gordon, Barry Peel and a dozen or so lads from the Golden Lion, my dad's old local at the end of the market place. We were all sitting in the Fleece Inn singing silly but innocent songs, when a giant of a bloke strode up and threw a pint of beer over us all shouting "Shurrup or stand up y'noisy bastards, thez norra fuckin' man among ye"

None of us knew the guy and he obviously did not know us. I suppose if we all jumped up we could have killed him though he did have three or four meaty pals in tow, but we were so stunned that nobody moved. He shouted to his cronies "I told y'they were a bunch o' fuckin' cowards" and strutted off, laughing loudly.

We remained silently wary of the size and aggression of the bloke and I later learned he was Sid Foster, who worked for SLD Pumps and lived at Burneside. I think he was married to the sister of Brian Mitchell, who was in my class at primary school. Sid was nineteen stones and a Cumberland & Westmorland wrestler. For the uninitiated, Cumberland & Westmorland is a bit like Sumo but the guys are not as fat and do not wear the big nappy-like contraptions, they wear long-johns with embroidered underpants on the outside instead! The dress is traditional and the participants, despite their fancy fighting attire, are usually big, strong, hard-working hill-farmers.

Things calmed and we left the Fleece to resume our tour of the town's pubs, down one side of the main street and back up the other. On the return leg we stopped off at the Angel, which is across the road and down a bit from the Fleece. After a couple or so pints we started drifting back to the Lion in ones and twos, and on leaving I glanced across the road at two mini-skirted girls on the other side. I noticed a commotion down the Fleece alley and recognized one or two of the Lion lads, so walked across the road and saw monstrous Sid kneeling on the ground beating hell out of some poor soul. I could only see an arm and a leg sticking out from under Sid's smothering bulk but Karl Schwarzer was standing by and I asked who was underneath.

"Baggy" he answered, meaning Paul Bagshaw whom I had known since primary school and who could remember more jokes than any person I know.

I said "So what are you standing watching for?" grabbed Sid's hair and yanked him backwards.

Sid jumped up like a man possessed and screamed "Who the fuck was that?"

Nobody, including me, uttered a word. He shouted again, whirling around to scan the growing crowd of spectators "Who was that, I'll fuckin' kill 'im?"

After another uneasy silence Curly Hillbeck said in his slow, laconic, Cumbrian drawl "It was little Mac, 'e'll knock yer fuckin' 'ead off"

My heart sank as all eyes turned towards me, including those bulging out of big Sid's bright red face. I squared up manfully as he lumbered towards me and as he came into range, peppered his football-sized skull with a dozen or so jabs, which bloodied his nose and swelled his eye but had no other effect than to enrage him further. He roared like a bull-elephant and charged at me. There was no room to move in the narrow, crowded alleyway and he easily clamped me in a crushing bear-hug with his chin stabbing down into my throat, forcing my head back. The ribs damaged years earlier by my father felt like they were about to crack again as he squeezed hard and at the same time tried to flip me sideways off my feet. I knew that if he got me down I was beaten and probably going to get hurt so I scrambled around on the paving like a drunken Fred Astaire, trying to stay upright. As he paused to take a few deep breaths and gather himself for a re-newed effort I managed to slide my right elbow out of his grip and get the heel of my hand under his chin. The noise from the packed alley was deafening as I gradually pushed his massive head back and he stumbled just one step towards the alley wall. He steadied though and gripped hard again, but I managed to jerk his head back against the wall and land a half-power headbutt into his teeth. He growled as he spat blood into my face but his grip again gave a couple of inches. I could sense that he was beginning to weaken as I knew a man of his size must, so ducked and pushed back off him, breaking his grip altogether, and let loose with both fists hooking into his ribs. He winced, clawed at my back and then tried to cover up as the punches thudded home. He had switched from attack to defence and was now at last, ready to be beaten. I popped up from my crouch and slammed a right hand into the side of his jaw. He lurched sideways and I followed him down the alley, bouncing punches off his head until he lurched to a halt next to the rear door of the pub with his back against the wall. His head was bowed as if in defeat but his angry eyes still glowered through their brows in defiance. I walked forward and threw a six-punch combination, ending with a right uppercut under the heart. He gasped and dou-bled over, but stayed on his feet. I knew the fight was finished and did not continue the attack, but remained in battle-mode just in case he rallied. Instead he put a palm up and spluttered that he'd had enough. I relaxed immediately, watched him warily for a few seconds, then turned and walked back up the alley, now more con-cerned about my appearance and feeling ashamed as always, that I had been fighting on the streets in public. The cheering crowd parted as I passed with head down and many hands clapping me on the back. I sat alone in total silence on the stone steps of my old home in the corner of the market place until perspiration and heartbeat slowed, then went into the Lion where I was hailed a hero and inundated with free beer. At the time I was eleven and a half stones, seven and a half lighter than Sid, and five inches shorter.

Barry Peel, who had accompanied us that night, was originally from Rawtenstall in Lancashire but by then married to Brenda Gill and domiciled on Hallgarth. He was a Lion regular, a friend, and a very tough customer. He came to the area with a construction company, decided to stay and by the mid-1960s was a plant driver working on the construction of the M6 motorway. He met there two fellow drivers, Big Glen (or more accurately 'Gren' for Grenville) Rose, a fighting man renowned throughout the North, and Malcolm Price from Merthyr Tydfil, South Wales, now a virtual working-class legend throughout the whole of Britain. Both were big, muscular and powerful men with Glen the tallest at just over 6'2"

In his book 'Street Warrior' Price describes how he knocked out Glen in the Dunhorse pub, Kendal, with a hefty punch. Price was an ex-boxer and I think this simple knockout impressed Glen with the dangerous ability of the genre, because several years later, Glen paid me for a time as his bodyguard or 'minder' though I think this may have also been a tactical move on Glen's part because at the age of sixteen, when Glen was twenty six, my brother Gordon had the courage to fight him. Gordon had gotten into some bother at a dance in the Parish Hall, had already fought off one bouncer, Melvin Crawford, but the most feared man in the area had been summoned to sort things out. He beat Gordon but I, at the age of fourteen, warned Glen that night that I would come looking for him one day, after he hit my brother when he was already down. Glen was unfortunate enough to have to live up to the reputation he had carved out for himself, as a man of extreme violence who had inflicted serious injury upon many, but I later discovered that in reality, he was also a relatively compassionate and generous bloke.

Malcolm Price was also twelve years older than I, but I got to know him as an acquaintance through his association with Barry. He also had a cumbersome reputation to maintain and obviously took this duty seriously. When I first saw him it was at Kendal's Town Hall dance, shortly after he arrived in the area. He was chasing a terrified victim, David Thexton; farmer Thexton's son, across the floor until David ran into a girl, Carol Hine, and fell down on top of her. Pricey hit David a few times on the floor and probably Carol as well but David, not at all a fighting man, managed to regain his feet.

73

A crowd had gathered though, blocking his escape route and Price threw some more punches at him. From where I was standing, up on the balcony and too far way to help, none of those punches actually landed and I have to say that it was probably because Malcolm was swinging wildly in the roundhouse manner and not at all like a trained boxer. I was however, relieved for David's sake because Price was undoubtedly capable of killing a normal non-combatant with his pile-driver punches and uncompromising mental approach. The second time I ran into Malcolm was in the Cock & Dolphin pub in Kendal, where I had gone with Howard Rainey to speak with ex-pro welterweight champion, Jack McCabe, originally from Bamber Bridge, Lancashire, who was the landlord.

Howard was an ex-heavyweight of note who had been an Olympic reserve and once beat Al 'Blue' Lewis, who fought Muhammad Ali in Ireland. He was originally from Sheffield, Yorkshire but his boxing career took him to London where he fought for the famous Fitzroy Lodge club as a youth. After retirement from the ring he moved north again and settled for several years in Ambleside, Cumbria, where he revived the small boxing club behind the Golden Rule pub and where we became friends after he called round to my house one day. Howard was a big, amiable man who did not worry about reputations and valued friendship more than respect. He coaxed me out of retirement by paying me from expenses and I had several more fights, winning all of them until the last. Other considerations were then more important and I had decided to retire again after one more contest, in Manchester. At the weigh-in though my opponent's trainer recognized me from earlier campaigns and withdrew his man. I was both disappointed and relieved, and adjourned to the bar to celebrate retirement again. As I started my third pint Howard rushed over and said he had found a substitute. I told him I'd had a few beers but he said that was ok as the sub did not have my experience, that I would have to go easy on him and definitely not unleash a right hand – he had promised the opposing trainer. Foolishly I agreed and entered the ring after finishing the pint, feeling slightly the worse for wear. My new opponent, a black kid called Manderson, rushed out at the bell swinging leather. I easily evaded his charge, backed him into a corner and was about to curtail proceedings when I noticed Howard waving frantically from ringside and remembered his instructions. I hesitated, took a step backwards and Manderson saw his opening. He landed a big right on my jaw and down I went. I stupidly jumped straight up, missed him with two punches that would have knocked him cold if they had landed, and he caught me again with a jolter. This time I rose to one knee and composed myself during the 8-count. When I stood he rushed in again but I clipped him with a left hook to the chin. His initial impetus carried him forward though, careening into me, and we both fell ignominiously to the canvas. 'Last one up's a cissy' I thought, recalling Max Baer's reported quip during his 1934 world heavyweight title win over Primo Carnera. Scrambling to our feet we resumed hostilities but the inexperienced referee jumped in and wrongly invoked the three-knockdown rule, awarding the fight to Manderson amid a near-riot amongst the spectators. I was angry but knew it was my own fault, well mostly anyway. It was not a spectacle I felt proud of and wish my ring career could have ended more appropriately, but that's life I guess.

As we entered the almost empty and silent lounge bar of the Cock & Dolphin we saw Malcolm at the far end of the room. He was alone, shuffling around in a corner shadow-boxing and other customers seemed too afraid to even speak amidst a very strained atmosphere. We were a little surprised and watched the performance whilst standing at the bar. Howard eventually shook his head and laughed "Well, I've seen it all now"

Malcolm looked over and seemed to be aware of our presence for the first time. We stared back at him until he sidled over and said, in the accent of South Wales "I suppose you think I looked stu-pid over there do you?"

I nodded as Howard answered "That sorta thing doesn't do much good for the reputation of boxin' if that's what it was supposed to be"

Rainey was several inches taller than Price but Malcolm looked up at him with a gaze that conveyed an intention to kill. Howard stared right back and stood up to his full height.

"Yous two done a bit have you?" asked Malcolm with his eyes flicking between mine and Howard's.

I do not think for a moment that Pricey has ever been really frightened of anybody in his life, apart from possibly his father Les, but he was wary and made the decision that day not to pursue the matter further. He relaxed, became relatively affable, and we had quite an amusing conversation about his shadow boxing-skills and lifelong interest in ornithology. As many others, his preferred path in life had been distorted by unfortunate circumstance.

"By the way" said Howard as we prepared to leave after finding out that Jack was away for the day "That left hand needs a bit of work, why don't you come down to the gym and let Bob here sharpen it up for ya?"

Pricey said he would and we arranged to pick him up from his digs on Kirkbarrow where he lived with his girlfriend, Pat. He was not in though when we called, and never did make it to the gym – probably forgot or found something better to do.

Howard, who was a qualified plumber, and I, took on some extra building work together when the boss of a small building company, Tony Walker, also from Hallgarth, asked us to build steel-reinforced bases for some houses at Bowston, near Burneside. As we completed them over several weekends another builder, George Colby, asked if I could find him a plasterer.

"Why don't we do it?" asked Howard enthusiastically.

"Er, 'cos neither of us is a plasterer?" I answered.

"No but I've done it before" he said and eventually convinced me to give it a go, him plastering and me labouring to him. We went to the site and discussed money with George, an ex-farmer:

"Weel tha knows, I wasn't plannin' on payin' a reet lot ferrit, things bein' what they is these days"

"Well we're not doin' it fer nowt George" I countered.

"Nay, nay, course thas nut but let's keep it civilized is all a'm sayin' We don't wanna be robbin' each other now do we lads eh, tha knows? We're all wukkin lads"

"What y'got in mind George?"

"Well, I was thinkin' about three 'undred fert' lot"

"Four 'undred"

"Three twenny-five"

"Three seventy-five"

"Three fifty"

"What about tax?" I asked.

"Nay nay lad I disn't bother wi' tax an' seck-like tranklements, it'll be cash in 'and tha knows, pound notes"

I fell silent for a moment as if struggling with a decision I was already happy with, but Howard must have misread the situation "A'll tell y'what" he suddenly announced thrusting out his plate-sized hand "We'll do it fer three-thirty"

George and I looked at Howard in surprise, then at each other in bewilderment before he grabbed the massive fist with both of his own "Done" he smiled.

At least Howard proved he could plaster and we finished the work without a problem. He eventually returned to London where he became a full-time professional trainer, and coached Colin McMillan to a world title which he unfortunately lost due to a serious shoulder injury. Pricey ultimately returned to Merthyr to pen his memoirs but David Thexton, whilst working at a local factory in preference to pursuing his trade as a bricklayer, climbed onto the factory roof to retrieve a cricket ball and fell through it to his death.

Glen Rose, who over the years became a friend and upon whom I did not exact the revenge that I had long planned, sadly died of cancer. During the year before his fatal illness was discovered, I had occasion to issue a stern warning to one Philip James, an instructor of the Korean martial-art, Tae-Kwon-Do, who held a 7th grade black-belt in that discipline. Several of his sycophantic followers had embroiled themselves in an argument with my brother John, during which one of them made the provocatively stupid statement that a martial artist could beat any boxer. This childish, alcohol-fuelled banter took a serious turn when my name was mentioned in comparison to the awesome fighting skills of their leader, Phil. Although he was a few years younger than me I knew him because we both trained at the Lads' Club gym off Sandes Avenue, he doing his high-pitched instructing in the deadly arts and me just pounding away at the heavy bag in the corner. I had a discreet word with him regarding the behaviour of his companions but made the mistake of doing it in the presence of one of them. Phil obviously felt that he had to protect his reputation, that ubiquitous stumbling block, and display some bravado in issuing a virtual challenge to me. I arranged to meet him at the gym early the following Sunday morning, when all was quiet. We would both bring £500 cash, a paltry sum considering the risks involved but the most he would agree to, and the winner would take all. No rules of engagement would apply and the fight would end when one protagonist was either dead or unconscious, or verbally submitted. I knew that Phil would not show alone and so asked Glen to attend and ensure there was no interference.

On the preceding Friday evening I was out with my wife, sister and her husband, and called into the Chinese carryout in Stramongate. The place was packed but we found a seat on the bench as we waited for our meals. I suddenly noticed Phil pushing his way through the crowd towards me and tensed to repel an attack, but he put his hands out in a gesture of peace and sat down beside me "Mac" he said "I'm not comin' on Sunday"

"Well I think that's a sensible decision Phil" I opined "Any particular reason?"

"I've bin asking around about you, and I don't think it's a good idea for me"

"That's fair enough Phil, what about the money?"

"Please don't make that a problem, I've backed out publicly an' that's enough humiliation"

"Ok Phil, we'll say no more about it, just make sure y'keep a rein on yer pals"

"Thanks Mac, I will"

I forgot about the matter immediately but unfortunately, also forgot to tell Glen the fight was off. He went down to the gym as arranged and then up to the house to see if we had changed the date. I felt bad about not showing him sufficient respect to update him on events, and apologized to him for that.

The next time we met at the gym Phil watched me on the bag for a while, which I found a little disconcerting, before asking if I could teach him how to punch correctly. He said that three of his protégés had recently been in high level competition and all had made it quite easily, to the final of their weight divisions. In each of the finals though, the Kendal competitors met opponents from a club in Preston, Lancashire, and all lost against them. Phil's pupils were undoubtedly better at long-range fighting he reported, where they could use kicks but as soon as the Lancastrians got inside which they inevitably did, they pulverized their opponents with short, stabbing punches just like the ones he had seen me throwing at the bag. He discovered that the Preston fighters were all ex-amateur boxers from a club in Bamber Bridge, quite possibly the one where Jack McCabe began his illustrious career.

In my experience boxers usually take up the sport to channel their aggression because they can fight, whereas martial artists often start training because they cannot fight and wish to learn how to, after watching ridiculously staged films, the action in which would be suicidal against even an accomplished street-fighter. Actions and movements can be learned to a degree but what actually makes a true warrior, that which goes on in his head and his heart, cannot be. It's a matter of genetics.

I happened to watch the World Karate Championships on tv one evening. There I witnessed some of the best martial-artists on the globe pawing, pirouetting and cuffing at each other in contests which invariably ended in floor-level scuffling, in exactly the same manner as can be seen outside many British pubs at closing time. One idiot expressed his opinion that 7-stone Bruce Lee (primarily an actor) if still alive would easily beat 17-stone Muhhammad Ali (a professional world heavyweight boxing champion!!) If poor Bruce was still alive I fear it would not be for very long, if his fate was left in the hands of his adoring but misguided fans. A very tall Japanese martial arts expert was once pitched against Ali in a 1970s televised contest. Ali quickly frightened his bigger opponent with a flurry of fast punching and he fell to the canvas from where he contented himself with trying to kick Ali's legs, without even attempting to rise or fight in any effective way. The embarrassing debacle continued with Ali appealing to the Jap to at least show some manful opposition, until it was mercifully curtailed and thankfully forgotten.

The misconceptions continue purely because of the film industry, which can make fictitious scenarios rivetingly-interesting to a large percentage of the world's population, and turn otherwise boring, untalented people into film stars!

Fighting in competition is not a thing which is done for fun or enjoyment, it is too painful and physically demanding for that. At its highest levels it is done invariably, after fame has lost its importance, for money, and anybody who does not earn money from it is not at the highest level. The fighters who are paid by far the most to exhibit their skills and excite audiences with their gladiatorial prowess, are boxers. If a fighter is not a boxer – he is undoubtedly a lesser being.

Eight

"Travel broadens the mind
We'd heard it said
So set off cycling
To the Med"

(Author – 2007)

MY FATHER'S MOTHER WAS from a renowned Glasgow family, the Lockharts, but it is thought she might have inherited a percentage of gypsy blood from somewhere along her lineage. She read palms and tea leaves, was a small-time money lender and the driving force behind her family's move south from Scotland after her husband Duncan came home from the Great War. Perhaps it was the nomadic wanderlust in her bloodline that imbued me with the sometimes overwhelming urge to roam, that I have always felt. I have learned to stay put at various times in my life because not to would have compromised its overall quality and dictated who I might spend it with. Remaining in one place, one job or one relationship for a long period has never been easy for me, and I have always sought some other interest or occupation to curb my tendencies to break free. I acknowledge grudgingly, that wandering aimlessly around the world is not a valued asset in a husband or partner. However, after my first trip abroad the urge was stronger than ever and before the year was out I was off again, this time with Stuart Clegg who was as much a wanderer as I and had returned from his adventures in Switzerland.

I had known Stuart since we were both twelve and first heard him before I saw him, belting out a drum solo from his attic room at Ferney Green. We became good friends and by mutual commiseration plus backing tracks from Bob Dylan, helped each other through the difficult early teen years. His father died around this time, leaving his only son to grow up in an all-female household with his mother Annie, two older sisters and one younger, also named Anne. I never realized until recently how the untimely loss of his father had probably affected him.

We were both cycling to keep fit in the early 1970s, both up for any challenge and bored with Kendal, and decided to go to Morocco – by pushbike!

We set off in December and reached Wigan before replenishing our energy with a few pints after pitching camp. We got into the routine of pedalling for a few days then catching a train to some agreed point on the map. We crossed to Calais on the ferry, rode through Paris and south towards the Spanish border, camping at Perpignan. Then up and over the Pyranees, during the descent of which I fell off being slightly drunk, and sustained some cuts and bruises before catching a train from Barcelona to Valencia. From there we spun south through the costas, camping on beaches and drinking local wines for a few pennies per bottle. We swam in the Med on my 21st birthday. Most of the time we had no idea nor cares about even what day it was, and life just passed quietly by without burdening us with any of its problems. By the time we reached Marbella cycling had become not our favourite mode of transport and we caught another train ride to the industrial port of Algeciras, the most southerly major port on the Spanish mainland. Tarifa is a few miles further south but nowhere near as big or busy. The Spanish trains were alive with squawking chickens, children selling bric-a-brac from the corridors and platforms and even the odd goat or two sharing a cabin with us. We obviously looked rough after being out on the road so long, but always smiled and people invariably smiled back. One old woman asked Stuart to hold a small pink pig wrapped in a blanket, which she had been rocking on her knee like a baby. He obliged graciously but I don't think he enjoyed that experience too much. Looking out of the windows we could see black-clad women washing clothes in streams, picking fruit, toiling in the dry, dusty red soil and loading the produce of their labour onto the backs of small grey donkeys. Motor vehicles were rare away from the cities and towns. Spain was perhaps taking its first tentative steps towards the thriving economy it enjoys today, but was still very much in the unyielding grip of General Franco's dictatorship. Spain had been discovered though, and tourists were beginning to bring much-needed income to the holiday resorts springing up from the arid wastes of Andalusia and dozens of coastal villages.

We cycled triumphantly round to La Linea and up to the gated border with Gibraltar. When attempting to cross however, we were stopped by armed guards because the border had recently closed as part of Spain's dispute with the UK over dominion of the Rock. So back we pedalled to Algeciras and tried to sail to Tangier in Morocco, but the Moroccan border authorities on board ship would not allow us to embark, describing us with distaste as "hippies" We did look a bit road-weary. Eventually we sailed to the Spanish-controlled port of Ceuta, nestling several miles east of Tangier under the shadow of Mount Hacho. The town lies on the northern tip of the peninsula stretching out towards the Rock, between which points there was obviously a land bridge at some pre-historic time, before the Atlantic rose to divide the two by forming the Straits of Gibraltar, or the Estrecho de Gibraltar as the Spanish prefer. From Ceuta we travelled overland by bus to Tangier but on the outskirts of Ceuta we had to get off, walk a few yards over the Moroccan border and then reboard. As we trudged from one country to the other, a stunningly beautiful arab girl who was standing watching us said something to me which I did not understand. I shrugged and she said in broken English "Do you know the time?" She reached out and gently touched my left hand, which I turned so she could see the face of my watch. She smiled and nodded but did not let go. I smiled back and she whispered "Are you American?"

I said "No, British"

She looked up at me through half-closed lids and I realized Stuart was staring at her with his mouth half-open.

The bus driver shouted at us and revved his rickety engine.

I whispered "We gotta go"

She took half a pace forward, reached up and kissed me very gently on the lips. I was keen to develop the situation but the bus was starting to move with Stu hanging from the doorway.

I returned her kiss, turned and jogged for the bus. She stood watching as we pulled away, motionless, beautiful, not smiling now.

"Jesus" Stu said as I plonked down next to him on the torn and dusty seat "She was gorgeous"

"Was she ever" I said "Think she was on the game?"

Before we left Spain and were killing time until our ship sailed, we drank local wine in a small rural bar not far from the port, and got slightly drunk. We were discussing the relative plight of the Spanish people who, under Franco's rule had apparently missed out on the whole of the 1960s social revolution, and at the very mention of his name the locals became quiet and left us alone in a dark corner. However, we did get a few smiles on leaving when we said loudly "Adios, amigos y hermanos, Franco es un porco gordo, viva Espana" meaning something vaguely like 'Goodbye friends and brothers, Franco is a fat pig, long live Spain'

By now we were so sick of pedalling or even pushing our bikes that Stu seriously considered an offer from a campesino on the roadside who wanted to swap his donkey "Well it's got four legs hasn't it?" Stu reasoned "You just have to lead it along with all the bags on it"

He had a valid point but we decided against. It might have been fun but slow and difficult to get the animal on trains, boats etc. Just as we were considering these grave problems over a bottle of wine in the town square, seven or eight children sidled over. Their unanimous opinion was that the bike way out-valued the donkey for fun, and they obviously admired our machines with all the fancy equipment and camping gear hanging off them. After a while they were called to go "comer" pronounced com-err (to eat) and trudged away waving back at us. We watched in silence until they reached the corner which took them out of sight into the village. Just before they disappeared Stu nodded at his bike and said "Whadya think?"

"Why not?" I answered.

He shouted after the kids, who stopped on the corner. He waved them back and started off-loading his gear onto my bike before wheeling his machine over to stand it gleaming and unburdened in front of the children, who stood looking confusedly from him to the bike. "Howd'ya say it?" he asked.

I said to the kids "Es para usted" (It's for you)

The children babbled excitedly amongst themselves but would not touch the bike. Stu took one of the kids hands and placed it on the crossbar, repeating "Es para usted"

The kid asked "Para mi?"

I answered "Para todos" gesturing to encompass all the children present.

The babbling started again and they all gathered round the bike. Eventually, after much reassurance from us and incredulity from them, they were convinced and communally wheeled the bike off like a prize bull to the ring, amid shouts of "Muchas gracias senors, viva Inglaterra" (Many thanks gentlemen, long live England) I think word of our exit from the bar the previous night had spread.

We settled back to finish the wine but about twenty minutes later at least thirty adults came marching into the square from the village, pushing the bike before them and leading a flock of sheepish children behind. They strode directly up to us as we lounged on the ornate fountain steps and presented the bike with dramatic, open-hand gestures and heads held high like matadors. Some of the kids were crying and it soon became clear that the adults thought they had stolen the bike from us. We shook our heads and said "No, es para los ninos, un regalo" (No, it is for the children; a gift)

The kids stopped crying and looked up at the adults, who stopped gesturing and looked confused. A deeper-toned babbling ensued but we finally convinced everybody that Stu had given the bike to the kids and would not take it back. The adult confusion turned to extreme surprise, then smiles of appreciation as they shook our hands before marching off again across the square. We assumed that was the end of the matter but just as we drained the last drop of wine, the whole parade wheeled round the corner again straight for us. This time they were carrying meat, bread, fruit, and lots more wine. Some of the older women carried kitchen chairs and cushions to sit on. They made it clear the food was for us to take on our journey but we refused it at first saying "No es necessario" but finally agreed to accept if they would all stay and share it with us. We sat around the fountain with the old ladies to the front so they could see what was going on and ask lots of questions. The commotion attracted others and before long virtually the whole village was camped out in the square, including the local policeman who had a large pistol strapped to his waist in a brown leather holster, and who shook our hands at least four times each when we agreed that Real Madrid was a fantastico football club. A party atmosphere developed with everybody chatting, neighbour to neighbour, relative to relative, friend to friend, but when Stu or I tried to answer a question or say something in Spanish they all stopped and listened intently, and applauded loudly whether they understood or not, which would have been most of the time. We ate, drank, laughed and talked about the different worlds we lived in, and at that time we certainly did, till long after midnight. Some of them even came down to the harbour the following day to give us more food and wave us off.

I sold my bike to a bloke in Ceuta, and when we got off the bus in Tangier we sold most of our camping gear too. We were sick of camping almost as much as cycling and digs were cheap in North Africa. We stayed for about a month down by the docks and got to know quite a few locals, including the guy next door when he wailed to Mecca each morning from the flat roof between us.

As we left our room one morning a kid of about ten kept pace alongside us with a tray round his neck like a cinema ice-cream seller. On the tray were little wraps of chewing gum, sweets and single cigarettes, and he asked in broken English if we wanted to buy something. I said no it was too early in the morning but flipped a coin onto his tray anyway. He danced away and must have told his friends because soon we had an entourage of little ice-cream sellers trooping along behind, but they disappeared when we entered a café and the waiters chased them. Next morning the same kid joined us again and chattered away as we walked along the quayside. He had·a slight limp and his name was Azu. He hobbled along smiling, talking animatedly, whistling pop tunes and gave us some chewing gum. Apparently the coin I had given him was worth not far short of his weekly earnings, though I did not realize that at the time. We took him to the same café and calmed the waiter when he tried to chase him. We bought him a big breakfast and he sat with pride and pleasure on his face as we treated him with respect and importance – obviously an approach he was unused to and I knew how that felt. He was still with us that night when we went for a restaurant meal and later slept outside our door on the ceramic tiles. We invited him to sleep on the floor inside but he would not, saying it would be disrespectful, and eventually started sleeping outside our window on the communal wailing-roof. We gave him blankets and a pillow and let him use the shower in the mornings when he got up, which was always at least an hour before us. One hot afternoon as we trudged along the harbour and he skip-hobbled about twenty yards in front of us, bodies darted from the shadows of an alley. A gang of older youths grabbed him, pinned him against a wall and rifled through his pockets. The youths were startled when we came hurtling down the street and ran off leaving Azu on the ground.

"You ok?" I asked.

He looked up with his big gappy-toothed grin and nodded, so we picked him up between us and carried him down the street on our shoulders.

When we told him we were leaving he cried and said he would save up his money to come to "Hingland" and we would have taken him with us if it was possible to get him across the borders, maybe get his leg sorted and give him a better start in life. But it was not. We gave him £20 towards his savings anyway, which was a small fortune to him. He stood on top of the dockside wall hanging onto a broken flagpole, crying and waving until we were out of sight on a ship taking us to Gibraltar. I hope he did ok.

We got a room above Smokey Joe's Café, just off Main Street, dumped our gear and wandered around for a while. The landlady of the Horseshoe pub offered me a few pounds to be around when the Ark Royal docked later that week, as the three thousand strong crew had been at sea for six months and their landfall was likely to ignite a certain liveliness on the streets. Stu collected glasses and we carried on doing odd jobs there for quite a while, even after the nervously anticipated landing. Actually things were quite dull apart from the odd boisterous frolic, and there was no trouble at all at the Horseshoe. The shore patrols trawled the streets from about two in the morning onwards, gathering drunk and incapable sailors and recording allegations of their damage to bars and restaurants.

One lazy Saturday afternoon we were sauntering down Main Street without a care in the world when I saw a familiar, fuzzy-haired head bobbing along in the crowd on the other side of the road. I said to Stu "Christ that's Golly isn' it?"

Stu looked in the direction I was pointing and we both shouted "Golly"

The fuzzy head turned round but so did a hundred others, and was soon lost in the throng.

It did not seem to bother anyone at the time, least of all him, that he was called 'Golly' shortened from 'Gollywog' because of his afro-style haircut and swarthy complexion. His real name was David Scarboro, from Windermere, eight miles north of Kendal and he was wholly English as far as he knew. We were not sure it had been him but later in the day on our way back to Smokey Joe's, we bumped right into him on the street. After initial surprise we all headed for the Horseshoe. Golly asked where we were staying and his nose wrinkled when we told him. He said he could get us a better place for free and we would also be doing him a favour. Our new residence turned out to be a yacht moored in the harbour. It was not seaworthy but was comfortable, complimentary, and had all the facilities we needed. It, in return, needed protection from thieves attempting to steal it or parts from it. The vessel obviously did not belong to Golly and we didn't pursue the issue of ownership or entitlement, but manfully provided security by lying out on deck in the sun with a never ending supply of lager from the marina shop. Our favourite line with the ladies that summer was "Would you like to come back to our yacht for a drink?"

I had thought about Dorothy and the baby for some time. Were they ok? Were they managing financially? I had not paid any maintenance since being away. Did they need anything – did they need me? Was the baby healthy? Had Dorothy found someone else and what would my feelings be if she had? I had to face the fact that I was likely to feel guilty and unhappy. Once that reality had been established, I had to assess what I was doing and what effects my actions might be having now and in the future, with regard to what I truly wanted from life.

We were lying up on deck in the late afternoon, half asleep as we bravely guarded the yacht from any passing pirates. The sun was dipping in the west, seagulls chattered in the distance and the boat swayed and creaked gently on still water. Other vessel-owners had enquired about our security services and our languorous life could have gone on, probably for years if we had wished it to. I took a long sip of lukewarm lager and said "I'm goin' back"

After a long pause Stu took an even longer swig and replied "Thought we were goin' to India?"

"Maybe next year" I lied.

When I made my decision I did not know whether Stu was going home with me, but a few days later there we both were, all packed, a note left for Golly along with my transistor radio which I forgot to take, and ready to go.

Back in Kendal I started work on the Fellside Flats site and resumed the rugby training I had started to maintain fitness when I retired from boxing. I was quick and agile but never sufficiently interested or weighty enough to be valued as a player, and therefore content to trundle around in the lower teams. I did however, once run four tries in for the second team whilst playing loose forward. I was dropped the following week when other players returned from their Christmas break so never took the game seriously after that.

Soon in the social whirl again I was invited to a nurses' party at a house near the hospital at the top of Captain French Lane. I went into town first and had a few pints with Irish Tommy Lynott, with whom I set off to the party later in the evening, each of us buying a four-pint can of beer on the way. Just inside the house lobby they had a table set up like an admissions desk. All very orderly and efficient. We put our cans down on the table, smiled at the unattractive nurse behind it and went through to the party. But the party was not very party-like with only twenty or so people there, the majority being blokes who were standing around talking football and car engines. I made the quick decision to leave and looked for Tommy but he had disappeared, so headed for the door, picking up my can of beer from where it still stood on the table. The girl said with an attractive lisp "Sorry but you can't take that"

I said "I just put it here thirty seconds ago"

She replied "I know but you can't take it back once you've handed it in"

I looked into her eyes and knew that here was a person who lived by rules, any rules, and that further discussion would prove pointless. I turned again for the door "Watch me"

A few yards down the road two blokes came running after me "You're not taking that" said one and made a grab for the can.

I moved to avoid him and he threatened "Don't fack as around bampkin"

He sounded like a southerner and I think a little smile flickered across my face as he stepped forward and made another grab for the beer. I nutted him between the eyes without letting go of the can. When he got up they both retreated to the house and I went on my way. A few seconds later the door crashed open again and half a dozen figures came running out, silhouetted against the full moon just peeking over the top of Gillingate Hill. This time I put the can on the ground as they encircled me, and for a moment it felt as if we were going to dance round our handbags in true northern tradition. The ensuing fracas did in fact take the form of a dance

Robert MacGowan

as they all came at me at once, and I grabbed the nearest collar and held its owner at arm's length in front of me, using him as a shield. In the surging melee I went with the flow as much as possible to save strength and energy whilst they pushed, pulled, swung and kicked but hit each other most of the time. I hung on, going with each surge and floating around in a violent moonlit waltz. My feet were moving fast, maintaining balance so that every time a face appeared in front of me I was in position to throw a quick punch at it whilst still hanging onto the heaving throng. This went on for a few minutes, me knocking them down, they getting up and me knocking them down again as I bobbed, weaved and hooked to the rhythm in my head. The whirling mob began to thin out. I did not feel tired nor any pain but I did feel sweat, or what I thought was sweat, running into my eyes. I wiped the moisture away with the back of my hand and it came away dark in the dim evening light. I realized it was blood and that what our twirling feet were crunching around on was broken glass strewn across the road. With adrenalin pumping through my bloodstream, mind and body in battle mode, I had not even felt the blows but my attackers had smashed several bottles which scarred me forever, over my head. When I realized this I started to get angry. The dance was over. As I started throwing punches with real force the little army fell over itself in hasty retreat back to the nurses' house, locking the door behind them. All went silent as the blood dripped from my chin onto the new suede shoes I had bought in Puerto Banus. I walked to the garden across from the house and pulled a revolving clothes dryer from its ground-socket. Using it as a lance I jabbed several holes in the cheap front door and then speared it through the lounge window. I was planning further vengeful mayhem but the female screams of panic from within brought me to a halt. I stood a few moments, becoming aware that surrounding windows were open and the spectacle had been witnessed by many, before turning back down the hill. As I picked up the can of beer I heard footsteps running and turned wearily to face an attack once again. But it was Brian, Tommy's mate who was manager at Grosvenor House Papers in Stramongate. He had been at the party and pulled me into a nearby garden, whispering hoarsely that the police were on their way. We hid under a low tree as the siren wailed into earshot and its accompanying light flashed blue over Beast Banks. The van

89

stopped outside the riddled door and two officers got out, looking around warily with their batons drawn. The van's radio crackled in the background. We stayed under the bush, giggling like school-boys playing hide-and-seek as the policemen looked at the shards of glass in the road, the damaged house, talked briefly to the occupants and then drove off. I said I was going home but Brian took me to the nearby hospital. When we entered the waiting area I thought there had been a major car crash or some other disaster. There was standing room only though I was offered a seat, which I declined. Eleven men and one woman waited in the room with assorted black eyes, cuts, bruises, split lips and missing teeth, but I did not realize until Brian told me, that they were all from the nurses' party. All were very respectful and apologetic. The woman was horrified when she saw the bloody state I was in and vigorously berated her wounded companions, who sat with their heads down. Multiple lacerations had covered my head and shoulders almost completely in blood which was now caked dry. Silence returned to the room as a nurse entered and asked if I had been in the same accident as the rest of her casualties. All eyes turned to me hopefully as I nodded "Yes" They were well aware that I could have had them prosecuted. After the glass was removed and some hair shaved off, over forty stitches were inserted into my scalp.

Nine

"When I recall the joys of being a father
There really is nothing that I'd rather
Mostly I think, being a dad
Is extremely good, not bad"

(Author – 2007)

ON RETURNING TO KENDAL I heard that Dorothy was seeing some-one so did not interfere nor try to contact her. I was disappointed but glad that she may have found happiness. However, shortly after the nurses' party and when my shaved hair had nearly grown back, I was sitting in the White Hart having a quiet drink on my own prior to a date when she came in with a bloke called Somers, whose brother I knew from Grammar School. They sat at the other side of the room but she kept looking over and smiling, and looked more beautiful than ever. I smiled back and just as I was about to leave they both came over, sat down and started chatting. I thought they were just being friendly until Somers went to the bar and Dorothy kissed me passionately on the mouth. I kissed her back with enthu-siasm and Somers must have realized that there were still serious feelings between us because he disappeared.

We started going out again and this time it felt right. I was living in a town flat but Dorothy would not move in until we were mar-ried, and I wanted to marry her. She'd had her name on the council housing list since Stefan was born and fortunately was offered one a few months later on Hallgarth. When it was clear we had some-where to live I asked her to marry me and she agreed. We married in the summer of 1974 when she was twenty, I was twenty two and Stefan was four.

Married life started out relatively well. We improved the house, bought a car, went on holidays and did the things that families do. Life was normal and I was content but the urge to wander, to experience and discover was still with me. One avenue of escape from life's routine was the drawing which I had always loved to do. After re-decorating the house we needed pictures for the walls and sought something different or original. On seeing high-street prices I decided to do some ink sketches of local buildings and on taking them to the Kirkland art shop for framing, the owner asked if he could buy them. Pictures of old, historic Kendal apparently sold well to the many thousands of tourists who visited the town each year en-route to the Lakes. I continued supplying him at a meagre profit to myself and a local pet-shop owner, George Stobbart, saw some in the window. George asked me to do an oil painting of a deceased trail-hound he had owned 'Gun Runner' whose race earnings had paid for his house on Fellside. I did the portrait from a creased photograph and framed it for him. He liked it so much that he put it on show in his own shop window in Highgate, opposite the Kendal Bowman pub. The following stream of enquiries led to an ever-increasing backlog of commissions including portraits of dogs, cats, budgies, babies, horses, houses and even the local prostitute, Mary O'Neill. Several older people brought in black and white photographs of deceased pets and asked if I could do oil paintings from them. For one elderly lady I produced a coloured portrait of her beloved black and tan terrier. She cried when she saw it and said I had brought the little fella back to life for her. After that I became quite expert at the task. As I sold everything to order we still had no pictures on the walls but as I had now started painting in oils, I completed example portraits of Dorothy, some of her family, Stefan, and my parents. This led to a third avenue of income in addition to the ink drawings and joinery work.

At that point art did in fact interest me far more than building, with which I had become bored but which was still my main source of income. Though very time-consuming I was loathe to give up painting and drawing and many thought it was what I should really have been concentrating on, instead of 'wasting my time knocking nails in' I spent a period producing as many pictures as I could to supply the art shop, near the Cock & Dolphin, selling ink drawing copies directly to the tourists, oil and ink portraits to individual customers, and exhibiting at local galleries. An oil portrait of my brother John wearing a faded denim jacket brought critical acclaim locally and commissions, when accepted for exhibition at my first attempt by the prestigious Lake Artists' Society summer show in Grasmere. Things were going pretty well and I was able to gradually increase my prices, but the lack of regular income with Stefan still young and Dorothy only working part-time, eventually drove me back to the building sites. The acclaim and success of my artwork though, prevented me from taking joinery or construction as seriously as I needed to, for many years. Life steered me in a different direction and ultimately I am glad that it did, but even now I often wonder how far that initial drive would have taken me had I been able to sustain it for long enough to establish a career. My determination and capacity for work would surely have earned me a reasonable living.

I was content to remain at home during most of my spare time where I enjoyed being with Stefan and Dorothy and we went for a considerable period without even a disagreement, then one day we fell out over something trivial, had a mild argument and she took off to her mother's house. I could not believe that she would leave home over something so minor that a few weeks later neither of us could remember what it was, and made the mistake of allowing her back without a word. Taking off to her mother's thereafter became a weapon she used regularly to get her own way. It gradually caused serious damage to our relationship and I think also to Stefan's perception of life and family unity. Once, when he was still at junior school and we were on holiday in Spain he said "Dad why can't it always be like this?"

We were sitting on the harbour wall looking out to sea, just the two of us. "What, you mean sunshine and ice-cream?"

"No just peaceful and all having fun together"

"Mmm, well, maybe 'cos we're on holiday and there's no work or school to get in the way?"

I picked up his blue plastic bucket from the wall and placed it upside-down on his head, like a hat with the handle as a chin-strap, it fitted perfectly.

"Yeah, I know" he said, adjusting his new headgear "It's just that being here makes me feel like everything's alright and I don't need to worry about anything"

I was quite stunned at what my little son had said "What do you worry about?" I asked him softly.

"Oh, you know, you and mum arguing sometimes and when I can't see you 'cos we're at Burneside and I never know if we're goin' home or not"

I watched an eagle-sized seagull swoop down on the stub of ice-cream cone Stefan had thrown onto the sand. It snatched it up in its sharply-cranked, albatross-like orange beak without landing but lost its grip a few yards into the air. A perfectly aerodynamic backward somersault allowed the bird to catch the cone again in mid-flight, before flying off with a deep-throated squawk.

"Show-Off" I said, nodding at the gull.

Stefan smiled and looked up at me.

"Look Stef" I said, putting my arm round him and pulling him close "You don't have to worry about that kinda stuff. We both love you mucho and things'll be ok pretty soon" I said hopefully and kissed him on the cheek. "Should we go back to the hotel and play bar-football 'til it's time for tea?"

"Ok but I'm reds" he answered, standing up on the wall.

"Come on then Reds, winner gets another ice ream" I said, bending slightly so he could climb on my back for a ride.

Partly because of the unease at home at that time and partly because of boredom I started going out at weekends, and one night when Dorothy had run off again to her mother's, dragging Stefan with her as usual, I took revenge by sleeping with Marie who worked behind the bar at the Kendal Hotel. I enjoyed the excitement and release as it took me back to a time without worries or responsibilities, and it lead to other encounters of a similar nature.

Once, when Stefan was about seven and had been taken on one of the frequent short breaks to his grandmother's, he came home on his own when I was at work and left me a note. He must have planned his visit, which he kept secret from his mother, well enough to obtain a door key. The note said simply "I love you dad" I kept that little note on a crumpled piece of lined school paper close to me for over twenty years, until I lost it in a hasty house move. When I look through old books or documents I still harbour the hope of finding it again one day, and sometimes imagine the little note that my son wrote to me all those years ago, lying bedraggled on a rubbish dump somewhere, waiting for me to find it and restore it to a place of pride and remembered love.

Clockwise from top left: Father; Mother; Gordon; Robert

*This and following page shows illustrations for sale
to Lakeland tourists*

Ten

"Danger is so thrilling when it's someone else at risk...We know boxing is a dangerous game; some boxing performances combine great skill and beauty but the point for the spectator is to see men expose themselves to the sort of pain and risk that most of us could not endure for a moment"

(David Robson – Daily Express – 2006)

IT WAS A BAD time in the building industry and work was hard to find. As a family we were never in debt but often had to live on a tight budget, and I was as ever, always alert to any prospect of earning more money. Sometimes I had to sign on the dole but could always make a bit extra somewhere. I classed it as survival in a time when many did not survive too well. Usually I would do private joinery jobs or a bit of bouncing, and continued with portrait commissions.

With no regular joinery available I took a labouring job with Nuttall Civil Engineering, who were blasting a tunnel through Shap Fell to accommodate the large-bore pipe which now supplies Manchester with Lakeland water. We worked twelve-hour shifts doing various jobs including moving rock from the tunnel face on Haglund Cars pulled by small locomotive engines. Inside the tunnel ground-water dripped constantly from its rocky roof and the reek of fumes from each gelignite blast stung the eyes and throats of the men working there. Outside, winds blowing across the Cumbrian mountains fanned icy sleet onto the Fell, the ascent of which was infamous for stranding and even killing unwary motorists before the M6 motorway offered a safer, more manageable route over the steep and often snowbound incline.

When first starting the job I was ordered by the Irish Shift Boss, Danny, to drive the locomotive to the rock-face whilst the regular driver took his break. I was offered no operating instruction but did what I was told, it looked simple enough. On my first trip I crept tentatively down the tracks through the stinging, lung-damaging blast fumes to the tunnel face. It was 2am on a freezing February morning. The two linked Haglund cars were loaded by Irish and

Polish miners using mechanical Emco shovels, and the loco dragged the combined 88 tonnes up the gentle slope to the tunnel-mouth. The track then changed direction to the left and the gradient gently dropped as it eased away to where the tracks ended at steel railway buffers, looking over a steep descent of tipped rock fragments. The tip was probably 30 metres high and it was part of my job to extend the railtrack as the debris piled up and stretched out into the yawning chasm towards the adjacent fell. The waste rock actually formed a new mass in the undulating landscape, altering its natural contours forever.

As the locomotive and following freight cars moved away, now downhill from the tunnel-mouth, they gradually gathered momentum. I pulled the large hand-brake lever up in attempted restraint but it had no effect on the increasing speed. I was totally alone outside the tunnel in the howling wind and sleet, though the area was lit by spotlights during the long night-shifts. The driving rain lanced almost horizontally into my face and thudded into my oilskins like machine-gun bullets, as I alighted from the loco's footplate and looked round the engine for some form of slowing mechanism that I had not yet noticed. I even tried pushing the massive weight back up the slope manually before re-boarding and yanking vigorously on the brake again. Still no effect and still the metal leviathan gathered velocity, although still less than fast walking speed. It was now nearing the end of the tip and I watched mesmerized as the gleaming buffers loomed into view from the surrounding mist and blackness, wondering whether they could hold the approaching mass but knowing the moving weight must be too great. As impact became imminent I pulled everything moveable in the loco cab during the last few seconds, and finally stepped off the foot-plate as steel crunched and creaked against steel. The 4-inch, square-section drag-bar buckled under the massive force of two fully loaded cars and slowly wrestled the engine off its tracks. Once past the point of balance the loco lurched sideways and slid down the rocky slope of the tip. It crashed, banged and sparked its way to the bottom of the man-made ravine and lay there steaming and groaning like a wounded rhinoceros. Its orange safety-light still whirred, flashed and cast moving, animal shadows on the surrounding rock. The buckling and snapping of the drag-bar had at least slowed the cars and they trundled to a gentle halt against the buffers, which remained unmoved amid the commotion. I leant against them watching the dying locomotive and listening to the growing cacophony of frantic voices behind me.

I was exonerated of blame because I had not been trained in usage of the locomotive or its dead-man wheel, which has to be turned repeatedly to tighten the brake, and had not even been hired as an official driver. Sufficient torque has to be maintained to slow and control the mountainous loads, but not acutely enough to jerk the cars off track.

Later in the contract a derailment broke a foreman's pelvis and there were dozens of other injuries. In those days, health and safety at work was a fine concept, but little more than that.

A bloke from Manchester with the same name as the Yorkshire Ripper, Peter Sutcliffe, also drove Nuttall's infamous locomotive. Peter was driving down to the face one night and its trundling vibration along the tracks loosened rock from the tunnel roof. A weighty piece hit him on the head, dazed him and probably compounded the effects of the cannabis he smoked on night-shifts with his pal, Richard 'Drunk' Harrison. He staggered across the footplate and fell onto the rails in front of the engine, where he lay on his back staring up at the jagged roof. The dead-man brake had stopped the loco a few yards from the tunnel-face and 'Heavyhead' as was his nickname, began moaning "Cave-in, cave-in" in warning of what he thought was the unfurling of a major catastrophe. The miners drilling to place gelignite glanced nonchalantly round at him lying face-up on the rails, bleeding profusely – and carried on drilling. He was neither Irish nor Polish, nor a legitimate miner, so lay where he was until ice-cold ground-water dripping through the rock strata revived him, and he was able to walk back to civilization. He left Kendal, scarred around the head, after the Shap section of the tunnel was finished but the Union Steward, Steve O'Toole, found him on the south coast where he delivered a cheque for several thousand pounds awarded to him in compensation.

The tunnel drive through hard rock, as most of its type, was manned predominantly by Irish labour who openly supported the IRA, and a significant amount of gelignite went missing. I personally found several sticks and a few detonators stashed in a hole in the tunnel wall!

My father, despite getting on in years, also worked on the tunnel as a concrete-finisher for a time, but by then I had already left. I worked with him on several other contracts for short periods and during a lull when work was scarce took him, Eddie Mahoney and Steve O'Toole to work on a private contract I had acquired at Thornton Cleveleys near Blackpool. Strong March winds had damaged a lot of property at the time and we carried out repairs and alterations to a large restaurant owned by Franco Messina from Sicily, for whom I'd done renovation work at his restaurant in Highgate, Kendal.

I have never understood how any reasonably intelligent person can think it fair for builders, miners and other manual workers to retire at the same age as those who sit comfortably at desks in heated offices, but as my father grew older and arthritis set in, he took a less punishing job with a local contractor. I was once told a story about an incident that occurred during refurbishment of the Catholic church on New Road, Kendal:

Mid-morning on the first day of operations, Father Flanagan entered his clerical domain and squinted in the gloom, blinking repetitively as rays from the rising sun lanced through the stained-glass of the east-elevation windows and reflected off dispersing dust clouds. He peered at the various building workers as they moved about the church interior, before nodding in agreement with some decision known only to himself and proceeded down the aisle "Now den" he said to my father as if to a small boy "Y'must make doubly certain to protect Himself" he instructed, nodding at the six feet tall effigy of Jesus on the cross, screwed to the wall behind the altar "When yez are in here making your mess. Make sure He comes to no harm or damage at all and disn't get all covered over in dust and durt"

My father looked round at the priest from beneath the flat cap he was wearing to keep the grime out of his hair "Don't worry Father, there'll be no damage" he replied.

"No and der better not be because I know what youse builders are like when nobody's watchin' yez so I do"

My father ignored the insult and carried on working.

"And fer Jaysus sakes man, take off dat hat in de house o' de Lord" the priest shouted before scurrying back down the aisle, muttering to himself.

My father turned to look at the priest as he disappeared into the sacristy, before pulling the hat down tight over his brow.

Late in the afternoon the clergyman looked in again on his way back from enlightening sinners at the St John Boste social club, on the corner of Kirkland and Gillingate. He waved a hand in front of his face, swirling white dust in the air, before making his way through the nave to the altar where my father and a few others were hacking damp, rotten plaster from the wall "I see yez are hard at it boys" he said jovially, his cheeks slightly flushed.

The men stopped work and looked round at him. My father leant his shovel against the wheelbarrow he was filling with plaster rubble and took his hat off, slapping it against a thigh to shake off the accumulated dust "We're doin' our best Father"

The priest coughed and flapped his hand again "Yes, yes I can see yez are boys, yez are doin' well, very well indeed. And tank God ye got Himself out the way before knockin' me walls to bits" quipped the Father, nodding at the clearly-defined cruciform dust-shadow on the wall where once the effigy had been.

My father nodded in return, smiling tolerantly.

"I trust yez have Him somewhere safe an' sound?"

"Don't you worry Father, he's well out of harm's way"

"Ah lovely, lovely, dat's me boy, dat's it boys, carry yerselves on wid de good work den"

The priest tottered away humming an indistinct tune to himself and the little band of plaster-hackers looked at each other. Casting one last glance at Father Flanagan's retreating back, all eyes then tilted in unison, upward into the high ceiling-vault. There, dangling in the dappled light of the clerestory, twirling gently in the updraft, hung the effigy of 'Himself' secured to the rafters by a length of blue industrial pull-cord looped neatly in a noose around its neck.

One Sunday afternoon I was with friends in the Fleece Inn lounge. It was before the introduction of all-day licensing hours and someone suggested going for a drink after closing time to a particular open-air dog show out in the country. A pub which we shall call The Snooty Fox, just over the Lancashire border, was staying open all day to host the show so off we all went in Glen Hoyle's car. Inside the pub I talked with Glen, who also worked on the Shap Tunnel, and his mate Brian Fleming, a hod-carrier, both of whom were originally from Rochdale, Greater Manchester. We chatted about nothing important, drank and played the odd game of darts.

We had been there for a while when two blokes came in whom the Rochdale boys knew but I did not. One turned out to be Tom Dearden, a well-known landscape and portrait painter who exhibited at the Royal Academy in London and was one of only two British recipients of the Gold Medal from the Paris Salon, though Tom did not even bother turning up to collect his. The other recipient was John Constable, who did. Tom's companion was a big, ex-professional fighter from the Manchester area I was told, called Paul Costello who, though still in his twenties, had given up boxing for a more leisurely life in the countryside when his parents bought the Derby Arms at Witherslack, just south of Kendal. Tom lived half a mile from the pub.

The afternoon went pleasantly well though we did not see many dogs, and evolved into various other forms of competition. These included darts, dominoes, press-ups with feet up on the bar, and arm wrestling. I won the press-up competition and Paul easily won the arm wrestling. He and I were playing darts and chatting when an argument broke out between Tom and Brian. Evidently a discussion had sprung up about Paul and I, as we had both boxed. Tom insisted that Paul, who was 15 stone and over 6 feet tall, would beat me easily in a fist-fight whereas Brian stated optimistically that I was a harder hitter and could knock Paul out. I said nothing as the argument continued but I could see Paul was becoming irritated. I said "Paul don't let it get to you, it's just craic, it doesn't mean anything"

He did not look at me but went to confer with Tom, and I sensed danger signals. Glen took me to one side and said "Look it's up to you but we think y'can take him an' we want to see it done 'cos he's a bully and once slapped Brian's cousin around"

I replied "He's a big fit lad and he seems ok to me, and I aint fightin' him just to settle someone else's score"

Glen said "Tom's got money and he's backing Costello. We'll guarantee you fifty quid win or lose"

"That's not much Glen"

"No but it's guaranteed, if you win we make more – a lot more"

"What's Paul say?"

"He's well up for it, thinks it'll be a walkover"

"Does he now?"

"Aye, he's always lookin' for somebody to knock about an' keep his reputation up"

"Reputation?"

"Big thing with him"

"Bit of a bully as well?"

"Definitely"

Unusual for a boxer I thought for a moment before answering "Oh well, I'm game if he is"

I was still comparatively light-hearted about the situation and not really convinced it would end in violence, but Paul began pacing around the bar throwing punches into the air just as Brian said "We'll put an extra hundred quid down says Bob knocks Paul out"

Paul spun round with a snarl, slammed a fist onto the table, knocking most of the drinks over and as the whole bar lapsed into silence he hissed "I've never been knocked out in my fuckin' life and that little bastard won't do it"

Violence crept closer. He scowled a "Let's go" at me and made for the door.

Those who still had un-spilled drinks finished or carried them, and every occupant of the bar filed outside onto the sun-baked tarmac of the car park to the immediate right of the front entrance and in full view of the main road. The road actually ran past the front of the pub and parallel to it and the throng of people emerging from the bar, added to those coming down the lane from the dog-show soon blocked it. People from the halted traffic abandoned their vehicles to join the crowd of onlookers and soon there was a tailback stretching over the hill and out of sight. Paul took centre-stage and immediately stripped to the waist, revealing a muscular torso. He was well-known in the area as a fighter and the general expectation was that I was about to be pulverized. I tried to think myself into a martial mood but was disgusted at exhibiting myself in such a manner merely for money, though at this stage pride in my ability and that little dash of fear, particularly of an unknown opponent, helped to generate adrenalin.

A friend and neighbour of my father, Derek 'Coidy' Ward (John's father) was appointed referee and brought us together to hear his instructions. He said we should not bite or kick each other but most else was ok. Paul flexed and bobbed around in front of me as I said "You don't have to do this Paul"

He replied flatly "You're fuckin' dead"

Coidy slapped his hands together in front of us and shouted

"Commence boxin"

Paul came straight at me behind a long lead and obviously knew what he was doing. He kept ramming out a stinging left which popped off my forehead and kept me out of range of landing any punches of my own. I tried moving in from either side but could not get past his lancing jab and scything right cross. His punches were hard and heavy and a sardonic grin spread across his face as he gained control of the fight and gradually forced me into defence. This continued for some minutes and I was beginning to tire. The head blows caused dizziness and disrupted both my visual and mental focus. He was sharp and well-drilled and whenever he sensed I was about to attack invariably moved to his right, away from my strongest punch. I tried to exploit this consistency by intercepting his move and catching him with a left hook, but he foresaw this and shuffled his feet quickly in a neat change of direction. As he did so however, his hands dropped slightly and I instinctively flicked a left into the opening. He pulled his head sharply back, causing me to miss by an inch or two, but his evasion left him momentarily off balance: I slid my left foot forward and pushed off my rear, right foot, creating the pivotal torque to land a perfectly straight right onto Paul's uplifted chin, and send him to the tarmac. I am told that both of his feet actually left the ground at the same time, and he did seem to float in mid-air for a moment before crashing face-up onto the ground, dispersing a cloud of blue-grey dust. Coidy stepped between us and pushed me back as, surprisingly, Paul sat up like a mechanical toy and scrambled to his feet. A momentary shiver of fear ran through my brain and into my legs as I marvelled at the man's recovery and how fit he must be. He put his big fists up defiantly and went into a crouch, but his eyes were unfocused and I realized he was still dazed. I looked to the referee but Coidy waved me on. This was the first point at which I heard the roar of the spectators, and therefore the first point at which my survival instinct began to relax enough for other thoughts to intrude. I put my hands down and said "Coidy he's gone, look at his eyes"

Coidy shouted "I'm the referee, do ya wanna fight on Paul?"

Paul scowled at me and nodded.

Coidy said "Fight on" and brought his hands together.

Mine stayed at my sides as I nodded towards the still glassy-eyed Paul and said "Come on Coidy"

But the crowd bayed for blood and the referee asked again "Do you want to fight on Paul?"

This time he shouted his reply "I'll fuckin' kill 'im"

A re-energized roar went up from the crowd at this and I realized the fight was not finished yet. Paul was recovering quickly now and came shuffling towards me, measuring the distance between us with his darting left lead. I kept my hands down and moved away from him but he continued to advance. For a fleeting moment I considered just turning my back and walking away, but was not then equipped to deal mentally with that action and would not be for many years to come. I chose instead to end things as quickly as possible, took time to pinpoint my target, and exploded a second straight right on the bony ridge of his sharp jaw. Paul collapsed from the knees and I knew there was no way he would get up unassisted this time. I helped carry him back into the bar where we laid him on a bench, and bought him a pint when he awoke. He did not come fully around for half an hour but I watched over him constantly. Today, calling for an ambulance would be routine but then it was never even considered.

Paul and I swiftly resumed our pre-fight friendship and he told me long after he had moved home to Barrow-in-Furness, where I happened to be working at the time, that I had actually done him a favour that day. He was aware that he had become a bully, did not like that image of himself and said it had taken what I had done to shake him out of it. He knew his fighting days were over when he woke up the morning after and asked himself 'Do I want a rematch?' The answer he gave himself was a definite 'No'

Word soon spread that 'money fights' were taking place in the area and opponents came from all over the North and as far south as Cornwall. I remained undefeated at any weight for eight months until the van in which I was travelling to a fight was pulled over by police in Cheshire. No complaint had been made but we were told that what we were doing was illegal, police throughout the country were aware it was going on and we would eventually be prosecuted and possibly jailed for it if we continued. I fulfilled my existing commitments and retired from the scene without a loss, even though the prize money involved had risen considerably. Some people that I respect are still involved in this activity and have asked me not to mention their names here nor any details of their involvement.

I had been in trouble with the law previously, once receiving a suspended prison sentence for punching the landlord of the Kent Tavern, Kendal, who took a swing at me after I complained that his drunken wife had spilled beer over Dorothy and Gillian O'Toole (Steve's wife). As a consequence of this court appearance and letters to the involved brewery, the landlord was discovered to be an out-of-control alcoholic and sacked. When I attended the court-hearing a woman approached me in the corridor and asked if I would be willing to accept community-service instead of a custodial sentence, such as this type of charge was likely to attract. I answered positively and she said that as I was a joiner (she had my antecedents with her) would I be prepared to build an all-weather play cabin for the orphans at Barrows Green. I told her I would be delighted to and could supply all the tools and equipment needed. Somebody must have told her I was sure to be jailed because she could not wait to tell the little orphans. However, when the facts emerged in court the bench recommended a suspended sentence and did not even award any costs against me. Outside the court, at Kendal Town Hall, I looked for the orphan woman and asked the usher if he knew of her whereabouts. I was keen to build the cabin for the kids but although I left a message at the court office, I never heard from her again.

Eleven

AFTER THE SNOOTY Fox fight Tom Dearden and I became good friends and discussed much about life, including art. He was a truly gifted landscape and portrait painter who had yet to make the best commercial use of his talents. He had though, acquired or been acquired by, a commercial agent in Lytham, near Blackpool on the west coast of Lancashire. We visited the agent with some of my pictures, which interested him though they were not of my best because I sold those to order, and he offered to represent me in the sale of my work. At first I was excited by this prospect but eventually realized that I could not afford at that point, to commit the time necessary to achieve success nor more importantly, to maintain it. Tom was slightly disappointed but if truth be known, I think he was more interested in my pugilistic abilities than those I possessed of an artistic nature. He has remained a lifelong friend who at his peak, was a better painter than most of the old masters.

I arranged to meet him one afternoon in the Derby Arms at Witherslack, the pub owned by Paul Costello's parents, near Tom's home 'Faraway' In the morning I went walking in the countryside with Brian Fleming, Glen Hoyle, a few of their friends who were visiting from Rochdale and two other men, one being Gary Middleton who is a nationally known breeder of the famous Patterdale Terrier. Several of these tough, fighting-breed dogs, some owned by Brian, accompanied us as we tramped across open scrubland in the Winster area to the east of Windermere Lake, on what I naively believed was simply a walk in the fresh air. The dogs ran around sniffing at holes in the ground and at one became very excited, yelping and jostling to squirm down it. It became evident that the hole was the entrance to a badger's sett, and that at least one of the animals was in residence. The dogs worked in relay scurrying back and forth down the hole and their subterranean encounters with the badger could be felt as a series of thuds which reverberated through to the grassy surface upon which we stood, as the animals writhed in combat a few feet below. The men took turns with a small foldable spade, digging directly down to the point of bestial confrontation. Eventually Brian lay down on the fresh soil above the newly-excavated shaft and reached in. With a grunt from him and a yelp from the dogs, he dragged out a thrashing grey ball of fur and held it up in the air at arm's length by its short, stubby tail. The captured animal's struggles subsided as, like a triumphant hunter, Brian held it high. The dogs jumped and snapped but the beaten animal remained still, apparently resigned to its imminent and violent death.

The normal procedure at this point would be to break one or two of the badger's legs or even its back, so that the dogs might have a chance to outfight it and increase their future courage in the face of these formidable, bear-like creatures from the same genetic family as the ferocious weasel and murderous American wolverine. Men and dogs closed around their suspended prey like a pack of hungry hyenas. The badger watched its attackers through an upside-down eye, surely knowing that resistance was futile. All that moved was its heaving chest and bristly grey fur, rippling in the soft breeze. Its mouth opened slightly revealing the tip of a pink tongue, and its front paws came together as if in prayer. Prayers won't help it now I thought, remaining stationary as the mob moved in for the kill. I watched, recording, riveted to the spot of ground upon which I stood, mesmerized by the stricken animal's bright little eye within its black furry stripe. It appeared to be looking straight at me through a gap between its massed assassins. The dogs jumped higher, yapped louder and salivated profusely in their crescendo of excitement. I watched in fascination as the circle of men closed and Brian's hand wavered under the strain of his trophy. He grasped the tail with both hands now and as he turned back to the audience his eyes also met mine, as I stood alone looking on.

"Let it go Brian" I mouthed softly.

He looked directly at me. The badger twitched silently.

The crowd also turned to look at me, still on my spot, and one of the visitors frowned as he asked "Wha' did you say?"

"Let it go" I said, still looking at Brian.

"You fuckin' soft or summat?" snarled the newcomer.

"Let it go" I said loudly enough to invoke a stunned silence.

All now stared in my direction and my hands dropped to my sides in readiness.

"Leave it" Brian shouted to the mob "Grab the dogs"

Within seconds the little badger was free and back down its hole – alive and well if a little shaken. Brian looked at me and smiled, and shook his head in apparent amusement. The potentially volatile situation calmed and settled, and we trooped silently overland to the Brown Horse pub where alcohol that day at least, soothed egos and did not spill over into alternative violence.

Later, in the Derby Arms, I conversed with Tom by the bar before his mother and sister came in. I had not met them before and was introduced.

"You must be Helen's friend?" asked Mrs Dearden.

"Who?"

"Helen Rigg, as you would know her then?"

"Yes I know Helen" I answered, remembering that Tom's parents lived next door to hers on Thornleigh Road in Kendal.

"Do you ever see your son these days?"

I looked at her in confusion.

"Alistair" she clarified.

"My son?"

"Er yes, I'm right here aren't I Tom? At least Mrs Rigg's sure he's your son"

Tom was talking badgers.

"I was never told that" I said.

"Oh I'm sorry, I thought it was common knowledge – that everyone knew"

"No, I was never told"

I later got in touch with Helen, who by then lived and managed pubs in the Midlands, and we met one evening a few months later on Windermere Road. She got into my car and we drove to a quiet place on Kendal Green, where I recounted what I had been told by Tom's mother. She handed me a photograph which in the dim light, I thought depicted Stefan.

"It's Alistair" she said.

"But he's dark" I said in reply.

"Yes he was only fair when he was very young, don't forget you haven't seen him for twenty years"

"Twenty years... Where is he now?"

"He lives in Australia, he's got a good job, a family and a degree in Computer Science"

"Australia...Christ!"

I looked up from the photograph into her eyes, which peered deep into mine.

"You were with Dorothy" she said "You didn't want me"

I stared at her blankly.

"And anyway, I thought you knew"

"How?" I whispered.

"Do you remember when I lived on Hallgarth and Terry was knocking me about?"

"Uh-huh"

"And you came round to the house?"

"Yes"

"Well you did that to protect Alistair didn't you, because he was your son?"

"I did it to protect you, you were the one being hit"

She fell silent and looked down at the photograph of her son, now a young man, still in my palm. She reached out and touched it, and in doing so took my trembling hand in hers.

"I thought it was because of Alistair" she breathed.

I looked out of the car window at a young couple walking past, holding hands and laughing, about the same age as we were when Alistair was born.

"What did you tell him?"

"I didn't really tell him anything. By then I was settled with Robert and Alistair just grew up calling him 'Dad' Robert was happy with that and I just thought it was for the best to leave things as they were"

"So he has no idea?"

"No, I never told him and I don't think it would do any good now. He's got his own life and family and still thinks of Robert as his father, whether or not he knows anything of the truth. I never had any more children you know, so it's important to Robert as well"

I nodded and watched a lone raindrop trickle down the windscreen.

In the ensuing silence I drove back to Windermere Road and dropped her off where she asked me to.

"Keep the picture" she said, as she looked at me for the last time – with tears streaming down her face.

Throughout the long hot summer of 1976 I worked on the building of the Keswick By-Pass for Tarmac plc, constructing timber shutter-moulds for the concreting of Greta Bridge, once the largest of its type in Europe. I remember 'accidentally' along with many others, dropping my hammer into the river Greta below and diving into the cold, fresh, mountain water to retrieve it. At weekends I would strap Stefan's little helmet on his head and take him all over the open countryside on the motor-bike I owned at the time, a Honda 400 Dream. I would box and wrestle on my knees with him, make shiny, silver-painted wooden swords with leather-look handles that were the envy of his friends (and some of their fathers) and play war games on the carpet with marbles as cannon balls which defeated vast armies of little plastic soldiers. Years later when Stefan was about twenty he came to see me and over tea we discussed current politics. He was very aware of international current affairs, was a vegetarian and an active anti-blood sports campaigner. He suddenly stopped mid-sentence and said "Do you remember that game we used to play with soldiers and marbles?"

I replied "Yes, it was good wasn' it? Me and my brothers invented it I think"

He replied "Yeah, it was brill, I could just fancy a game now and buggar the anti-war campaign"

I taught him how to draw using light and shadow instead of simple outlines, and also the rudiments of chess, and whilst he was still at junior school the teacher asked if anyone knew how to play – he was the only one in the whole class. When he was older he practised against the computer and became very good – way too good for me!

One afternoon when he was about eight, he came home from school with three other kids and a serious look on his face. I was upstairs painting in the back bedroom. I heard him enter the kitchen and watched from the window as he re-emerged with two bottles of tap-water. He then went back in and came out with two pairs of boxing gloves from the under-stairs cupboard. He handed a set to one of the other lads, Mike Ainsworth, who was over a year older than Stefan and several inches taller. He and Stef then took their jackets off and squared up to each other on the back lawn, whilst the other two took up their respective positions as 'seconds'

I watched from the upstairs window with amusement as I thought they were merely playing, but it was soon obvious that they were not. The bigger lad charged at Stefan, raining blows on him and I was about to shout down when I saw that Stef had tucked his chin in behind his shoulder as I had taught him, and was stalwartly weathering the storming attack. When the incoming tide of blows ebbed he jabbed out a perfect left lead which bloodied his opponent's nose, and quickly followed up with several more. Mike recovered quickly though and charged again, but once more Stefan covered up and countered with his own crisp punches in reply. Time after time Mike charged but Stefan stood firm, retreating a foot or two occasionally but always remaining poised and coming back to trade punches. The lawn was ploughed and churned into mud by now and both boxers were tiring, the heavy going underfoot slowing them considerably. I decided to halt the contest before the turf got any worse or a combatant was injured, but just then Stefan popped up out of a retreating crouch and loosed a ramrod-straight right cross. Mike spun around with his hands to his face as I ran downstairs to rescue him. Stefan did not pursue his advantage though but asked Mike if he'd had enough. Mike nodded and the contest ended. I was surprised and proud of the courage, determination and modesty shown by my young son that afternoon, particularly so when told that the fight took place as a result of Stefan being insulted and challenged by the older boy. Stefan never bragged about his victory nor as far as I know, ever spoke about it again. I never spoke about my exploits in his presence, nor anybody else's unless pressed.

When he was young I slapped him a few times as I had been slapped by my parents, when I thought it necessary to discipline him in a manner which he would not ignore. I knew no better then. If I could take those slaps back and replace them with hugs and kisses, I would, a thousand times over. When he was older and as big as me, I actually punched him when he was out of control at his grandmother's house and I had been sent by his mother to restrain him, though she later denied it as part of her coping mechanism.

These memories are now my nightmares and I live with the pain of their existence. My only consolation is that I know Stefan understood my weaknesses and forgave me. I loved him then, I love him now, and I will love him until I die.

Twelve

"Why are some teachers so horrible dad,
I thought they were supposed to help people"

(Stefan MacGowan – 1980)

THE BUILDING OF HEYSHAM Nuclear Power Station on the north western Lancashire coast was the biggest construction project in Europe in the 1980s, employing over six thousand operatives at the height of production and paying the best wages north of London. When the main contractor, Taylor Woodrow, laid on transport from Kendal I acquired a job there working with a gang of joiners from North Wales. They had transferred from the Dinorwic Power Station near Llanberis, west of Caernarfon on the rocky edge of Llyn Padarn, and were experienced shutter-hands. Dinorwic harnessed water-power from the mountain lake, or llyn, which at times of high electricity demand was allowed to fall through turbines, producing power at peak periods, to be pumped back up into the reservoir through the low demand, night-time hours.

I worked alongside the Welshmen and learned about their humour, nationalistic pride and historic hatred of the English. They wrote slogans on their safety-helmets which read 'Twl din pob sais' ('Arseholes to all Englishmen') but I was invited to visit their homes on and around Anglessy and did so several times. I think they made allowances because of my Scottish blood.

Apart from a brief period when I left to work on the Levens By-Pass for Dowsett, building road-bridges over the A590, I continued at Heysham for several years. Prior to returning from Dowsett I rang a contact I had made in Taylor Woodrow's site management team, Mike Carson. He said there was no problem with me coming back as a joiner, but they also needed foremen at all levels, so why didn't I apply? I said "Are you sure?"

"Yes why not" he replied "You know the site, and you can organize. Just apply as a basic foreman and see how it goes"

I said "What do I need to do?"

He said "I'll put you some bumf in the post, you still at the same address?"

As I put the phone down I had already decided against this proposition, and regretted agreeing as it might affect my return as a joiner. I was unsure that I could cope with the responsibilities of front-line management on such a large scale and was wary of the vehemence with which all managerial staff were regarded generally by the Heysham site operatives. There had been several physical attacks on and off site, with one foreman being beaten up outside a Morecambe pub and left with a broken leg. He had not committed the cardinal sin of venturing there alone, but did make the mistake of being delayed by a buxom blonde.

As I looked around for alternative employment a brown envelope arrived. It contained an immense amount of information about every aspect of Taylor Woodrow as a highly-profitable, multi-national, blue-chip company which actually began its operations in Blackpool, Lancashire, in the early 1960s. It also included two application forms, one regarding my experience, qualifications and background, the other concentrating on my honesty, integrity and financial status. Undischarged bankrupts would be rejected immediately and high credit-risks frowned upon because of the company's insurance requirements. I skimmed and left it all on the kitchen table but it did not leave my head, and I eventually asked my wife's opinion. I said I could not see myself as a foreman and just wanted to be one of the boys, easy-come-easy-go with no allegiance to anybody but myself and my family. She read through the information though and said it could be the chance of a lifetime, and that I might never have to scratch around looking for decent wages again. In the end I completed the forms, waited a few weeks then went for an interview with Heysham Phase II Project Manager, Peter Bradley, whom I liked immediately despite his reputation as a ruthless bully. He was Irish and had worked his way into senior site management from ground level, an achievement I admired, respected and filed for future reference. His brother Olly was still a general labourer on the site. Peter asked where I had worked previously and I told him basically the truth with some minor embellishment. I had built up quite a range of experience, was a good organizer and adequately literate. I showed him my trade qualifications and assured him that I had never been bankrupt nor in any debt. At the end of the meeting he asked if I had ever been in trouble with the law. I wavered a little but told him truthfully that I had been in court for a few bar room brawls. He laughed and said "That's not a problem, it's almost a requirement here. You any good at golf?"

He offered me a job that day and I accepted.

When I reported for work I met Sub Agent, Albert Welch from Peterlee, County Durham. He offered me his best advice on man-management and labour relations "Don't get too friendly wi' the bastards" and "I'll know yer doin' a good job when I see yer name on the shithouse wall"

It was reported that Albert ordered all the windows in the site toilet block to be broken out, so 'the bastards' didn't spend too long in there.

Building generally but particularly civil engineering, is a tough, demanding industry, usually carried out in appallingly harsh and dangerous conditions. Deaths and serious injuries have always been frequent occurrences. Within that industry I had entered a particularly brutal and confrontational regime which evidently needed to be so, to achieve the required deadlines and profits. At the site entrance a large sign recorded the number of injuries (and deaths) in the preceding month on each section. The foremen with the lowest counts got a bottle of whiskey for encouragement.

Once I crossed the proverbial threshold into management everything changed, including former colleagues' perceptions of me, and I was now one of those advised not to venture into town alone for fear of physical assault. Even on site we were far from safe and experienced foremen never stood for long below anything from which an object could be dropped. One supervisor who looked skyward in response to a shout from above was killed instantly by a 3" steel bolt which smashed through his eye socket from a height of 90 metres and exited through the back of his skull with his brain attached to it. The official opinion was that even if he had not looked up and the bolt had therefore struck his safety helmet, the impact from such a distance would still have killed him.

Wages were relatively good though, labour in demand and men were bussed in from many parts of Britain, except Merseyside which was black-listed because of its industrial militancy. Albert gave me a 4-strong gang of labourers one freezing Monday morning, with the instruction "Make 'em or break 'em"

They were all related under the surname 'Lancaster' but despite being named after the city which lay a few miles inland from the site, they were actually from Sunderland, on Wearside.

The Lancasters did not communicate easily with strangers and as a consequence had become marginalized, bored with the resultant mundane tasks and correspondingly morose. They were passed from section to section as no foreman wanted the bother of supervising them, particularly as they could be quite aggressive. I said to 'Uncle Ernie' Lancaster, who was about 10 years older than me "This is the end of the road for you lot one way or another"

"Whadya mean like?" he asked, affronted.

"You're in the departure lounge, you either shape up or I gotta ship you out"

"How's that like?"

"Nobody wants you, they say y'can't do anything and might as well hit the road back to Mackamland"

"That's 'cos we never gerowt decent ta dee, we're sick o' sweepin' up" said Ernie, his anger rising at last.

"Y'can't do anythin' but sweep up can ye?"

"Fuckin' right we can" he stormed.

"So what can yez do?"

"We can dee any bloody thing" they all chimed together.

"Like what?"

"Steelwork, concretin' anythin' but neebody gis wer a chance"

"So y'can place concrete can ye?"

"Why aye, course we can man"

"Ok then I've got a fire-break wall to pour in Reactor Hall 7 an' it's gotta be ready by Monda' mornin' eight o-clock, can y'do it?"

"Bloody right can wer" they chorused, more animated than I had ever seen them apart from one Saturday when Ernie had a good win on the horses.

"Can y'do it on time?"

"Why aye man"

"WELL GET THE FUCK ON WITH IT THEN"

"YAHOOO" they screamed in jubilation, scampering off to get all the tools and equipment needed for the job.

I brought my brother John into the gang to add some extra zip to proceedings and the massive wall, designed to withstand earthquakes and nuclear explosions, was completed on time after working two 'ghosters' (24-hour shifts) consecutively.

John was a qualified Chef and had just returned from managing hotels in South Africa. Whilst he was considering catering options I got him a job as a site labourer at Heysham to keep him busy. Obviously he entered the industry as a newcomer at the lowest end of the employee scale – pushing a sweeping-brush with a cleaning squad. Even so, he liked the macho lifestyle so much that he never returned to catering and has since travelled the world with civil-engineering companies, specializing in building airport runways and earning high tax-free salaries. He quickly progressed from brush-hand to General Foreman, and is currently working in Jamaica where he lives with his second wife, Sandra.

The Lancasters turned out to be one of the better gangs on section, their bonus payments went up significantly and they returned to the North East a far happier crew.

Harsh conditions breed hard men: One Christmas Eve afternoon in the mid 1980s I was recruited to a squad of staff to form a human wedge and force entry to a site cabin occupied by sub-contract steel-erectors, some from London and a few from Glasgow. They had smuggled whiskey onto site and were battering each other with the empty bottles. We broke down the door and entered a steaming bloodbath, with more bodies on the floor than were standing. As we gazed aghast at the gory scene, the mayhem stopped and a 6'3" Glaswegian smiled jovially at us before spitting blood at the wall and saying "How're ye daein boys, fancy a wee draam fer Chrasmas?"

I worked there when Margaret Thatcher carried out her whistle-stop tour of nuclear installations as part of her tactics to ensure that the country did not rely on coal and that the miners' union never wielded power again. I was put in charge of a gang who covered the route of her visit, painting out dozens of makeshift signs erected by the men bearing slogans less than kind to Maggie. When she reached my section she thrust out a gloved hand for me to shake, but I turned at the last moment and avoided an action which would have bothered me for the rest of my life. Colleague, Neville Jones, jumped into the breach and lost my respect forever.

Whilst I was putting in long hours at Heysham, Dorothy told me that Stefan was unhappy about something at school and asked if I would have a word with him. I did so and discovered that he was despondent about being singled out by a particular teacher, Mr Morris. It seemed that Stefan, along with some other boys had gotten into mischief on their way home from school, but Mr Morris insisted that Stefan alone had to report to him at specific times of the day, including early mornings and late afternoons. The afternoon reporting meant that Stefan had to walk home alone, often in the dark of winter when traffic was heavy, and would arrive over an hour later than usual. Morris himself would often not even bother to turn up as arranged and nonchalantly leave Stefan standing outside his office not knowing what to do. He was in fact a woodwork teacher, so hardly crucial to Stefan's education and did not actually teach him but was pastoral head of his year. He had just returned from a lengthy sick leave. I considered the situation to be unfair and told Stefan that he did not have to report to Morris unless I told him to, intending to contact the school to discuss and clarify the matter first. However, two days later Stef returned home from school with a letter from Mr Morris which stated unequivocally that he had to report as instructed every morning and afternoon, and that if he did not he would 'suffer the consequences' The wording of the letter, with its unspecified consequences and unqualified demand that Stefan must do the teacher's bidding whether justified or not, had an ominous tone which was threatening and it certainly upset the boy and his mother.

I finished work early the following Friday and stopped by the school on my way home. As I entered through the glass front doors a boy passed and ascended the open staircase that curved left and upwards away from the foyer. I asked him if he knew where I could find Mr Morris. The lad stopped mid-flight but as he did so a door opened to my left and a tall, woolly-haired man stepped out saying with a rigid smile "Hello, is someone looking for me?"

I looked up at him "Are you Mr Morris?"

"I am indeed, what can I do for you?" he asked with a condescending glance at my work clothes.

I was surprised by his height and ebullient manner, and annoyed that a man of his size should threaten my son.

"You must be responsible for this then are you?" I asked calmly, holding up the letter for him to see.

He stepped close to tower over me and peer at the sheet of paper "Why yes I believe I am, is there a problem?" he asked challengingly.

"The problem is this, you ever send my son a threatening letter again and you'll be back in your sick-bed for a long time"

He began his retreat.

I advanced.

Still holding the letter up I screwed it into a tight ball and threw it at him. It bounced off his high, narrow forehead as he withdrew into his snug office, where he fell inelegantly over his polished desk and landed in a heap of wrinkled grey trouser and fluttering paperwork on the floor. I smiled at the sole of his size eleven shoe, still hooked up in his blue swivelly chair, and sauntered back out to the car park whistling a merry tune.

The school responded quickly and decisively by sending us an official letter saying in no uncertain terms that Stefan was henceforth suspended from his studies, and asking us to attend a forthcoming meeting to discuss the situation. I arranged another early finish, drove the twenty miles back to Kendal where I picked Dorothy up from home and hurried to the school conference room. We were approached by a pleasant lady from the Education Authority, who had been called in to the fray by the school's headmistress to have her draconian actions officially endorsed as a matter of course. She informed us gravely that the outcome of the meeting could carry serious consequences.

The headmistress was present with her deputy and several others armed with pens, folders and pads. All looked suitably serious and cast superciliously condemning glances in my direction. The attendees were all introduced to us separately by their names, every one of which I instantly forgot. We all took seats around an enormous table, made up of several smaller tables pushed together, and the headmistress peered over the top of her finely-cut spectacles at me "Isn't Stefan present?" she asked, feigning incredulity.

"No he isn't"

"Well, why not for heaven's sake?"

"Well the first reason is that he's suspended from school without current dispensation, remember? The second reason is that he doesn't want to be here and the third reason is that I can't think of a valid reason why he should be, can you?"

"Why, yes I think it imperative that he hears what we have to say about his behaviour" she replied indignantly.

"Stefan will hear all about this meeting but in a way that's fair to him, and doesn't involve him sitting here already-condemned, listening to your misguided views about him"

A stunned silence ensued during which most most of those present concentrated on the little patch of tabletop directly in front of them. The headmistress stared at me with saucer-shaped eyes and a mouth slightly agape. Dorothy fidgeted nervously with her handbag but her gaze never wavered from the headmistress. The deputy finally relieved his superior's apparent discomfort by keeping his head low and cranking it sideways to whisper. She gathered herself for a retaliatory strike but I pre-empted it with a question "On the subject of appropriate attendances, can I ask why Mr Morris is not here?"

All heads scanned the room as if noticing for the first time that Morris was not present. The deputy dipped and cranked again for a brief, hushed exchange with the headmistress.

"Umm, where exactly is Mr Morris today Pauline?" she asked of a slim woman seated to her right, who immediately dipped and cranked in response.

"Erm, it seems he's not in school today" the headmistress finally announced.

"But why not?" I interjected "Surely you asked him to attend the meeting?"

Pauline stepped into the breach of the following silence to say "We didn't think it necessary for Mr Morris to attend as he has already made a statement regarding the incident"

"What incident?" I asked swiftly.

"Well" she snorted down her nose at me "The incident in his office when you attacked him"

"Oh yes, when I cudgelled him violently with a piece of paper, but what's that got to do with Stefan being suspended from school?"

The headmistress could not contain a little shriek of astonishment as she blurted "We think it has everything to do with Stefan's suspension Mr MacGowan, and I must say that we are extremely disappointed at your attitude towards this matter"

All eyes reverted to me in unanimous accusation and I let the ensuing pause linger before responding "And I must say that I'm more than a little surprised by your attitude, to your obvious mistakes as head of this school"

Her withered mouth fell open again revealing a tiny streak of red lipstick across her upper teeth, as I continued "Unless I'm mistaken, you brought my wife and I here today in an attempt to sit us sheepishly and obediently at this table while you reprimanded and shamed our son in front of us, his parents, and in front of yourselves, his publicly-paid educators. You're outraged that we didn't subject our son to that ordeal and yet you didn't think for one moment that it might be in the interests of justice to bring his accuser before him, and us"

Silence settled like a London fog "Furthermore" I continued with gathering momentum "Again unless I am very much mistaken, this meeting is not even about Stefan or his behaviour, it's about me and my behaviour. Nothing that he has done warrants his exclusion from school and in any case, I authorized him not to follow Morris's instructions as they had implications for his safety and well-being, obviously not regarded as remotely important by you, and certainly not as important as poor Mr Morris's fragile pride"

Heads stayed motionless but eyes flashed sideways as I continued, looking straight at the headmistress "So perhaps your real aim was to ridicule and revengefully subjugate me, in front of my wife and son?"

Pauline, showing more management potential than either of her managers responded quickly "We assure you not Mr MacGowan, but we did think that your threat to return Mr Morris to his sickbed was extremely uncalled for, he has after all had a rather difficult time of it lately"

"Well I'm afraid it's about to get a little more difficult for him Pauline" I bluffed "Because I'm going to challenge the legality of his actions, which I believe amount to threatening behaviour and harassment"

Pauline's mouth clammed shut as the headmistress's gaped a little more and the woman from the Education Department showed the first signs of life "Oh, oh I'm sure that won't be necessary Mr MacGowan, I'm sure if we all just calm down a little?"

"I haven't finished yet" I interrupted as she shifted in her seat and shuffled paper. The whole room came to attention like a class of boringly obedient pupils. Dorothy let go of her handbag and placed two clenched fists on the table.

"It's plainly obvious that you" I accused, looking straight at the forlorn headmistress "Have suspended my son from school for something that I did and not for anything that he did. You have therefore illegally deprived him of his right to an education under English Law, and I am going to sue you personally and also whoever is financially responsible for your professional mistakes, in compensation for long-term damage to his future prospects"

The silence compounded to a crushing density before Dorothy and I rose to leave. I had intended to smile smugly at that point but was surprised that my anger prevented me. The Education lady fluttered out after us "Mr and Mrs MacGowan could I possibly have a quick word?"

We stopped in the corridor as she caught us up "Phew, you certainly give as good as you get don't you?"

"I don't like bullies"

"No neither do I, but look I know you agree that Stefan's education is paramount here, so before you proceed against the school, which you have a perfect right to do I hasten to add, let me have a word in the right ears and see what I can come up with?"

"Oh, do you think you can help?" asked Dorothy, anxious to rebuild bridges.

"I'll try my best and am sure I can achieve a better outcome than what is presently on the table"

"Ok" I said as Dorothy nodded her agreement enthusiastically "We'll wait a couple of weeks but whatever happens, Stefan will not be subjected to any more threats, bullying or victimization" I said, quoting a few loaded words and looking serious.

"No problem, I'll be back in touch a-s-a-p, and by the way, I think you're right"

The following afternoon Dorothy received a telephone call from the woman, saying she had sorted the problem and thought we would be pleased with the result, also that there was a letter explaining everything on its way to us. The letter arrived two days later inviting Stefan back to school immediately, where he would no longer have to report to Mr Morris at any time and in fact would have no further contact with him throughout his school life. A new mentor was appointed whom Stef respected and got along with well, and who wrote him an excellent final report.

About a year and a half later, after I had been transferred to Scotland and then London and decided to look for alternative, local work instead, I took a temporary job at the Allen Technical College on Station Road, Kendal, tutoring carpentry and joinery. My duties were to teach first-year apprentices who had just entered the building industry, partly to escape the school environment as I had done. The job was easy, conditions soft and comfortable, remuneration excellent and I quickly decided that I never ever wanted to be a full-time teacher. One afternoon though was at least interesting. I had been asked to work extra hours demonstrating the features, controls and safety requirements of modern woodworking machinery (a subject I had to read up on that very afternoon) to a group of visitors. I opened the workshop door to a timorous knock at the appointed hour, and beheld a group of twelve adults. Poking out above the expectantly-smiling assemblage was a wiry head I recognized, that of Mr Morris. I smiled back courteously, ushered them in, showed them where to hang hats and coats etc, then went about putting the embarrassed and fearful woodwork teacher at his ease, by being as professional in my temporary job as he should have been towards my son when in his care.

Several years later I was told by my sister that Mr Morris had been in sole charge of a group of schoolchildren out tripping in a minibus that he was also the official driver of. The children had become over-excited and unruly, and Morris had tried vainly to bully them into silence by shouting and threatening them. Again this tactic failed to work for him and the children grew louder as Morris's reaction to the noise became more erratic. Eventually he stopped the bus on a secluded country lane, got out and abandoned the children to their fates. Although the kids had mobile phones they were completely lost, could not direct rescuers accurately to their whereabouts and were panicking as darkness descended. They were however, eventually located and returned intact to their worried families.

Morris was summarily dismissed from his post.

Thirteen

"Curled up tight on the cold, hard floor
Lying outside a police cell door
All the exits locked and bolted
In the foetal position – being assaulted
Officers grunting overhead
Am I about to – wind up dead?"

(Author – 2007)

DOROTHY AND I WENT out for a drink after work one summer's evening and made our way to the Roebuck Hotel in Allhallows' Lane. Apparently there had just been some trouble in the pub and staff were very jittery. After waiting at the bar for twenty minutes I eventually complained about the service as I was being handed our drinks, and the landlord shouted "Get out if you don't like it"

I ignored him and we stood out of the way in a secluded corner. However, a few minutes later the police arrived in answer to a call about the earlier trouble and the over-excited, under-experienced landlord pointed me out to them. It was the first pub he had managed. Two policemen came over and asked me to leave and I recognized both of them. One was Eddy Warburton, a fat lad from Windermere who used to hang around with the Liverpudlian hotel workers and who, according to Steve O'Toole who was one of them at that time, was a fine shoplifter before signing up to the force. Obviously he was well-trained by the scousers and never got caught. I knew his sister who was not fat at all, nor as far as I know, a thief.

It took a few seconds to figure out how I knew the other officer before realizing I had previously met him out of uniform. In the Kendal Hotel a few weeks earlier I was talking to Bert Boardley's mother about his training regime for the ABA Championships, and noticed a stranger who was obviously drunk. He was shouting obscenities at one of the bar staff (not Marie) with whom he was apparently acquainted, which was embarrassing for Bert's mother and therefore me in her company. I asked him to quiet down but he puffed his chest out belligerently as he lurched over to stand right in front of me. He was a big lad but I pushed him back against the wall and told him to come back when he was sober. Evidently though, his memory cells were working just fine because he clearly recalled me at the Roebuck "Remember me do ye?" he smiled sarcastically "I hoped it wouldn't be long"

His name turned out to be Bill White and he had recently been posted to duty in the town. I showed him the drink I had just bought and suggested that my money should be returned if the bloke who sold it to me now wanted me to leave. Bill looked around in frustration and eventually went over to the bar. The disrespect that he now detected from me was obviously interpreted by him as a personal insult. Add this to the tension already prevalent in the bar plus our Kendal Hotel altercation and it can be appreciated that the situation, although controlled by the police, was dangerously volatile.

He returned my money, I took a last gulp of lager and hand in hand with my wife, headed for the door with him right behind us. Outside, another fight linked to the first had drawn a crowd of spectators around the waiting police van, blocking our exit. Bill intentionally pushed me from behind into the crowd and then immediately grabbed me about the neck, swung me round and dragged me backwards towards the police van. Both he and Warburton were about four stones heavier than me and had been trained to use their weight effectively. Eddy opened the doors at the rear of the van as I reacted negatively to being dragged around the street, wrestling loose from Bill's grip as he lost his footing and stumbled to his knees. The inertia of his tumbling bulk propelled him forward until his palms met the tarmac and his helmet fell off and rolled across the road into the gutter, eliciting an appreciative roar from the crowd. Seeing his colleague down and possibly not realizing he had merely stumbled, Eddy charged at me, grabbed me by the throat with both hands and thrust me back against the rear of the van. He jammed his right forearm against my throat, choking my head back, and fished a pair of shiny handcuffs from his belt. Clicking one end onto his own wrist he then tried to get the other end onto mine, but although Eddy was big, his sedentary lifestyle had not made him strong. I did not like the idea of being publicly manacled so grabbed the open cuff and pulled it down to the floor of the van, just above knee-height. Obviously Eddy's arm and connected body came with it, leaving his enormous backside poking out at the crowd and causing great amusement.

White was back on his feet by now, re-helmeted and ready for action. Eddy huffed, puffed and struggled but did not take much holding down. I stood perfectly still and made no aggressive movements, realizing that I was in a precariously dangerous position. White grabbed the front of my shirt and screamed "Get in the fuckin' van" whilst trying to manhandle me sideways. I did not reply but got hold of his lapel with my left hand and pushed him back against the inside of the open right-hand door, holding him there at arm's length. And there I stood at the back of the police van, both arms out in lopsided crucifixion, holding two large policemen at bay and wondering what to do next. The audience laughed and shouted encouragement and some were actually clapping in applause. Then Dorothy was in front of me looking very concerned. She said I should go with them and she would see me down at the police station and I knew she was right, not least because I could see a nearby policewoman on her radio and assumed reinforcements were on their way. So I said to Bill "Stop kicking and punching and I'll get in the van"

"Get in then" he gasped.

I let go of them simultaneously, got in, sat on the left side bench and Eddy followed me, sitting next to the door. The policewoman also got in, sitting opposite me, and Bill clambered into the driver's seat clutching his helmet tightly. As we set off I nodded at the crowd through the rear window and asked Eddy if he should not take some names and addresses as witnesses. He hit me square in the mouth with the back of his left hand and shouted "Shurrup"

He was still out of breath, obviously embarrassed and very jumpy.

I wiped the blood from my lip and said "What, you scared of someone telling the truth about this farce?"

The darkness in the van prevented me seeing him half turn as he punched me in the face with his right hand and shouted "Shurrup y'little bastard"

For the first time in the evening I began to get annoyed and warned "Don't do that again Eddy"

He hissed "Yer ours now y'little twat"

He let go with another swinging right, half rising from his seat, but before it landed I butted him and he fell onto the steel floor of the van as it left Allhallows' Lane and drove to the top of Beast Banks, passing both the Fellside and Serpentine Road junctions towards the police station, turned right and stopped in the secluded darkness of a large, overhanging Beech tree below Kendal golf course. Bill got out of the cab, locked it and climbed into the back with the rest of us. He secured the back doors from the inside before all three officers set about kicking, punching, kneeing and scratching every part of me that they could reach. I had already realized that I was in a vulnerable position both physically and legally, so rolled up in a ball to hopefully withstand the attack. Bill and Eddy lashed out viciously in vent of their frustration though they were restricted somewhat by the low height of the van roof, and Ms McKenzie dug her nails into my neck until it bled. When they were all puffed out with their exertions the assault waned and we drove on to the station. I sat back on the bench and looked across at the wpc. She stared back and struggled to regain her breath. Bill radioed ahead for 'assistance' and when we arrived at the rear station entrance there was a reception committee of eight waiting with rolled-up sleeves. The doors opened and I was dragged out and flung face down onto the tarmac, where I received another brief kicking before being hauled upright and rammed into the station wall. I was also steered into collisions with a series of other walls on the way to the charge desk. Four officers including Bill then dragged me through the narrow corridors to the cells. Eddy went to get a band-aid for his nose. They hustled me along to a cell at the far end of the passage and then halted as the heavy steel door was unlocked. I was hit on the head from behind and pushed to the floor where I again curled into the foetal position. Bill and a pal then set about the job in earnest – previous action had obviously been a mere taster prior to this, the main event. Two watched, presumably in reserve or to protect the vulnerable kickers from my vicious retaliation. They booted just about every part of my anatomy until one stopped and all fell eerily silent apart from the rhythmic thud of boot leather on flesh, as Bill carried on his own personal mission. He kicked and kicked and kicked. One of his accomplices eventually said "This is fuckin' sick" and walked off along the echoing corridor.

Bill kicked until he could kick no more and slumped against the clammy masonry wall, gasping for breath. I knew that if I tried to fight back it could lead to my death, so lay there and listened, letting my imagination kill the pain and transport me to my armchair at home, with my son sitting on my knee smelling of soap and goodness in his Postman Pat pyjamas. Bill recovered and resumed his assault.

A voice said "Jesus Bill, you're gonna kill 'im"

In between gasps Bill said "So fuckin' what?" and let go another flying boot.

"Fuck's sake that's enough isn' it?"

Bill launched a last kick and fell back exhausted against the wall before staggering away, sweating profusely and fighting for breath. The remaining two hauled me into a vertical position, pushed me into the cell, locked it and left me alone for a long, painful night.

The following morning there seemed to be an air of embarassed confusion in the station. I was released without charge after being examined by the duty-doctor who happened to be my GP, Dr Jackson. He was openly shocked and disgusted when he saw my condition and went into the adjoining room as I re-dressed. I could hear him loudly berating the officers present, even though they were not the ones responsible as Bill's shift had finished at 2am. I made an official complaint against every officer present the previous night and an appointment with a solicitor before Terry Belshaw from CID, whom I knew from the rugby club, gave me a lift home – walking was painful.

Stefan cried when he saw me, even though I laughed through swollen lips and joked about it to reassure him, and he threw his policeman suit in the bin. Dorothy put both hands to her face and said "Oh god, oh my god what have they done to you?"

She had followed me to the station and waited for hours but they would not let her see me. There was hardly an area of my anatomy left without severe bruising and swelling, including the whole of my face and head. My groin area in particular was black with contusion.

The police and their internal complaints department manipulated the case for almost two years before anything official was allowed to happen. Throughout this period they threatened to charge me with all manner of crimes against society but unofficially via officers I knew socially, offered various deals. I was repeatedly told that if I dropped my complaint I would not be charged with anything, but I refused. I was warned by many that I would never beat the police in court, particularly with my background and no witnesses in my favour, and would end up in jail. Often I doubted the possibility of remaining free myself but had made my stand and could not back down. I would rather have met my attackers face to face and actually offered to meet them one at a time with gloves on, but that was never going to happen, not even when I increased the offer to two at a time.

I contacted all the people I could remember from that night to take statements, as I had been warned that the police were going to claim I was drunk and incapable of recalling what actually happened. I was told by Terry that the CID had been to every pub in town to interview staff regarding my level of capability, and the evidence indicated that I was sober and chatting pleasantly to my wife and others. They even remembered that I was wearing a tie with a white shirt, probably because that was not usual for me, I leant more towards the jeans and tee shirt look at weekends. I went over every detail of the night's occurrences and wrote it all down until it was lodged securely in my memory. Dorothy made a statement and insisted on attending court even though I did not really want to put her through that additional trauma.

We took two car loads of witnesses to Carlisle Crown Court for a jury trial that would last three days. I had elected for trial as opposed to being dealt with by magistrates, whom I knew tended to side with the police generally.

The old courthouse in Carlisle city was an awesome, intimidating place designed to deter offenders from re-visiting. On arrival I was officially arrested and placed in the custody of warders from Walton prison in Liverpool, which contained the cell they had reserved for me, assuming my conviction and custody were mere formalities. I was released each lunchtime to eat and again every night to go home, and then re-arrested the following morning before the trial re-started. I felt as if the jury would be unaware of this arrangement and that seeing me in custody every day, jammed between two burly jailers, would make me appear already a prisoner and therefore guilty. We found out where the jurors went for lunch, which turned out to be a nearby cafeteria for most of them. Dorothy and I went to the same place and smiled pleasantly to make sure they noticed us out and about unfettered. For the benefit of the rest of the jury I made sure that we came back a few minutes late on the second day after they and the warders were already in place. The tactic risked annoying the judge but I smiled apologetically and made it clear to all that I was still very much a free man.

At the start of the trial the prosecuting barrister strode over and stared directly into my eyes from a few feet away. I reasoned that he was trying to intimidate me into becoming nervous and so appear guilty when I was responding to his questions. I looked straight back at him. My confidence declined steeply though as he read out his version of the case against me in all its contrived detail. The judge peered sternly over his bifocals as he listened to the prosecution's tale of me throwing poor innocent policemen about the streets, and then knocking myself against police station walls and floors in a maniacal, drunken rage. The landlord's testimony followed and the jury's quick, sideways glances turned to slower, accusatory stares and at a brief break in proceedings, one of the warders turned to me and said "I think you'll be coming with us tonight son"

At one point the landlord stated that when he came out of the pub he saw Warburton and me at the back door of the police van, and Eddy appeared to be leaning in, fastening my wrist to the van floor. The judge later picked up on this observation.

Things brightened a little when Bill and Eddy rumbled consecutively up to the witness box. I did not realize why at first but their appearance caused murmurs and tittering amongst the jury. Dorothy later told me "It was their size, everybody had just been told that you'd flung them around like rag dolls and then they appear and they're both twice the size of you. You looked like a little lost boy sitting there compared to those two lumps"

McKenzie also made a brief appearance but said almost nothing, none of which condemned me very much and hardly any of it corroborated Bill and Eddy's tale. This caused a few furrowed brows in the audience and a flurry of note taking by the judge, who asked her to speak up twice as she continued to gaze at her feet. I did actually see her again once, long after the case was over. I was standing by the juke box in the White Hart and although I was not smoking she came over and asked me for a light for her cigarette. She was blonder and prettier out of uniform and I would have liked to discuss that night with her, but I just smiled and let the moment go with a shake of the head. I think she probably regretted her actions and I have always thought how being a police officer must brutalize a woman's femininity. Imagine making love to a woman who helps beat up captive people.

Most of the first day of the trial was taken up by the prosecution making its case against me and overall, things looked pretty grim. It was a quiet journey home that night.

On the second day my witnesses were called and basically followed our plan of saying what a fine chap I was, in staunch denial of the claim that I was drunk on the night in question. The prosecuting barrister attacked Dorothy over some little detail she could not remember about the night's confusion "Oh you can't remember" he echoed "How convenient"

Dorothy looked at him as if he was something she had just scraped off the sole of her shoe.

"Is that right, you can't remember?" he pressed.

The judge intervened "The witness has already said that she cannot remember this particular incident, and the submitted evidence suggests that the reason for this is that she did not actually see the incident you refer to"

I began to allow myself the first little inkling of hope that the judge might just see past the screen of lies offered by the police.

Two of my witnesses were Tommy Lynott, my companion at the nurses' party, and his wife Linda. Tommy wore a big coat for his appearance and looked like a gangster. The prosecutor said to him "You know the defendant well don't you?"

Tommy nodded and said yes. The prosecutor asked "Have you ever seen him drunk?" but my barrister raised an objection which was sustained.

The prosecutor then asked "You would know if he was drunk or not though wouldn't you, knowing him so well?"

Tommy nodded again, expressionless "Yes"

"And he was drunk that night when you spoke to him wasn't he?"

"No he was not sir"

"But you knew he'd had a drink didn't you?"

"Oh yes I knew that alright"

"Ah, and how did you know that?"

"Because he had a drink in his hand when I was talking to him" said Tommy in his big brown coat.

The jury actually laughed out loud and the prosecutor looked slightly embarrassed.

At the end of the day I was called to the stand and briefly gave my version of events. I was then set about with gusto by the prosecutor who went through every detail of my testimony hoping to trip me in a lie, but I had rehearsed well and was almost word-perfect in my responses. He persistently tried to create an image of me in the minds of the jurors of a mindless, violent lunatic and liar "Do you expect this court to believe?" he shouted whilst pointing towards wpc McKenzie "That this young woman simply took it into her head to attack you in the back of a police van for no reason?" He stared at me with a gaping mouth and bulging eyes.

"No I don't think that" I replied calmly, holding his gaze "I think she saw what her colleagues were doing and felt obliged to join in, as new recruits are encouraged to"

"Felt obliged to join in" he repeated in a virtual whisper, looking at me intently before turning to shuffle papers on his desk. After a moment he attacked again by trying to explain away the injuries to my lower body; claiming that they happened as I was being pushed against the rear of the police van, in a prolonged attempt at arrest. The judge stopped the trial here and ascertained the exact height of the van floor in relation to my injuries. The two did not correlate. The judge asked me about precise details of the van interior, such as what the seats and doors were like, and the exact size of the window panel between the cab and the rear compartment, and sent out for corroboration on these points. He was obviously deciding whether or not I was drunk and causing mayhem all the way to the police station as was claimed, or whether I was sober, calm and aware enough to record such details accurately. The reports seemed to indicate that I was truthful in my statements so far. He then asked for verification as to whether there was a facility for chaining prisoners to the floors of police vehicles, as indicated by the Roebuck landlord, and was told there was not. "It might seem then" he volunteered "That the defendant's claim to have been standing perfectly still whilst holding officer Warburton to the van floor – is actually true"

The prosecutor squirmed and once again I allowed myself to think I might have a chance of winning. But he was certainly no fool and the jury would not easily accept that Kendal police force was an institute of liars. He gathered himself to reply "You've got your story well-rehearsed haven't you, even from day one at the police station. Did you sleep much on the night you were arrested?"

"No, not much" I answered.

"No, I'll bet you were lying in your cell all night planning this fabrication down to the last detail in order to get yourself out of the mess you were in?"

"No sir, I was not doing that because I was not in a mess. I was and am innocent and it appears to be your clients' evidence which is in a mess"

The judge asked what I meant by that.

"The prosecution is insulting the intelligence of the court by asking you to believe these injuries were self-inflicted by me throwing myself at walls and floors" I replied, pointing to the photographs laid out in neat rows on my barrister's desk, directly below the jury "They were caused by policemens' boots" I spat in the direction of White and Warburton.

The court stilled before lapsing into isolated whispered discussions as the judge ordered an adjournment. I stepped down from the microphone-assisted witness-box and slumped back onto the worn and shiny oaken bench, bracketed by the two prison guards like a pair of beefy bookends, and tried to gather my thoughts. My mind was in a whirl but I had one distinct advantage that I kept reminding myself of, the truth. I looked up but the judge was busy scribbling notes. To my left the jury avoided eye contact and engaged in private little conferences. In front of them my lawyers were in animated, muted discussion as was the prosecution team opposite. To my immediate left a court reporter typed furiously with intermittent twitches of his thick ginger eyebrows and opposite him the press scribes scribbled just as vigorously. For the first time since the case began, nobody looked at me. Or perhaps someone did? I turned to look behind me, high into the public gallery and saw Dorothy, sitting forlornly alone. We exchanged a private little smile of mutual encouragement as the judge re-entered. Both barristers approached the bench for a three-way whispered discussion before the judge nodded his agreement to some proposal by my barrister. Were things going so badly that he was trying to plea-bargain?

On re-convening, a previous witness was re-called to the stand. PC Culgaith, a trained dog-handler and person present at Kendal police station during my initial incarceration there, was slim and quite nimble and slid easily into the judicial spotlight where Judge Brown eyed him amicably. He was told that the court simply wanted to expand on a few of his previous answers. Nothing at all to worry about the judge reassured the constable.

It was established that the officer had not been present in The Roebuck nor in Allhallows' Lane or the police van or the rear yard of the police station, but had seen me being brought into the station via the back door. The judge asked "Why do you think the prisoner was brought to the rear entrance?"

Without hesitation Culgaith answered "Because there's more room and it would avoid congestion in the main entrance which is often busy on Friday nights, as I'm sure the court will appreciate. Maintaining civic order on our streets is not an easy job"

He had prepared and was impressive. Faces lightened receptively in the jury as the judge nodded with a smile "Uhum, carry on" he said, peering at the defence team.

My barrister stood as if suddenly thrust into a daunting situation, adjusted his cockeyed wig, pulled the front of his gown into place, coughed several times and asked with extreme politeness "Congestion which would be exacerbated by the, what was it, eight or nine officers?"

"Yes, about that. Eight I think"

"And they were all necessary to restrain this one prisoner?"

"Yes sir he was very violent"

"How did this violence manifest itself"

"He was thrashing around and trying to hit the station officers"

"With his fists?"

"Er, fists and feet, he tried to kick them as well"

"Did he try to hit or kick you?"

"No"

"Did you see him actually strike any of the officers"

"Yes, er, no, not me personally sir"

"But you were watching closely, as well you would if your colleagues were in danger?"

"Yes"

"And you would have assisted if necessary?"

"Yes of course"

"But your assistance was unnecessary because he never hit anyone to your knowledge and none were reported injured, apart from pc Warburton?"

"Not to my knowledge, no"

"But he was thrashing around and trying to injure them?"

"Yes he was"

"And he was also very drunk?"

"He appeared to be drunk from where I was standing"

"And where were you standing constable?"

"At the end of the charge desk"

"So you had a clear view of everything that occurred after the prisoner was brought into the station?"

"Yes"

"And in previous evidence you say that you also followed the prisoner down to the cells, in the company of three other officers?"

"I did"

"And presumably four officers were required at that stage because of the prisoner's continuing drunken violence"

"Yes, you know, just in case"

"Just in case what constable?"

"Well, just in case we were needed"

"Just in case you were needed if the prisoner became violent possibly?" asked the barrister, with raised eyebrows.

Culgaith remained silent and after a pause during which the judge made several notes, the barrister continued.

"Isn't it true that you left the cell block before the prisoner was locked up?"

"Erm, er yes I think I did"

"You think you did?"

"Yes I did"

"Why was that?"

"I didn't think I was needed any longer and there were still three officers present"

"But you decided, did you not, because of what was going on in that dark, soundproofed basement that you did not want to be present there nor to be a participant in what was being perpetrated by your colleagues against a defenceless man?"

A loud and frantic objection from the prosecution was sustained.

Unperturbed, the defence continued "Yourself and other officers have stated that whilst in the station charge-room, the prisoner was too drunk and violent to be processed correctly, is that your recollection?"

"Yes sir that is my recollection" the constable replied confidently, standing to his full height.

Following another brief pause for wig adjustment and water, the barrister said from beneath a furrowed brow "I have here a copy of the police operational handbook, which includes procedures for arrests in situations like the one you describe. What, in your understanding would be the normal procedure for officers in this type of situation?"

"Erm, to restrain the prisoner as soon as possible to minimize danger to the public or to the officers themselves, or even to him"

"Physically restrain?"

"Yes"

"How?"

"Well, erm, by force when necessary"

"Is there any equipment specifically designed for restraining violent prisoners?"

"Er, yes"

"What is that equipment?"

"Handcuffs"

"Yes handcuffs, do you carry handcuffs?"

"Yes of course"

"By regulation?"

"Yes sir"

"Is that true of all officers on active duty? We know that pc Warburton certainly carried his that night"

"Yes"

"Was the prisoner handcuffed before he entered the station?"

"I don't know I only..."

"Yes yes but you saw him enter the station did you not?"

After a pause "Yes"

"And was he handcuffed?"

"Er, no but I believe officer Warburton had made an attempt to handcuff him"

"But he was not handcuffed when you saw him, despite the presence of eight or nine officers?"

"No sir, not when I saw him but ..." mumbled Culgaith, possibly realizing where the barrister's questions were leading.

"Did you see any officer attempt to handcuff the prisoner at any time either immediately outside or inside the station?" demanded the barrister, cutting him short.

"Er, yes I believe I did sir, at the charge desk" stated Culgaith.

"Oh" exclaimed the barrister "Could you then provide the court with the name of that particular officer as it is not included in your original testimony?"

Culgaith's head jerked downwards as he mumbled something indecipherable.

"Could you repeat that" asked the barrister, peering over his gold-rimmed bifocals at the police constable in the witness box.

"Um, sorry, no I didn't see exactly which officer it was ...you know ...amongst all the action that was taking place at the time ..."

"I see" quipped the barrister as the judge's pen flourished back and forth across his jotter, glinting like morse-code under the bright courtroom lights.

The barrister took time to regain his breath, re-adjust the troublesome wig once again and sip more water before continuing. He glanced quickly at the mound of paper on his desk and asked "There's another measure recommended for use with violent prisoners is there not?"

After a silent pause "Yes sir"

"And that is?"

"Use of the truncheon"

"Yes, use of the truncheon. And did you see a truncheon being used by any officer that night?"

Another pause.

"No, I did not" Culgaith replied resignedly.

"And presumably you did not employ your own truncheon?"

"No, I did not"

The judge laid his pen down on the desk before him, removed his spectacles and looked directly at Culgaith.

"Why was that?" asked the barrister.

A long pause ensued during which Culgaith twice glanced towards his colleagues watching from the wings. The court waited in absolute silence as the officer froze before the headlights of impending justice. His head again slumped forward as he gazed shoe-ward and mumbled incoherently. I watched from my prisoner's seat, I the accused, fascinated by and even sympathetic for the trapped policeman.

The judge said something to the court usher, who in turn asked the witness to repeat his last statement. Culgaith straightened and looked directly at the judge "I must admit that I have seen more-violent prisoners" he repeated.

"Have you now?" pounced the barrister, looking towards the jury "Have you indeed?" he emphasized as the judge retrieved his pen.

After three days we retired to a small holding room to wait for the verdict. One of my guards lit a cigarette but smoked only a third of it when the door opened and the usher announced "They're ready"

The guard looked at me in surprise as he stubbed out his cigarette and tucked the end into the top pocket of his blue, prison officer's shirt, wisps of grey smoke emanating from it as we trooped back to the courtroom in single file. As we resumed our designated seating the jurors glanced across at me blankly. The fight was now over, my survival instincts had relaxed and I felt strangely weak. I was now at the mercy of fate and would go docilely, wherever it led. I stood groggily when ordered. The usher asked the jury foreperson whether they had reached a verdict upon which they all agreed. She answered "Yes"

A unanimous verdict then. Absolute silence reigned as I floated up above the courtroom and looked down upon it from the ceiling, just left of the ornate, cut-glass chandelier.

"And what is the verdict to which you are all agreed, Guilty or Not Guilty?"

The foreperson looked down to her right, straight at me, before directing her answer clearly and confidently at the judge "Not Guilty"

One of the prison guards squeezed my arm with a smile as I twisted round to see Dorothy, already tottering down the gallery steps in tears towards me. Judge Brown tapped the desktop with his gavel to control the rising surge of sound and declared "You are free to go Mr MacGowan, and you have my best wishes"

I got to the end of the bench as Dorothy fell into my arms.

Outside the court three of the jurors waited for us to emerge and said they knew from day one that I was innocent and it was obvious that the police were lying. The judge had confirmed that in his opinion, they reached the correct decision.

Before we even left the court building I was approached by a police representative who attempted to persuade me to drop my complaint against them, but I pursued my grievance and was eventually awarded a few thousand pounds in compensation. Warburton spent time at a police rehabilitation centre in Yorkshire to recover from his 'traumatic experience' and White retired with a publicly-funded pension on grounds of 'ill-health' I have often wondered just where exactly he retired to, but am probably better off not knowing. However, if you ever happen to read this Billy boy, don't rest easy 'til I'm dead.

The illegal beating I received from Kendal Police was officially described by doctors as 'Severe to the point of being potentially life-threatening' I was back at work after three days and at the weekend limped down to the Black Swan to discuss the legal situation with my father and uncle Duncan. As I passed the old Central School on Fellside I glanced up at the small patch of scrubland area to its left and remembered a day the previous summer when I had also passed that way: A young policewoman came rushing down the steeply-sloping, cobbled lane shouting "Help, can you please help me sir?"

I looked past her to see that she was being pursued by three thuggish-looking youths in tracksuits and hoods, and stopped immediately. The wpc ran behind me and held onto my arm as she peered back at her pursuers with round eyes, like a hunted doe. She stood on tiptoe to look over my shoulder at the gang, who also stopped and lined up in front of me. I turned to face them square on, the terrified policewoman fox-trotting along behind me, and said "I don't know what's goin' on here boys but yez better away hame fer yer teas before somebody gets hurt"

"Says fuckin' who?" replied their apparent leader, whacking his left palm with the baseball bat he carried in his right.

"Shurrup fer fucksake" interjected one of his accomplices "It's MacGowan"

"Oh, oh fuck sorry Mac, I didn't recognise ya" the leader apologised, backing into his cronies in hasty retreat.

Apparently the three youths plus others including a number of girls, had carried out several thefts from old peoples' homes and holed up in a little den they had formed amid the bushes of the scrub area high above the road. In there, out of sight, they smoked the cannabis bought with the loot. The young wpc tracked them down but over-enthusiastically confronted them on her own, whence she was promptly set about and chased into the street. I accompanied her back up to the leafy den from where I cleared out its remaining occupants and stood guard over her as she gathered various elements of evidence she needed to avoid the old-folks being robbed again.

Fourteen

"So we shall still see you,
Be it peace or war,
Still in all adventures
You shall go before,
And our children dreaming,
Shall see your bayonets gleaming,
Scotland's warriors streaming
Forward evermore."

(Alan E Mackintosh – 1916)

AFTER THE COURT CASE, the fight against the injustice of which had united us with a joint purpose, Dorothy and I remained close for a while but eventually something annoyed her and off she went again without a word. I realized that I had never felt secure in the relationship and resented her for making so unstable, what could otherwise have been so good. I constantly felt at her mercy with minimal say about what was best for our son. I wish I had been stronger by putting his needs first, though I was never quite sure what they were or should be, above my instinct to keep the family together. By this time I felt little guilt about seeing other women, particularly those who allowed me to feel wanted and non-apologetic. I was unsure of how to make the most of my life, by being faithful in the hope of future happiness, or to take what life had to offer as and when it did. The answer to this question is no doubt different for each person but for me, I felt that the latter course of action was the only one possible if I was to remain at all true to myself, and that if I failed to follow that course, my life would eventually become one filled with regret and loneliness. I still respected my wife though and continued to concentrate all my efforts into making her and our family unit happy in the long term. If I strayed, which I did, it was on rare, singular occasions which did not keep me out all night nor interfere with our family life, at least to a certain point.

I met solicitor's daughter, Julie, in a work-related situation where I was in a manual role and she was in dire need of a strong male presence. She was ten years younger than me at twenty one, very attractive, spoilt by her wealthy father and as a result carrying out the inevitably disappointing search for her unrealistically ideal man. Cut loose from her father's ties and illusory goals for his only daughter's future, she drifted with the tides and currents on the heaving sea of human relationships, in desperate need to find again the comfort and support of an unconditional love centred upon only herself.

The affair strung out for several months because we kept seeing each other at work, whereas normally it would have been over in a matter of days. Eventually I broke it off but the break went unheeded by Julie, who tried to carry on in denial as if we were a committed couple and eventually revealed all to Dorothy. The revelation triggered Dorothy's first long-term period away from home and a definite cathartic turning point in our lives. I did not blame her for leaving that time but as always, she eventually returned. After that, if we had even the slightest difference of opinion my guilt about infidelity, compounded by my absence during Stefan's early years overrode everything, ensuring her emotional dominance over me in every conceivable way. Eventually I simply accepted the blame for anything and everything that might present itself as a problem in our life, and this acceptance became the norm for both of us. I often asked myself whether things might have been different without the affairs I was probably addicted to from my teenage years, and think that I would probably have just shrivelled up as a person under the ever-increasing burden of guilt that my marriage had imposed on me, in a vain attempt to become the person I had been in my wife's imagination. We did however, survive twenty years or so together. I remember once watching her preparing food in the kitchen I had recently built. She was humming distractedly in tranquil, Sunday afternoon oblivion when she sensed I was there. She turned to smile at me for a long moment, her perfect profile framed by the window and backlit by summer sunlight before whispering "I love my life"

If we could have maintained those moments forever we would never have parted. I too loved my life then, and also her. Stefan was happy, we operated reasonably successfully as a family and I had no plans beyond extending and consolidating that situation.

Although I did not completely agree with the ethics of governments selling their stocks of council houses, we took advantage of a substantial discount scheme and bought 47 Hallgarth Circle at our first opportunity, provided in 1981 by Margaret Thatcher's domestic policies, and busied ourselves improving the property into an attractive home. Dorothy was extremely painstaking in her care of the abode which provided her with a focus, glossed over our troubles and for the most part we jogged along in relative contentment. A friend, Alan Mitchell, once said he regarded us as the 'perfect couple' and thought that was also the opinion of most other people who knew us.

Stefan left school in 1986 intent on becoming an electrical engineer, an occupation he had an obvious flair for. His bedroom was wired up like a NASA control pod and commencing when he was twelve, cars driven by grown men pulled up outside the house for Stef to install radios and other electrical components, a service he duly charged for. Contacts were made via Citizens' Band radio, also installed directly to his bedroom by himself. His intelligence and practicality should have assured a prosperous future for him but unfortunately, the political climate at the time ensured that jobs of any type were scarce. He was bitterly disappointed when he failed in his quest, and thereafter looked at the world through more cynical eyes.

Taylor Woodrow's Power Station contract at Heysham ended the same year and I transferred to short projects at Halbeath, near Dunfermline in south east Scotland where I slept in the site office in order to send more money home, then to Robert Maxwell's proposed printing plant, opposite Victoria Station in London. I soon tired of the work-drink-sleep-work routine of being away from home, and of city life, preferred to be with my family despite any imperfections therein and eventually left the company in favour of a return to the North.

Whilst in London I was told there was a labourer on site who shared my surname. I later noticed his signature, spelt the same way as mine, when checking weekly timesheets but never actually met him for over two months. When I finally did we chatted for a while, mostly about the job and he told me he was from County Cavan in central Ireland. I met him again a couple of weeks later in a pub after work with several colleagues. We conversed again and I said I thought the way we both spelled our name was in the Scottish trend, my father's family being from Glasgow. He said no, it was the other way around, the Mc was Scottish as opposed to the Irish Mac, which originated from a prominent Gaelic clan name. He said his father, Padraic, then 88 years old, was an accomplished historian having worked for the Irish Records Office and if I wanted to hear the true story of my ancestors, he would take me to the pub he frequented. The labourer, Diarmuid, moved to England in 1976 in search of better prospects and married his lovely wife Jenny in Liverpool, the port of his disembarkation, before following the wage-trail to London. When the worry of his long-widowed father surviving on his own became intolerable for Diarmuid, he moved him to England too. Although old Pat was not initially overjoyed at this move across the water, he soon settled to his new lifestyle and almost grew to like his English neighbours, all of whom quickly got to like him and his easy-going, humorous philosophy on life. I said I would like to meet the old gentleman but thought no more about it until I bumped into Diarmuid at work a few weeks later. He had mentioned me to his father, who had grunted in acknowledgement, which was evidently a very good sign and I found myself in his company a few days later.

I bought Pat the obligatory pint o' the black stuff, which he initially ignored, and sat meekly opposite him in the seat Diarmuid had reserved for me. I avoided eye contact as instructed for the duration of the first pint and bought more Guinness before Pat cast a piercing eye in my direction. "So yer a MacGowan are ye?"

I nodded silently and smiled.

"Well" he said, sipping his pint and wiping the creamy froth on the sleeve of his tweed jacket "A'll tell ye a wee tale"

He then began his recital of a story which impressed me with its cohesion, literacy and attention to historic detail. This is my version of that story:

The earliest known inhabitants of the land that is now Scotland were the Picts, named from the Roman word picturam (picture) and so called by the Roman force occupying what is now England, Wales and most of continental Europe, because the men of the far north painted themselves for battle, usually with daubs of blue pigment. The people of what is now Ireland were named Scoti and after their arrival in Pictland via the Western Isles, must have had a significant impact on the warlike natives as the modern word Scotland obviously derives from the Roman name for the Irish race. With the

Irish settlers came the Ghabhains, the metal-smiths and arms-makers, who found much demand for their skills within the embattled clan system which, because of the largely non-arable terrain of the Scottish highlands, flourished on war, pillage and local rivalries over cattle and land. So much did the Ghabhains prosper, selling their skills and wares to whoever would pay most, that they remained a close family sept and never evolved into a full blown clan showing allegiance to any particular laird nor wearing his plaid.

The Gowan sept, whose name evolved directly from Ghabhain or Ghobain with Mac being added to denote the 'son of' Gowan, first became prominent as the O'Gowans (the 'O' signifying 'grandson of') They are first recorded in Ballygowan on the west shore of Strangford Lough, County Down – not to be confused with Ballygown, on the east shore of Loch Tuath, Isle of Mull, the latter name deriving from the first after being transported there by migrating Scoti, who quickly spread to the area around Breffny, near the present Leitrim border. The Ghabhains were most commonly associated with the Clan Donald, particularly in the Western Isles, probably because they were the most expansive clan and therefore the source of most profit. Although the 'Mac An Ghabhains' (MacGowans) would not sacrifice their fierce independence and advantageous financial position as providers of tools and weaponry, they always responded to the MacDonald call to arms and fought alongside them against other clans in defence of their interests, and also in unity with other clans against invaders of their common homeland.

The united clans defeated disciplined British armies on many occasions, often when vastly outnumbered, but unfortunate political circumstance, disunity, apathy and foreign interference finally caught up with the Scottish people at Culloden, near Inverness, in 1746. The clan system and much of the highland way of life itself was ended forever by the Duke of Cumberland's post-battle slaughter and subsequent clearances of the highlands and warrior traditions. Most Jacobite rebels were tortured and executed along with their families by the English, assisted by foreign mercenaries and regiments of lowland Scots. Thousands of highland men, women and children were sold as slaves to plantations in America and other parts of the British Empire, in addition to the many hundreds of delinquents, strays and homeless waifs from all parts of the country already in bondage, who set the unfortunate model for African slavery. It is likely that not many MacGowans were present at the crushing Culloden defeat however, as the main body of the clan had returned to Ireland over a century earlier:

King James VI of Scotland, later James I of England, patronized Scottish Catholics to solidify his political power base whilst preparing his eventual challenge for the English crown, with unity being almost impossible between a Protestant England and Catholic Scotland. But the clan chiefs were aware that James would eventually fly his true Protestant colours to appease the more powerful English contingent and that this would herald a significant downturn in the fortunes of Catholics in Scotland. One possibility for ensuring clan prosperity was emigration to Ireland where Queen Elizabeth offered tracts of arable land to colonists. She wished to weaken the Irish nation and render it ripe as the first annexation to England's Empire. With green acreage on offer and serious opposition removed, thousands of English settlers flocked to Ireland following the execution of the 14th Earl of Desmond in 1583, and the ratification of the Munster Plantation in 1586. Native unrest spread and many feared a violent backlash against the English immigrants, not least because the newcomers openly regarded themselves as racially superior to the Irish. Ireland was clearly in turmoil and with no clarity as to how the upheaval might resolve itself, presented a potentially rich pasture for those with an entrepreneurial spirit.

The prospect of armed conflict was hardly deterrent to the MacGowans, it represented guaranteed income. The clan sailed for Dun na nGall (Donegal) in June 1587, navigating through upper and lower Lough Erne to disembark at a point near their ancient homeland, to which they gave a derivative of their historic family name, An Cabhan, later abbreviated and anglicised to Cavan.

Elizabeth's restoration of Protestantism to England brought with it a new period of antagonism with Catholic countries, including the world's most dominant military power at the time, Spain. Continuous political bickering put these two most westerly European nations on a war footing and when in 1587 Elizabeth ordered the execution of iconic Catholic, Mary Queen of Scots, King Philip of Spain assembled an Armada to re-establish credibility.

In July 1588 the Spanish invasion fleet set sail under the command of Medina Sidonia, carrying 10,000 sailors and 20,000 troops.

Intending to join forces with the Duke of Parma's land army in the Spanish Netherlands, Sidonia reached the western approaches to the English Channel on 29th July.

The Spanish galleons were large and cumbersome, having been designed to transport personnel and equipment to land battles as they established their own Empire. They were easily harried by the swifter and more manoeuvrable English warships, whose gunners were trained in delivering rapid-fire, repeat salvoes, to prevent them entering the channel ports. The English fleet was commanded by Lord Howard of Effingham aboard the Ark Royal, assisted by captains including Sir Martyn Frobisher, and Francis Drake on The Revenge. The English vessels outnumbered the Spanish by more than 60, and also outgunned them at the Battle of Gravelines, between Calais and Dunkirk, on 30th July. The Armada was scattered along the north European shoreline before reforming to counter attack, but west winds gusting through the channel blew the fleet eastwards and into disarray on the North Sea. Sidonia avoided further conflict by sailing north, rather than re-enter the heavily defended Channel. He steered a wide course round the north of Scotland, only putting in at relatively safe havens such as Flannan and St Kilda, but many ships were lost. Once past Cape Wrath and the Butt of Lewis the Spanish captains hoisted full sail for home but out in the open North Atlantic, strong west winds again forced the galleons east, towards Ireland's rugged shore.

Between the 14th and 25th September 1588 a further 17 Spanish ships were wrecked along the full length of the west coast of Ireland from Donegal in the north to Kerry in the south. One, the Castillo Negro, was even lost on the east, Antrim coast. On the 20th September alone the Juliana, La Lavia and Santa Maria de la Vision were driven ashore by heavy storms off County Sligo, and the San Esteba and Amuniciada damaged on rocks off Clare. The resultant wreckage and its promise of easy pickings brought the natives out in force to the water's edge. There is speculation that they might have helped engineer these shipwrecks by strategic misplacement of warning beacons, but no firm evidence survives. The Irish were not at war with the Spanish, both shared Catholic beliefs, and they assisted survivors to dry land whilst plundering their ships. There were however, other forces in action. Several detachments of troops were on their way to the west coast from military bases set up to facilitate English expansionism. The men-at-arms leaving Belfast were reinforced by a squadron of Prussian mercenaries, recently demobilized from their armed protection of the Protestant Huguenots in France, and now in place as a deterrent to Irish forces opposing English occupation. The English thirst for Spanish blood was exacerbated by the recent threat to England posed by the prospective invasion, and the lure of gold bullion thought to be stowed aboard the galleons to pay Spanish troops in Holland. The Belfast force made its way quickly west on the most direct route, to Sligeach (Sligo) where at first light on 18th September the massed troops were assembled in serried ranks at the head of the wide path leading to the shore. As hulks from the stricken Armada lay helpless in the surf, English and Prussian soldiers prepared to descend upon them like vultures on easy prey.

News of approaching Spanish ships had also reached the Cavan men, who were always interested in any venture which might add to their income. Their most direct route to the west coast would bring them to the headland between Donegal Bay to the north and Sligo Bay to the south, and as the richer pickings were likely to be on the more open, Sligo side, they veered south without hesitation.

The Belfast detachment left the level ground at the head of the pathway in tight column formation, with the battle-hardened mercenaries leading the march. As the high dunes engulfed the rear of the column, proceeding as quietly as possible to maintain the element of surprise on the bedraggled, half-drowned Spaniards, the early morning silence was broken only by the shrill shrieks of circling seagulls, as if in warning to the unsuspecting victims. The west wind, softly whistling through the tall sea-grass, carried all other sounds east before it.

The leading Prussian officer, eager for the upcoming slaughter, strode breast-plated and with blade already drawn, to the crest of the path before it dipped again past the estuary sluice gate and onto the shore proper. He glanced back from the hillock at the following column but his gaze was dazzled by the sun rising in the east, now visible above the headland. As he turned back to the shoreline his view was blocked by the massive frame of Conlan MacGowan, silhouetted against the waning moon. Conlan stared down at the neatly manicured officer from above his wild, dark red beard, and drew the four feet long, five inches wide claymore from the worn leather strap which held its considerable weight to the side of his body, just behind the left elbow. The officer squinted in disbelief. Intensifying orange sunlight glinted off the awesome weapon as it whirled through the air and reflected bright gold off the Prussian's domed helmet as it fell to the cobbled path, still encasing his head. The column had halted behind its leader but the majority of following soldiers were unaware of his decapitation. The helmeted skull rolled back down the path, where the first troops in line moved their buckled shoes and wide knee-breeches in a rhythmless dance to avoid contact with its gore. As the concertina effect shortened and thickened the column, a deep roar emanated from the dunes to each side of it, as kilted ambushers rose from the silver sand to begin their terrible onslaught. The confused soldiers hesitated fatally in their attempts to avoid the swift and savage attack, and were swept aside as nothing by the highlanders. Those who fled were caught and slaughtered mercilessly, and within minutes the whole Belfast regiment lay butchered on the scarlet sand being picked over for anything of use or value.

The shipwrecked Spaniards were led to safety by the Scots but were then stranded and unable to make a safe escape for several months. Many remained permanently in Ireland and were integrated into local communities. They were protected and concealed from the English by the Irish villagers, and in particular by the settlers from Cavan who never ceased in their attempts to forge trade links with Spain. Unfortunately the Spanish authorities, whilst respecting the famous fighting abilities of the Scots, snobbishly regarded their weaponry as brutal and unsophisticated.

"And" declared old Pat as he drained his final pint for the day "Just look yourself at any west coast man and see isn't he a black-lookin' fella?" Pat nodded to himself and peered at me through bloodshot, watery eyes "Aye, they're black-lookin' alright so they are, same as yourself young fella, and that's the Spanish blood in 'em from the auld Armada so it is son"

This statement reminded me of a comment made by the Special Branch officer I had to show round my section of the Heysham site prior to Margaret Thatcher's flying visit. There were hundreds of Irishmen on site and he noticed that some were fair-skinned with red hair, and others sallow and jet-black, but all equally as thick, he opined. His observations were cut short though, as we entered the wire cage of the Alimak hoist and began our rickety, juddering ride to the 90-metre level platform of the nuclear-reactor building. The open cage commenced its normal clattering, shaking and vibrating ascent, the ground receded and the officer turned deathly white. He flattened back against the rusty mesh and closed his eyes, teeth clenched and fingers gripping the metal frame to each side of him, shoulder-holster peeping out from his jacket. As we lurched to a halt a few seconds later with the ratchet-shaft swaying in the wind, I kicked the gate open and stepped out onto the concrete deck. The officer seemed to be frozen to the spot as he looked in horror at the 18-inch gap he had to step across from the moving hoist to the building. The Alimak operator, a Limerick man, concealed a smile as I held out a hand to virtually pull the policeman out of the oscillating cage before he scuttled from the edge to place both hands against the two metre-thick concrete wall, where he bowed his head and parted company with his breakfast.

"Jesus fuckin' H Christ" he exclaimed, wiping his mouth with one trembling hand and fumbling for cigarettes with the other "D'ya havta do that every day?"

"Yeah, most days" I answered with a smile "Usually more than once but y'get used to it"

"No fuckin' way I'm getting' used to it" he stated unequivocally "There must be another way down?"

Ah well, it was good to know old Maggie was being so well protected by our valiant special forces.

Fifteen

"Being diligent and productive
Tranquility becomes seductive
But do not be fooled by fickle fate
An enemy is at the gate"

(Author – 2007)

I JOINED THOMAS ARMSTRONG Ltd who, with bases in both Newcastle upon Tyne and Flimby, near Maryport on the west Cumbrian coast, were recruiting for projects across the north of England. I applied for the post of Site Agent, a considerable hop up from Foreman, and was fortunate in the fact that I contacted them just prior to their start of a project in Kendal, to install the large-bore, over 1m in diameter, off-site drainage pipe for the new Westmorland General Hospital on Burton Road. The pipeline route crossed three fields, two main roads, involved the construction of several pre-cast concrete culverts, the part-demolition and reconstruction of a road crossing and bridge, to disperse into the fast-flowing River Kent, immediately adjacent to the busy Low Mills extension of the K Shoes factory.

My prospective new job presented more than one challenge and I did not realize until after I had applied that my Area Manager would be an ex co-pupil from Grammar School, Colin Briscoe. In further coincidence, Colin's parents lived right next door to us on Hallgarth Circle. These facts did not secure me the job though and Colin was certainly the most nit-picking of the three-man interview squad, probably recalling an earlier misconception of my character. I was confident though, knowledgeable about construction and was offered the Kendal contract, a company car, a pile of contractual documents and a handful of coins for use in public telephones. Colin escorted me on a tour of the site and offered one piece of advice "Make a profit"

I started by ordering site cabins and a contract telephone line. The year was pre-mobile 1987.

The site area was criss-crossed by the meandering Natland Mill Beck water course and the project was made additionally difficult by the fact that it had been priced during summer months, when the stream was a mere trickle. However, the Natland Road culvert crossing took place in winter when the trickle had grown into a raging torrent requiring men to work up to their armpits in freezing water. The client, South Lakeland District Council, had little sympathy but I completed the project successfully, made 15.4% profit which was very respectable for the industry, and realized for the first time that I was capable of more than supervision. I was required to set out accurately using a surveyor's level and theodolite; a skill I had picked up from the graduate engineers at Heysham, prepare monthly financial accounts for invoicing the client, who employed a dedicated team of scrutineers trained to defer until the following month any accounts not accurate to a fine degree, price-compare and order materials, control sub-contract payments and a variety of other equally demanding duties. At one point during this contract the council inspector, Geoff from Ulverston, asked where I had done my training as an engineer. He was surprised to learn that my background was in joinery and said that when he checked the levels of the new inspection chambers, some were within 2mm of the given heights, which he said was extremely accurate in site conditions. All data levels throughout Britain relate back to nominal sea-level at Newlyn, just outside Penzance in Cornwall, looking out over Mount's Bay. References calculated from this governing datum point are cleft into structures throughout the country and used as Bench Marks, from which engineers and architects work out construction heights for all new projects. Under this system, derived from the national Ordnance Survey, the heights of all structures in the UK can be checked and verified at any time. Setting-out therefore has to be very accurate as demolition orders can be placed on anything built in the wrong place or at the wrong height.

During this period I employed Stefan as a 16-year old labourer after he left school, to provide him with focus and earnings before he fell into the insidious benefits trap. He proved to be an excellent worker, both conscientious and energetic. He was also surprisingly strong; one afternoon just before he left school and I was attempting to clear a blocked drain at home, I dug down to the sewer in the rear garden and stitch-drilled into the top of the pipe to create rodding access at a point where no provision existed. I cleared the blockage and released the build-up of foul water but got the rods stuck in the drain. I tried for hours to dislodge them but without success and had all but given up by the time Stef sauntered home. He was fifteen at the time, slightly bigger and heavier than me with large powerful hands. Nonchalantly gripping the visible end of the rod with both of them he gave it one mighty tug – and it dislodged, gliding smoothly out of the stitch-hole with a resounding pop. I was known to be strong in relation to my size and it was a shock, albeit a pleasant one, to realize that my son had grown stronger than me.

Whilst the drainage project progressed Armstrong also won a subsidiary contract to widen part of Burneside 'back road' which I controlled concurrently. In addition to this the company had a standing contract with British Rail, or whichever part of its descendant conglomerate maintained tracks and properties at the time. The requirement was to preserve the routes of disused rail lines in a condition of safety for members of the public who might venture onto them. This involved clearing paths and rights of way which crossed railway land. Bridges, fences, gates etc had to be kept in a good state of repair and I was asked to find a contractor to carry out some works on the Cumbrian section of the old Tebay to Darlington line, though the actual track itself no longer existed. The work site was over a one mile walk from the nearest point which could be accessed by road, near the Croglin Castle Hotel at Kirkby Stephen, itself a good half hour's drive from Kendal. The walk traversed fields, slopes and fences before even reaching the old railway cut, so it proved impossible to persuade even one contractor to make the initial journey to price the work. It soon became clear that finding a reputable and reliable company to take on the contract would be impossible, so I devised an alternative plan as it was not within my nature to report to an employer that I had failed at anything. I checked through the contract details, invented a contractor and put in a price on his behalf just below the sum submitted by Armstrong and accepted by British Rail. I had already been told that I was not expected to make any profit from the maintenance works, as they were mere 'loss-leaders' which brought in larger, more lucrative contracts. I was instructed to get the work done by whoever I could as long as it was up to standard, without actually losing money.

Stefan and I picked one grey but dry Saturday morning from a diminishing autumn stock, and loaded up the car with sand, cement, a ladder and wheelbarrow on the roof, nails, tools and fencing timber, before heading out of town at 6am resembling a family of hillbillies leaving Oklahoma for richer pastures in the 1930s. We turned off the A685, drove to the end of a muddy farm track and then pushed and carried everything we needed along the now-grassy and defunct, rail route. I quickly repaired two fences before joining Stef, who had made a good start on cement-pointing weather-perished joints in the nearby stone-built foot-bridge. It remained a pleasant morning as we trowelled in the mortar and chatted about life's generalities. In the late afternoon however, it began to rain heavily and we responded by ramming the mortar home with our bare hands to finish the job faster. We were both soon saturated and squelching around in the half inch of rainwater trapped in our boots, but kept going and even burst out laughing each time we looked at each other. We finally finished the repairs, loaded up and trekked back to the car. Shivering with cold by the time we reached Tebay, the unanimous decision was to stop at the Cross Keys pub where we ordered pints and sat drying by the lounge fire. We spent a good three hours there, talking, laughing, playing darts, and I gave him the equivalent of two weeks wages for his efforts that day. Never once had he shown any sign of quitting or even discomfort and I could not have wished for better company.

For a while after completion of the Kendal contracts I supervised a road-construction job just outside Preston in Lancashire, but Armstrong had run out of local work and I was about to end up 'on the road' again, working away from home and living in digs. To avoid that I acquired a job as Site Manager for Dyke Brothers of Windermere, to build a block of luxury flats at Millans Park, Ambleside and again took Stef with me. We finished the flats on time and moved to the re-construction of a holiday centre at Silloth, on the Solway coast. This was a multi-million pounds refurbishment project which had run into trouble under its previous manager. We sorted the problems out and again completed on time, just, and began the conversion to luxury accommodation of the old Stock Ghyll bobbin mill, again in Ambleside. Stefan was becoming a valued colleague and well on the way to carving out a career for himself. I was actually planning a programme to train him into a site-supervisor but even at that time I could sense that his heart was not in the type of work he was doing, he had not yet experienced the harsh rigours of working outside ten hours a day through the long winter months, and I was also uncomfortable about committing him to a lifetime in such a dangerous and gruelling industry. For the moment though all was tranquil and I plodded steadily and reasonably successfully along, unaware that life was about to take a significant turn for the worse.

Sixteen

"Some men lead and some men follow
In self-pity, others wallow
But there's always, a reason why
Some men live and some men die"

(Author – 2007)

AT SILLOTH I EMPLOYED a foreman called John McCrindle, a re-nowned fighting man from the south of Scotland, to help restore the order and control necessary to complete the problematic project. He lived in Kendal with Shirley, caretaker of the Zion Church in Highgate.

I discovered John was frequently drunk on site and regularly booked in 'dead men' ie; claimed wages for operatives that did not exist, and pocketed the extra money. He was already earning a good wage and had use of a fully-financed company vehicle. I confronted him with evidence, he confessed and begged for leniency, and I allowed him to keep his job on the assurance it would be carried out correctly and efficiently in future. I issued him with dire warnings and instructions on how the company required him to behave, and eventually transferred him to the Stock Ghyll development when Silloth was complete. Now closer to home where I could monitor him effectively, I discovered that he was incapable of following instructions, his personality demanding that he conformed to his hard-man image instead of asking necessary technical questions, and repeatedly made rash, costly decisions. Eventually I was virtually forced into his dismissal because two of my other supervisors refused to work with him. John in turn refused to accept the reasons for his sacking and concentrated his frustration into a bitter grudge against me. The overwhelming hatred that evolved in his mind reached boiling point two years later and landed me back in Carlisle Crown Court.

I met a girl, Elaine, at Silloth, with whom I had a brief fling and about whom Dorothy found out, though I never admitted to it. This time she seemed so upset that I really did feel guilty and that perhaps there still was some genuine love left between us. She left for a while as usual and I decided that if she returned I would really put in some work at being a better husband. This resolution was seriously put to the test at Stock Ghyll, where I employed my father to do odd jobs and spend an hour or two in the Sportsman bar at lunchtimes, where he inevitably became popular. The old mill and adjacent buildings, which originally turned abundant timber from surrounding forests into cotton bobbins, had previously been converted into a variety of cheap flats, one of which was still occupied by the landowner's daughter, Kim. Before work started an excavator had been sent to dig some trial holes so that the ground could be analyzed for foundation design. Kim, perturbed by the intrusion and disturbance, hurled stones at the machine until excavation terminated. Foreseeing future trouble for myself in managing the upcoming project, I stopped off on a reconnaissance mission one afternoon en-route back to Kendal from Silloth.

Kim turned out to be a blonde, slim and attractive ex-policewoman with whom I had quite a nice chat outside her flat. She promised not to throw any more stones but I knew she was volatile and demanding of respect, so stopped by regularly to keep in touch. She mellowed considerably and smiled at me a lot from her window as I trundled about the site pretending to do something complicated. Her father, a very nice man called Mike, eventually re-housed her in another of his properties, on Ambleside's main road north, the A591, opposite the local church and football pitch. After I set up on site I began to notice on my way to work every morning that Kim was always looking out of her window when I passed, and I would smile and wave. But I did not smile in a jovial or neighbourly manner, I did it in a restrained, shy way, hinting that there may be something secretively shared between us. She visited site often, as both her sister and parents lived at separate houses on its boundary, and our mutual flirting intensified. One mid-summer morning the door to my site office opened and she entered dressed in tight, skimpy shorts and a figure-hugging top. I resisted the temptation because being aware that I had really hurt Dorothy bothered me, and now she had returned home I wanted to concentrate on rebuilding a future with her. I continued to hold out against Kim's advances but we did not stop flirting. She asked me to accompany her to a charitable function where she was giving a speech but I declined. She telephoned me at work the following day to say that I had missed a good night out and added "To show you how good, look out of your office window at the back"

I looked but could not see anyone or anything.

"What am I looking at?" I asked.

"In my dad's garden"

I looked again but still saw nothing. Some washing fluttered on a clothes line and as I focused on it I could make out several items of black ladies underwear. I said into the phone "Do you mean what I think you mean?"

"Yes, that's what I was wearing last night"

"Jesus"

"See you later"

I was seriously tempted but made time to talk myself out of it. She came to the office that afternoon, virtually naked but for a few skimpy items, and started unbuttoning my shirt. I said "Whoa, it's too hot in here and a stray bricklayer might walk in"

"It's nice and cool in my bedroom"

I was weakening fast as she leant back against the office door and pulled me to her – just as I saw the boss's car pull up outside. "Oh shit" I said as she straightened up and smoothed her hair. They passed each other in the doorway and he said matter-of-factly to me "Are you fucking her?"

"No" I replied honestly.

"Well if you are don't let Mike know, he hasn't signed the contract yet"

I told Kim I was married and wanted to stay that way but she was not deterred. She found out which pub I frequented and showed up in the Rainbow one Friday night looking stunning in a short, black skirt. Even after several pints I still resisted.

Breeding and showing Spaniel dogs was a passion of hers and she asked if I would accompany her to a weekend meeting in Wales. She was taking her caravan. I said no but on Friday afternoon she put a note bearing the venue address through my car window, open because of the summer heat, including directions and a phone number. I did not see the note because the breeze blew it between the seats, but unfortunately Dorothy did whilst rummaging for something or other and all hell broke loose. I swore my innocence but because of my poor track record she did not believe me.

While the ensuing fallout fell I received a letter from the tax office asking if I 'would like to reconsider my answer' to some question or other on one of their forms. I had forgotten to declare the interest on an investment account and they wanted blood. The same week Stefan said he was packing in his job, leaving home and going to live in Leeds. I asked why and he answered that he just wanted a different lifestyle where he could pursue his musical interests with friends who already lived there. He was a keen guitarist and had not the slightest interest in becoming a builder, and I couldn't criticize him for that. On a later visit to Leeds his friend Steve, who always had a little sheepdog with him, told me that he had accompanied Stef to a large outdoor concert on the city outskirts and one of the professional groups invited Stef to join them on stage for a couple of numbers. Apparently they knew him from previous events. Steve said Stef got up to a big cheer from the crowd, played well and was surrounded by well-wishers afterwards.

Dorothy took a paracetemol overdose when Stefan left home – two separate and individual actions which she routinely blamed me for. They pumped the drug out of her in hospital but she never got over our son's decision to leave. He was eighteen years old at the time, quite a normal age to fly the nest, but the complications and dynamics of our tripartheid relationship lifted his leaving into the realms of the disastrous in her mind. One reason for this was the secret worry she had about him, the cause of which she foolishly kept from me, which was to prove so catastrophic for all of us in the not too distant future.

The effects of my previously philanderous lifestyle, which had been compounded and intensified by her recent, understandable suspicions, must also have contributed to the mental turmoil she was plunged into by Stefan's decision not to live with us any longer, though he assured her that neither of us was the reason for it. I treated her very gently, with understanding, and cared for her as a priority. Her health improved considerably but mine began to falter. The build-up of stresses from various sources at this point began to tell and as my family threatened to disintegrate before my eyes, the reason for bearing and withstanding those stresses also began to disappear. I lost weight along with my appetite for the fight to preserve family life as I knew it, spent more time away from our unhappy home, and consequently drank more. I fell into the habit of going to the Rainbow after work where previously I looked forward to the comforts of my own home. It became a meeting place for colleagues and people looking for jobs or sub-contracts etc, often being referred to by them as 'The Office' I spent more time than usual there one Friday afternoon, in protracted discussion with roofing contractor Alan Pogson, the brother of Janet, with whom I went out for quite a while and was waiting to meet in the White Hart when Dorothy re-entered my life. We left together and he sped off in his white Sierra XR4 Sport, as I drove slowly and perfectly correctly out of the car park a few minutes later. The police car waiting in the shadows let Alan go, and instead followed me to a point where I was ambushed by two additional police vehicles. Alan and several others from the Office later pointed out that John McCrindle was in the bar that afternoon and at one point had disappeared for twenty minutes. The result was that I was breathalyzed and taken to magistrates' court. Whether McCrindle was involved or not in my capture had no bearing on the fact that I should not have driven after drinking all afternoon – I had no excuse for it and told the magistrates so. They obligingly banned me for eighteen months and as a consequence of this and the fact that I had lost interest in performing my job even efficiently let alone well, I also became unemployed. A few days later Dorothy left home again saying she wanted a divorce.

I could feel myself sliding downhill and was insufficiently concerned about the descent to attempt any arrest of the fall. I continued to lose weight to a maximum of three and a half stones, leaving me emaciated in comparison to my previous physique. I smoked too much and often sat in the pub all day, particularly on Saturdays. Some people looked at me with pity, some with concern, and others with a gloating smirk. If I cared, which I probably did, it hardly registered in the exhausted and confused jumble of my mind.

One Saturday afternoon I was joined in my gloom by ex-boxer Patrick Kennah, son-in-law of Mary Toal, my father's live-in ladyfriend. They were originally from the Wishaw area of Scotland, south east of Motherwell on the outskirts of Glasgow. Shortly afterwards, Mark Postlethwaite and his girlfriend bustled into the bar in an apparent state of panic. Mark's father ran a pub in town, the George and Dragon on Branthwaite Brow, and Mark had abused himself for years with drink, drugs and general lifestyle. His party trick was injecting neat vodka into his veins and I often wondered what manner of event turned his life in the direction it had taken, and was I in the early stages of such a turn? His life constantly teetered on the edge of impending disaster but he was a likeable bloke, respectful towards my father and myself, and was currently making a valiant attempt to get his affairs in order. He had found a girlfriend, got her pregnant and was in the process of acquiring a flat for them all. He was a painter and decorator to whom I had twice given a job, though I don't think he ever quite managed to work a full week. He obviously had more important matters at hand.

Mark and his girl were both very nervous and he was actually shaking, though that was not uncommon for him. He came over and hesitantly sat down as Pat asked "Whit's the matter Marrk?"

Mark stammered "Nick's just 'ad a go at us and pushed 'er" She was heavily pregnant.

"Who, Alan Nick?"

"Yeah, the bastard"

"Whit ferr?"

"Well, I owe 'im money from way back but there's no need to 'ave a go in the pub and push 'er around is there?"

"Which pub?" I intervened.

"The Kent ant' worst thing is she's left 'er 'andbag wi' our keys an' cash 'an everythin' in it"

"So you've no money?"

"No"

"And the handbag's definitely in the Kent?" I asked, looking at the girl. She nodded with saucer-eyes.

"Yes" added Mark "Int' bar ont' table nextut' front winda"

I thought for a moment whist fumbling in my jeans for some money.

"Get yersels a drink and I'll go for the bag before it disappears"

Mark grasped the note in trembling fingers "Thanks mate, y'know A'll pay y'back"

"Yeah right. Don't leave here till I get back. If y'show up at the Kent yer on yer own"

"I won't, I won't, A'll keep well out of it"

I drained my glass and left.

Pat followed.

Alan Nicholson comprised about seventeen stones of muscle and beer-belly. He had a simian brow, big arms and shoulders and was very strong. I had employed him on the hospital drainage job where he tossed stone paving slabs around like quoits. He was a simple, open man though sometimes a bit heavy-handed, and also worked as a bouncer. I liked his humour and rumbustious approach to life most of the time.

When Pat and I entered the Kent it was obvious Nick was slightly drunk. He had three or four sycophants hanging around him who appeared to be still celebrating the glory of Nick's magnificent victory over the frail and dying Mark Postlethwaite and his pregnant girlfriend. Nick was singing between bouts of laughter echoed by his cronies, but waved across at us. I nodded back but the handbag was nowhere to be seen so I said to the barman, Eric Nicholson "I believe Mark Poss's girlfriend left her bag here?"

Abrupt silence enveloped the room, apart from the juke box still warbling obliviously away to some long-forgotten tune, and the smiles faded from both Nicholson faces. Alan turned full square round to face me as his followers scuttled behind him "What's that got to do wi' you?" demanded Nick, flicking his cigarette butt across the room.

I remained perfectly still, continued to face the bar and said softly "Be quiet Nick, you've done enough today, I just want the girl's bag"

"Fuckin' bag stays where it is 'til that little cunt pays what he owes me"

Nick was obviously agitated and prepared for confrontation but I knew he was drunk and decided to take control of the situation before it got out of hand. I walked across the room with hands pocketed in a non-threatening approach. Onlookers moved aside and watched intently as the atmosphere electrified. Nick slowly and purposefully placed his glass on the bar and let his massive hands hang loose and ready by his sides. I stood a yard from him and looked into his hooded eyes "You shouldn't bully people who are smaller than you Nick, I've told you before"

He thrust out his big chest even further than his belly and snarled "He fuckin' owes me money"

I continued "And you shouldn't knock pregnant women about"

Although it had to be said, the statement challenged Nick's manhood, the central point of his existence and sole source of pride in himself apart from his just reputation as a workhorse. The bar remained in absolute silence as he attempted to preserve his image "Well you can take the little bastard's place if y'want" he openly challenged.

"Ok" I shrugged without moving my hands from my pockets, and butted him between the eyes.

He staggered backwards into his supporters, wavered, buckled at the knees but did not go down, his immense strength and pride kept him upright, and as he was drunk I did not follow up. He rallied, straightened, faced me square on and said to the room "Give him the bag"

I thanked him, apologized to the barman for the disturbance, and left.

Pat followed.

Seventeen

"I knew a man who hid from the sun
And in his mind he carried a gun
And when the day became more shady
He drew the pistol but missed the lady"

(Author – 2007)

IN 1942 AS WAR had raged throughout Europe, Jack Davison Jnr came wearily but gladly home on leave from service in the Royal Navy. After a well-earned night out on the town he went back to his parents' house with two new pals to whom he had promised suppers of true English tea and toast. They were Canadian soldiers also on leave before rejoining allied resistance to the German forces in Belgium. One of the two was Alexander Jay Lucas from the town of Airdrie, west of Lake Sullivan in the province of Alberta. He had been born and raised on a prairie cattle farm and was a genuine cowboy.

Their rowdy arrival caused quite a stir along Lound Road and in the household where Jack's parents and five sisters awaited his return. The servicemen were ushered into the front lounge whilst the sisters busied themselves excitedly in the kitchen, listening to the resonant laughter from the three comrades-in-arms filtering through from the adjacent room. The laughter subsided abruptly as a platter of perfectly toasted bread was taken into the room, because it was carried by the most beautiful girl Alex Lucas had ever seen, 16-year old Edith Davison. There was an instant attraction between them and they walked out together several times over the coming weeks. The development and blossoming of their friendship was cut short however, when the young soldier was transported back to front line action, from where he returned directly to Canada after the war and marriage to a local girl. A few years afterwards Edith was also married with a life contained in Kendal town. Forty years later, when both marriages had run their respective courses through death or disaffection, Edith, then in her fifties and weary of life, received a telephone call. It was from her sister,

Winifred, who needed to see her.

"Have you seen this?" she asked, handing Edith a folded copy of the Westmorland Gazette.

Edith scanned the page in confusion before looking inquisitively at her younger sister "What?"

Winnie extended a finger and pointed to a little square of text under the heading 'Canadian GI seeks his war girl'

It had been inserted by A J Lucas of Alberta, Canada, who was trying to contact Edith Davison of Kendal. The sisterhood got in touch with Alex, who flew over immediately to meet the woman he had last known as a girl, half a lifetime ago, and when he saw her again he knew instantly that he had made a good decision "I loved her then and I love her now" he often drawled in his West Canadian accent.

They married in England and thereafter set up home in Alberta where they spent many happy years together, travelling widely and enjoying life to the full.

Alex died in Canada and Edith brought his ashes back to England when she returned to be close to her family. I helped her scatter them in the sea off South Shields, a place they had visited often and about which Alex had said "I could live here"

Edith keeps the memorial plaque I made for her in the lounge of her Kendal home. It reads: 'In loving memory of my dear husband Alexander Jay Lucas of Alberta, Canada – A good man – laid to rest at Littlehaven Beach, South Shields, Tyneside on 15th January 2000 – Walk with God'

He had at least made it into the new millennium.

My own life was descending to street level again and inwardly at least, I felt ashamed of that fact. Dorothy had not returned and I felt the loss of her and Stefan, whom I rarely saw. I was drifting through life with no direction, no purpose and dwindling interest in the future. I shopped once a month and bought a week's supply of food. After one such post closing-time trip I was carrying two plastic carrier bags full of canned food and red wine when it started to rain heavily. I had walked all the way from town after drinking at the Ribble Club and was still quarter of a mile from home when the plastic bag handle cut into the flesh of my hand. I had damaged a finger two days before on a broken glass from which I was draining neat whiskey, and the weight of the bag forced the wound open again. Blood ran down the slick plastic to the inside of the bag, and rain ran down my forehead into my eyes. It seemed as though nature itself had turned against me and I began to feel for the first time in my life, that numbing shroud of hopelessness that turned alcohol, drugs and solitude into havens of comfort.

When I reached the cold, lonely place that was home and waded through the mess that I had allowed to accumulate over the preceding months, feelings of desolation and loneliness overtook me. I flopped into the one uncluttered armchair and opened the bottle I had left by its side the night before. I lit yet another cigarette and flicked the match uncaringly onto the carpet, from where it sent a spiralling wisp of silver-grey smoke towards the ceiling. I watched the bloodied match for five minutes, wondering whether it might erupt again phoenix-like, into engulfing flame. I sat almost motionless for hours, staring into space, hearing but not listening to the sounds of normality outside my darkened cocoon, and I think a tear of sadness rolled down my face, imitating the previous rain which had seeped into the clothes I still wore, before I fell into a deep sleep and dreamed a recurring theme:

A shadow closes from behind as it pursues me through a dark, narrow alley – I run, terrified – a hand grasps at my neck and at the last moment I turn and punch in desperate defence – the shadow, now a man, falls – a darker shadow spreads on the ground beneath his head – I continue to flee – hiding in corners and secret places – I can hear a wailing police siren in the distance – I have killed a man and am being hunted – for murder – there is no hope of escape – no future apart from prison – my life is over.

I awoke after midnight still in the chair, struggled wearily to my feet and went outside to breathe fresh air. The moon and stars were bright in the overhead blackness. Gazing up I imagined myself standing as I was, but viewed from a distant point in the sky. A lone being looking towards the constellations – a microscopic, barely noticeable and totally insignificant speck of humanity standing on the surface of a massive, colossal ball of – dust – part of a billowing cloud of tiny particles that drifted through an infinite, endless black void so immense that billions of gigantic dust clouds were lost in its vastness. What mattered my trivial problems – even on the single planet where I lived out my short allowance of time?

Far more prodigious troubles than mine existed – at least I had the greatest gift possible in the whole of that dark, meaningless space – life. Life itself and the freedom to enjoy it, which should surely both be treasured for their own sakes. I was lucky to be alive, of course I was, and free, and I would be thankful.

I went back into the house and looked around – perhaps the mess was not so bad after all. Starting with the whiskey bottles I commenced a major clean-up of my home and life. I washed mountains of crockery, clothing and bed-sheets, wiped every surface, dusted, swept and vacuumed, rearranged and tidied – I even scrubbed the toilet and oven. When morning light broke the house was pristine and I was ready in my trainers. I walked as quickly as possible the five miles of an old running route I used as a boxer, though then I did it in heavy work-boots so that when I took them off, my feet floated and danced as if weightless. It was good to be out and using my lungs and limbs again in the crisp morning air. I cleared my mind of all negativity and allowed in only the beauty of nature, the wonder of life on earth and the exultation of being alive – and being part of it all. My limbs swung vigorously and my heart pumped life-giving blood to them until I glowed with resurgent health. I had forgotten this feeling of well-being but would not let it go again. I held my head high and smiled at the early-morning people I passed – and they smiled back. I began to concentrate on what was good about me, what I was good at, and what was good for me – I would revert to the basics of my life – and survive.

The problem of not having a valid driving licence or personal transport now became less so. I ceased feeling sorry for myself and got a job with Sedgwick Joinery to help refurbish the ferry boats, Teal and Tern, on Windermere Lake. I was picked up from home every morning by Billy Riddell in a company van, and re-discovered the rewards of carpentry and long days of physical labour. The boats were anchored in dock for the winter and their steel hulls acted like refrigerators. The air inside was freezing but the manual exertion of work invigoratingly warming. We were employed to re-line the interiors with high-quality oak panelling, including the bar frontages, counter tops, corner moulds and friezes, columns, pediments and corbels. The work was interestingly precise but not mentally demanding, and I found myself absently whistling and even singing aloud throughout the day, as I had years before.

When I thought about the mess my personal life had become and the wasted years of effort, it was sobering and quite depressing, so I tried as much as possible to avoid those thoughts. I had cut smoking to evenings only, drinking to weekends and was healthier but still too thin, though I was eating better food. I resumed going out at weekends but in Kendal my reputation kept dragging me backwards. A family friend named James Toal, the youngest of Mary's sons, came to me one day and asked for advice. His wife had left him for another man, life was falling apart and he was being terrorized by the wife-stealer, Alvin Finch. Alvin was an ex-professional boxer who controlled some of the nightclub bouncers in Kendal and the Lakes. He was several years younger than me, and taller, but I knew him as an amateur when he was a nice kid. He had instructed James, a non-violent man, not to enter certain places and to address him with maximum respect if ever their paths should accidentally cross. Alvin was an old boyfriend of James's wife, Tracy, apparently still had feelings for her and did not want to be reminded of James's existence.

"Jesus Christ" complained James "E's teken mi wife, she's teken t'kids, A'm gonna lose t'ouse, 'e could fuckin' kill me if 'e wanted to, an' now 'e's tellin' me where I can an' can't fuckin' go"

I felt sorry for him. He was not the most reliable person on earth but was a likeable bloke and very attached to his family. I also felt somewhat involved as I was godfather to one of his two sons, and did not regard Alvin as the best father role-model. I said reassuringly "Alvin's ok, prob'ly just tryin' to impress Tracy, I'll 'ave a word next time I bump into 'im"

That time arrived the following Friday night in the Alleycats nightclub, where my brother John and I had worked as bouncers (or Crowd Control Engineers as John preferred) a few years before.

I was out for a few pints with Les Mitchell, Alan's brother, a bodybuilder whom I'd employed at Stock Ghyll as a labourer and with whom I had started training in an attempt to regain some healthy weight. We were chatting in the bar when he nodded and I looked up to see James walking straight towards me. He moved like a robot with his eyes fixed unflinchingly on mine. As he got closer I could see rivulets of sweat trickling down the side of his face to the collar of his blue shirt. I said to him "You been on the wacky-baccy or somethin' Jamesy?"

He kept staring straight at me and tried to speak without moving his lips. There was abject terror in his eyes. He whispered through the side of his trembling mouth "E's behind me, right be'ind me an' 'e's gonna fuckin' kill me 'e sez"

"Who is?"

"Fuckin' Finchy, don't y'remember I told ye?"

I looked past him and could see Alvin laughing and joking with a group of the club's bouncers. I asked James "What's the problem?"

"E follered me in 'ere 'cos I went int' Kent when 'e was there – 'e's just stopped 'cos A'm talkin' to you"

"You sure y'not imaginin' this James?"

"No, no, 'e took a swing at me outside but I ran"

I considered the situation for a minute, there were three bouncers with Alvin plus two hangers on, not good odds, but just as I was deciding whether or not he was really looking for trouble he shot a glance in our direction which told me that James's fears were not unfounded. I strolled over and tapped Alvin on the shoulder "Is there some problem between you and Jimmy Toal?" I asked with a smile, inviting an answer involving some misunderstanding and leading to peaceful resolution.

"Well it's not your problem unless you wannit to be"

His response surprised me.

"Are you challengin' me Alvin, 'cos maybe I do wannit to be?"

I do not think he wanted to say yes but he had put himself on the spot in front of his cronies, who now fell silent. He did not attack but spread his arms before him in a gesture of invitation. I knew that he would interpret a non-aggressive response from me as cowardice, which would increase his confidence sufficiently to press that advantage. As we were both ex-boxers I assumed Alvin would expect fists to be used so surprised him with a repeat of the headbutt I had landed on Alan Nick a few weeks before. Alvin's already contoured nose exploded into a cascade of blood as he fell backwards into his pals, who held him upright before thrusting him forward again. He lurched at me with a flying fist but as he came forward I caught him again with the head and this time, down he went. I stood back and sportingly allowed him to rise, which he did quickly but his eyes told me his heart was no longer in the fight. Instead he grabbed the nearest person to him, who happened to be one of the bouncers wearing a brilliantly-white shirt, and dulled its brightness by wiping his bloody face across it.

I learned after this altercation that Alvin had once tried to bully Stefan, who also had a fling with Tracy at one point before she was married, so did not feel too bad about the outcome. Alvin and I got along fine after that and he did not terrorize James again as far as I know.

Eighteen

"In Britain today a construction worker aged 16 to 24
is injured every 4 minutes,
Seriously injured every 40 minutes,
And killed every 4 weeks"

('Building Worker' 2006)

"In this industry today, 150 workers [3 per week]
are being killed every year by uncaring employers"

(Eric Tomlinson – UCATT – 1972)

WHEN REFURBISHMENT OF THE Windermere boats was finished I saw an advertisement in the paper for various construction personnel required by Haygarth Brothers Ltd, a local firm with about a hundred employees. They were not looking specifically for joiners but their advert told me they must have a significant amount of work on the books, and they had a good reputation as an employer. I telephoned and spoke to Frank Haygarth who asked "Are you't lad that ran t'ospital drainage job a while back?"

I told him I was and he said "Aye, we'll 'ave summat for you lad, A'll talk to Malcolm and ring y'back"

He did shortly after and told me to report to their office the following Monday. Haygarth Bros was a rural firm specializing in stone-walling and slate roofing, which had moved successfully into general building and was now venturing into the cut-throat world of civil-engineering contracting, an area I knew well. Nothing had been agreed regarding my actual job or wage and I had not bothered to ask. I was glad to have a local job in which I did not have to drive or think too much.

A four-strong team of us went off in a van to start a new contract at Barrow-in-Furness, a west-coast town historically dominated by Vickers' shipyard but fallen into decline with the rest of the British shipbuilding industry. Our job was to part demolish, part refurbish and add some new-build to a derelict hospital in transformation to residential flats. It was the first project for the appointed foreman and I helped him as much as I could with setting out and organization. We became friends and a while later I bought a car from him for Stefan's 21st birthday. Stef was upset when he saw the car because he wanted it but could not afford to run it, so we changed it for a chopper-style motor-bike which he chose. He and a friend toured the north on the bike that summer of 1991, busking to eat and camping out in the countryside. They chose fields where horses pastured, gained the animals' trust by talking softly to them, then rode around bareback in the warm evenings. Dorothy still has photographs, framed by myself, of this happy and independent time in his life.

The Barrow project seemed to be going well but I got a message from Contracts Manager, Roy Exelby one Friday, not to catch the van on Monday, the boss wanted to see me in the office. Fearing the worst I scanned the newspapers again at the weekend but work in the industry was scarce, many small firms having already fallen into bankruptcy. I waited forlornly in the company's yard on Monday morning until Malcolm Haygarth ambled out of the office "Hello Bob, has anybody told y'what the problem is?" he asked.

"No, didn't know there was a problem"

"Well it's this underground stream that runs through t'yard 'ere, it's an adopted drain but part of our sub-base 'as collapsed into it. We need to build a culvert"

Malcolm was undoubtedly aware that I had built large diameter culverts (which are essentially tunnels to channel water courses under roads or structures) at the hospital drainage project for Armstrong.

"Oh" I said in surprise "That shouldn't be a problem"

"Graham's 'ere wit' JCB to dig out an' lift t'rings in an' there's plenty timber for t'inside formwork. I'd guess you'll need concrete tomorrow or Wednesday so just let t'office know how much and they'll order it for ye"

"Ok Malcolm, A'll let y'know when it's done"

I felt exhilarated to know I had been effectively promoted already when I actually thought I'd been sacked, so set about the task with vigour. I had a quick word with Graham Magennis, the JCB driver and he began placing the concrete pipe sections along the drainage line, which was the route of the stream that had run for centuries carrying rainwater from the sloping approach to Kendal Castle, once home to Henry VIII's last wife, Katherine Parr. The rings were to be placed end to end and interlocking, the joints sealed and then covered in protective mass concrete to withstand vehicular weight from above. Malcolm had designed the joints to have timber form-work fitted in a wheel-shape to the inside, supporting the concrete above, and then stripped after it had set. This I judged would be awkward and time consuming and already had in mind a simpler method. I marked the new culvert's line and level as Graham com-menced the dig, then ordered two full loads; 12 cubic metres, of high-strength concrete for delivery in an hour's time. In the wood-store I found some bits of old, flexible hardboard, cut them into 500mm wide strips and soaked them to increase flexibility as Graham lifted the first ring. As each joint was formed I bent a strip of hardboard over the top of it, wedging each end into the sides of the excavated trench to keep it in place. Graham deftly placed the last ring and I was right behind him to cover the joint just as the first batch of con-crete arrived. We backed the load right up to the new culvert posi-tion and channelled the concrete straight on top, moving the lorry slowly along so the cover was even and simply needed some level-ling out and floating off. The same procedure was followed with the second load, then a quick clean-up and we were finished. It was just after 11am when I went over to the office where Malcolm asked "Problems?"

I replied "No, the job's done, what's next?"

I and a colleague, Alan Wharton, spent a pleasant few weeks erect-ing fencing at a country estate near Windermere, before I was put in charge of a squad to repair the roofs and fences of an outward bound centre at the far end of the Kentmere valley, just below the reservoir that feeds water to Croppers' paper mill at Burneside. The rock forming the steep valley is mainly slate and is riddled with old mine workings from when it and other minerals were recov-ered commercially for industrial use. The area is a desolate place in winter months once past the farms at the lower end of the ravine, and frequented by varied wildlife including deer, foxes, peregrine falcons, buzzards, badgers and even an adder or two.

With work well under way we arrived one misty morning to see that on one of the cliff ledges far above us, two domestic rams were marooned on an isolated promontory, probably after scrambling down from the upper plateau to feed on the lush, untouched vegetation there. They were obviously unable to make the return ascent and as the ledge was well over a hundred feet above ground level, three quarters of the way up a sheer cliff face, there was no hope of them reaching safety without assistance. I remembered how unpleasant being stranded on a lofty ledge was, so sent one of the lads to let the farmer know of his rams' predicament, and less than an hour later we watched a mountain-rescue vehicle trundle up the track towards us. Four figures alighted at the foot of the cliff, from where three of them spent half an hour climbing to the plateau. They secured ropes above the ledge and one man abseiled down to join the nervous animals, as we took turns watching the mini-drama through the theodolite telescope.

The climber on the ledge quickly made some adjustments to his webbing, grabbed the nearest ram by its horns and twisted the rope around them several times before hopping out into the chasm, taking the flailing animal with him. The bewildered ram became uncannily calm during its descent, relinquishing its fate to the rescuer, and they were lowered swiftly down to the valley floor. The ram was released and scampered away, shaking its head as if in disbelief at its miraculous escape. The whole operation was then repeated to bring the second ram down, before I had to insist that work should resume.

Just before we finished the Kentmere project one of the men noticed a patch of white high up on the fragmented rock scree at the foot of another nearby cliff. During our last lunch break in the valley, I and another of the team climbed up to investigate and found a dead foxhound. We spoke to the farmer again and its owner came to collect it after we pointed the way. He had lost the dog a week earlier and told us that he had been tracking a vixen which had repeatedly destroyed local poultry. He worked on foot with his pack of twelve hounds, because of course no horse could negotiate the terrain, and the fox had led them to the cliff top. It was misty as usual and visibility poor. The hounds followed the fox's scent and gave chase across the plateau right up to the cliff edge, where the fox jinked left to make her escape. Some of the following pack kept after her, some wandered around yelping in confusion, but the leading dog went over the edge in its blind pursuit, just as the wily vixen had intended.

Next came a return to the Westmorland General Hospital, where I had installed the off-site drainage. This time to take control of Haygarth's contracted installation of all the external works including car parks, roads, kerbing and footpaths. The foreman in charge, Neville, was at the time constructing a large overspill parking area to the rear of the main hospital, but had fallen into a surface-water drainage trench, damaged his leg and gone sick. The contracts-manager had taken over to cover the emergency and found something drastically wrong with the levels and gradients implemented so far. He asked if I could sort things out so I went through the engineering data with him, and then checked all the levels myself against the provided bench mark. I discovered that the actual levels as marked on site were correct, but no allowance had been made for the height of the 'traveller' (a mobile profile used to check depths regularly as excavation proceeds). These days this operation is carried out using rotating laser-levels and electronic total-setting-out-stations, but the project in question took place in the relatively low-tech 1980s, in a rural location. As a consequence of this mistake the car park excavation was beginning to resemble the tilted take-off deck on an aircraft carrier. I put the job right and completed on schedule.

One of the last tasks at this site was to paint divisionary lines on the tarmac surface to delineate parking areas, and because the design followed the shape of the available land to maximize space, the lining traced an odd shape with zig-zagging, curving kerbs at many different but connecting levels and gradients. The line-painting was sub-contracted to a specialist company but it was my duty to set out all the working points of reference, and I picked a quiet, sunny weekend to do it when I could take time to get it right – the lines would be there for all to see for a long time.

On Monday morning the sub-contractors rolled up with their convoy of equipment, and a bloke probably in his sixties de-cabbed with a bundle of architectural drawings tucked under an arm, a 100-metre tape in hand and a Woodbine hanging from his mouth. I watched apprehensively as he strode purposefully around the tarmac surface, a workmate hurrying the end of the tape from point to point at his command in the manner of a sheepdog trial, while he scribbled in a grubby notebook with a small pen from the bookie's shop. After forty minutes he strolled over to my site office.

"Who set the car park out?" he demanded.

"I did" I replied with resignation.

"Well son, I've been doing this job for thirty two years and this is only the second one ever that's been dead-right to the drawings"

Praise indeed!

I enjoyed working for Haygarth, had obviously proved my worth to the company and as a result was given considerable freedom and support in carrying out my duties, the demarcation of which was not rigidly enforced. I was by then an official site supervisor again but the days passed quickly and rewardingly because I was also able to work physically when time allowed, which was not the case with bigger companies.

My presence was requested at a site in the centre of Kendal, where we were sub-contracting the external works from London-based main contractor, Bovis, on the construction of new council offices and a multi-storey car park off Lowther Street. Bovis is a large international company and this project was managed from their Glasgow office, renowned for its tough tactics. Haygarth as a company was not used to the heavy-handed methods employed by many civil-engineering contractors, were following their instincts in trying to be as helpful as possible and being abused by the Glaswegian site management as a consequence. The original Haygarth foreman had gone sick with stress and refused to return to the site, the contracts manager and even the boss had supervised for short spells, and eventually installed big John Tyson as foreman to instill some steely control over their works, which were falling behind and losing money. Problems continued.

I arrived on site with a hangover one dismal, frosty Monday morning and spoke to the Bovis office secretary, a local girl. She told me that most of the time John sat in the office with his head in his hands, overwhelmed by his failed attempts to cope with the pressure exerted by the Glasgow boys, who applied it aggressively and mercilessly. Operations were directed by a project manager who wielded an unforgiving and ruthless approach to achieving success for his company. I had met this mindset before at Taylor Woodrow so was not as daunted by its effects as my predecessors on site – to the point where it had affected their health. In an early conversation one Bovis supervisor admitted that although they did not have a specific policy of bankrupting sub-contractors, they were conscious that if one did fail financially it was extremely unlikely that he would have to be paid, hence more profit for Bovis. Their methods at the Kendal project appeared to be to run their contractors ragged with technicalities and urgent requests for immediate action. Everything had to suit Bovis plans and programmes and never those of the smaller, more vulnerable companies who provided them with specialist services. This had been successful for Bovis to the point where Haygarth and others were operating flat out to maintain a position of simply satisfying and keeping pace with the main contractor's often unreasonable requests, and paying little regard to the interests of their own companies. The major financial problem in this unhealthy situation for the sub-contractors, was that they were not waiting for nor even requesting official written instructions from Bovis to carry out extra works and contract variations, of which there were many and even worse, neither were they recording additional outlay in the form of man-hours worked, plant employed, materials used plus consequential delays to their actual contract. Some companies had in fact carried out a massive amount of work that they would never be paid for, had already been denied significant payments on various technicalities, were leaving themselves vulnerable to delay and overrun contra-charges because the main part of their works had been neglected, and were carrying on apparently regardless in this financially-suicidal manner. Haygarth was at least aware of the dangers.

On my first tour of the site, which had a multi-million pounds contractual value, I found every single Haygarth employee engaged on undocumented extra works, most of them being actively, directly and contrary to contract terms, supervised by Bovis who were careful to keep their instructions verbal. I halted all work immediately, causing irritated frowns amongst the Bovis bully-boys and re-deployed all Haygarth operatives to works included in our official contract, apart from a few men that I sent back to the yard as unnecessary. After a short, stunned delay there was a rumbling outcry from the Bovis supervisors who came stomping into my site office demanding to know "Whit the fuck's goan on here son?"

I looked directly at them until calm prevailed before replying "If you're requesting extra works I presume you've brought the appropriate documentation, as described in clause 4(e) on page 22 of our contract terms and conditions?"

Grisly jaws dropped as the Glaswegians looked at each other from beneath deeply-furrowed brows, and then back to me "Whit feckin conditions, we havne time tae feck aboot like this mon?"

"It would actually save time for both of us if you brought the necessary paperwork with you when extra works are requested, one specific request for each separate task and don't forget that the contract allows us time to prepare and evaluate"

"Prepare and evaluate my asshole boyo, you'll be aff this feckin site toneet"

An hour later two of the boys were back after checking their legal position with the manager "Alreet, whors these bits ae feckin paper y'want signin?"

"No, you bring the paper, already signed and telling us clearly what you would like us to do. We then tell you if we are able to do it, and our preferred start date"

"FECKIN BASTARD"

They tried going directly to the operatives on site and resuming previous arrangements, but I had warned the men who then took great delight in referring all requests to myself. I noticed a make-shift scoreboard which was pinned up outside the canteen and previously read Bovis:10 v Haygarth:0, now read Bovis:10 v Haygarth:1. Eventually I got an efficient system up and running and was even given an office assistant to process the necessary paperwork. The documentation was in fact essential and turned what would certainly have been a financial disaster into a profitable endeavour. There were many heated arguments on site and at one stage Bovis asked for me to be replaced, but Haygarth replied stalwartly that if I went, so did they all.

We finished ahead of schedule, with additional profits from all the correctly-documented extra works, and a scoreboard reading of Bovis:10 v Haygarth:14. I was however, about to meet up again with another aggressive Scotsman.

Throughout all this time Dorothy did not come home and I did not take up with any other women, but my thoughts were beginning to veer in that direction. I had contacted her several times by telephone and letter but she did not respond and although I still loved her, I had no intention of letting life slip by in forlorn hope.

Nineteen

"...But then, the greatest song I'd ever heard
The singing of a blinded bird..."

(Spike Milligan – Circa 1985)

I FELL INTO THE habit of going out for a drink on Sunday nights
with Les Mitchell, his brother Alan and one or two other friends,
and our first and last port of call was usually the Rainbow. A trip to
the toilets late one summer's evening brought me face to face with
John McCrindle, who punched me in the mouth whilst I was otherwise occupied, cutting my lip. I was told that a few days previously
he had knocked cold 17-stone Richard Harrison with one punch
and was feeling even more confident than usual. People intervened
though, leaving me to wash the blood from my face and take time
out to let things cool down. When I re-entered the bar however,
McCrindle was waiting for me, hopping about like an unleashed
bull-terrier "Ootside noo" he snarled, making for the door.

The crowded pub was already alert and expectant as word of his
initial, successful attack had spread quickly, but now the room fell
into pregnant silence. Under scrutiny from the onlookers I shrugged
and followed him. I would have preferred not to be in that situation
at that time, particularly as I had drunk quite a lot, was under-
weight and trying to stay out of trouble, but pride had been brought
into play. It was dark outside and I was unsure which way he had
gone until he growled from the gloom "Up here cunt"

I followed up the alley towards the car park at the rear of the pub.
Halfway along there is a storage area built over the path creating
a totally dark, unlit tunnel. Adjacent to the Rainbow there stands
a small Quiggins Mint Cake factory with night-time security spot-
lighting and as I emerged from the tunnel at the far end, this daz-
zling light shone directly and blindingly into my eyes. McCrindle
had obviously picked this place for his second attack and possibly
rehearsed his manoeuvre at an earlier date. I heard feet crunching
on the gravel but not until the last moment did I see his bobbing
frame silhouetted by the spotlight behind him. In that instant I au-

tomatically rammed a straight right in the direction of the onrush-
ing figure. The punch caught him running onto it, increasing its
force, and he began his descent. Angered by his two underhand
attacks I delivered a follow-up left and a looping right uppercut
before he landed, sending his head crashing backwards onto the
ground. I knew immediately by his deep, staccato breathing that
he was unconscious. A dark stain spread quickly on the ground beneath his upturned face. I shouted to the gathering crowd to phone
for an ambulance, and stayed with my fallen assailant until help
arrived.

A less tough and fit person might have died I was told. John
did not but the force of the blows resulted in injuries so bad it was
said, that the police refused to believe I had not used a weapon
and charged me with Attempted Murder. His head had been jolted
back so violently they informed me enthusiastically, that a bone
in his spine had been chipped and although he had survived, he
might well be paralysed. This was a sobering shock for me though
in truth I felt little sympathy for McCrindle, but despite consequent
searches and investigations including my shoes being forensically
examined after a hair was found clinging to dried blood on one of
them, the police found no evidence of anything other than the truth,
that he had assaulted me in the toilets and I had later hit him with
my fists only when he attacked a second time. They knew that I had
stood in John's blood because I was still kneeling at his side when
they arrived in answer to the emergency call, and the hair turned
out to be canine. They suspected that I had picked up a heavy glass
ashtray or something else to use as a weapon as I followed him outside, but all witnesses confirmed that I left empty-handed, and that
McCrindle was definitely the aggressor.

The charge against me was commuted to Grievous Bodily Harm,
and McCrindle was charged with Actual Bodily Harm. He pleaded
guilty at the magistrates' court but I pleaded not guilty and elected
for trial at Carlisle again, where I eventually agreed to plead guilty
when the judge told me what the sentence would be. He was satisfied that we had agreed to fight, that no weapons were used and
that we were therefore equally responsible for the consequences. I
received the same sentence as McCrindle: Conditional Discharge.
John continues to wander around the pubs of Kendal without a dis-
ability except the one self-imposed upon his mind.

Shortly after this, late one warm but dull Saturday afternoon, I received a telephone call from my father. He was in the Rainbow with Mary and Dorothy, who wanted to talk to me, and asked if I would come down. I had waited over two years for her to return and was ready for a change in direction. After not seeing her for several months I had passed her twice in the preceding week on my way home from work. My driving ban had expired, I had retrieved the car from outside her mother's house and was mobile again. Unusually, she was smiling on both occasions.

When I entered the Rainbow she was smiling again and as soon as my dad and Mary left she kissed me passionately. Before long she was back home and I did not ask what she had been up to during our two years apart. I had remained more or less celibate and happy to wallow in my guilty self-pity. She seemed to have expunged something troublesome from her system, was more in control of her emotions and we agreed to move forward with a clean slate. We rediscovered slightly-modified versions of each other, went abroad on holiday and out walking together and re-engaged in a healthy social life. She still had a lot of spare time and often visited Stefan in Leeds, but always through the week when I was at work. She took food and provisions, cleaned his rooms, and we all got along well together on the occasions when she brought him back for a visit. The storm-damaged ship that was our life together seemed once again to have survived troubled waters and the future appeared brighter than for a long time. Unfortunately, we were about to receive the most tragic, traumatic and shattering blow of our lives.

Twenty

"My child is dead, and with my child my joys are buried"

(Shakespeare – Romeo and Juliet)

CHRISTMAS 1992 WAS A happy and settled one for us during which we enjoyed the present and anticipated the future with hope. Stefan visited for a few days with presents for his mother and I. He looked a bit unkempt but was obviously happy. He laughed a lot and spoke about his plans for the future and I could see the pleasure radiating from his mother's eyes at our open, amiable conversation. With my birthday coming up in January he also gave me a book about the second world war. It bears the inscription from him on the inner leaf 'To Dad, Happy Birthday 1993 – Love from Stefan, X' Paradoxically, we both admired military bravery and endurance but also agreed on the futile absurdity and colossal cruelty of war. When he left we shook hands at the door, a private little moment between the two of us, and he gave me a look which said 'I know there have been problems in the past but everything is alright now' There was genuine love in his eyes and I felt a powerful surge of love for him in return. It seemed like we had been to hell and back as a family but that nothing could ever go seriously wrong again. How wrong I was and how I wish I had hugged him close to me that day in December 1992, instead of saving it for a 'later' that never came.

Dorothy and I had our ups and downs over the years with me undoubtedly to blame for most of the downs, before our serious split in 1990 after sixteen years of marriage. The two years we spent apart seemed to heal the wounds and sweep away the debris and wreckage of the past, and when we reconciled it really did feel like a new, fresh start. Stefan remained in Leeds and although we still worried about him, we enjoyed a period of relative calm and renewed happiness. It seemed that we might still attain the elusive quiet and peaceful life together that we both wished for. We also received news from Stefan that promised to add greatly to our lives and contentment. His girlfriend Jill was pregnant and though only 38 and 40 respectively, we were to become grandparents. The expectant couple had already begun to collect pieces of furniture and picked prospective names for their child, and been promised a three-bedroomed house by a Leeds Housing Association. I visited them at home and thought Jill was a polite, well-spoken girl. She came from the London area and was several years older than Stefan. The rooms they shared at 65 Manor Drive, Headingley, were cramped and shabby but clean, tidy and reasonably homely. Stefan had actually bought some furniture polish before my visit, and applied it himself! There were off-cuts of green Lakeland slate stacked around the bed-sitting room, created by the business he was trying to carve out for himself making slate ornaments and jewellery. In partnership with a tailor friend, Steve (not Steve with the dog) they were also producing hand-crafted waistcoats of high quality with the unique distinction of having highly-polished slate buttons. The slate was similar to that once excavated at Kentmere near the outward-bound centre, but actually came from Langdale and was of a greener hue. The silken-fronted garments sold well to individuals but the entrepreneurial pair were trying to find regular outlets for their produce from within fashionable clothes shops. On a later visit by them to Kendal we approached three shop owners that I knew in town, the most promising being the owner of the up-market 'George Edwardian' boutiques, and all three struck up an informal contract to buy the waistcoats. They were impressed by the quality of the garments and also suggested other avenues and applications for their joint skills. It seemed they had a very promising future.

Acoustic and electric guitars, speakers and amplifiers adorned every wall of their lounge and his beloved computer vied with the large bed for prominence. A black and white cat languished upon a small table in the corner and Jill sat primly on a straight-backed chair with her hands folded righteously in her lap. She wore a plain top and long skirt, which unfurled as she rose to politely say "Hello" with her hand extended. We shook and she said she was pleased to meet me (she had already met Dorothy several times) in a refined 'English home-counties' accent. She looked a bit pale and grubby, obviously a life-style consequence, her black-dyed hair was lank and her eyes slightly yellow but I was impressed by her demeanour and courtesy. I thought she might even scrub up to look acceptably attractive. In any case, she appeared to have relieved Stefan of a recent moroseness which followed an accidental head-injury, and commanded a highly important position in our lives because of that and by virtue of being pregnant with his child.

We spent a pleasant day together in Leeds, and left with reinforced feelings that everything in our erstwhile tangled garden was definitely looking rosier. As we entered 1993 it looked like our troubles were over.

In the morning we went walking. The weather was cold and wet but we got back home feeling alive and invigorated by the harshness of the elements. In the afternoon we did some household jobs at a leisurely, therapeutic pace and the progression of the day acquired a quiet, serene quality. We moved effortlessly through the peace of the evening without expectation, needing only comfort and reinforcement from each other, troubles of the past forgotten, and took a long shower before settling down for an evening warmed by the cosy glow of satisfaction. Dorothy answered a knock at the door and reappeared a few seconds later with a worried look "It's the police"

My survival instinct whirred from standing start to defence mode as two uniformed officers entered the room, one of whom, Stan something or other, had been present at the police station on the night I was beaten up, but I remained at a loss as to the purpose of their current visit. I rankled slightly as one of them told, not asked, Dorothy to sit down, which they then did themselves without being invited. She remained standing. I watched silently with a creeping premonition of disaster about to befall us yet again. One of the officers asked her more politely to sit down and she perched on the arm of my chair facing them, protectively between us. My fears increased. The officers squirmed around on the sofa next to each other, adjusting too-tight clothing before looking directly at me with affected graveness "Mr MacGowan?" asked Stan brusquely. I nodded slowly, aware that he knew who I was.

"Yer son's dead Mr MacGowan"

The walls of the living room moved in towards me quickly and silently leaving the two policemen sitting outside the house – hovering eighteen inches above the garden rockery I had weeded two days earlier. They floated, still on the sofa, exchanging puzzled glances under a low sky which had become much darker than usual for that time of year. Air rushed through the room from outside, causing a hissing, swirling sound deep inside my head.

Dorothy said calmly "No he's not, he's in Leeds"

Stan replied from the garden in a distant, muffled voice "Yeh that's where they found 'im, lyin' int' street"

Dorothy emitted a strangled shriek, her legs gave way and she slid off the chair arm to the floor. I instinctively pulled her back up into a seated position and held onto her with both arms around her waist.

"No" she cried "You're lying. They're lying" she pleaded to me, and wailed the gutteral, heart-rending, timeless lament of the bereaved mother.

I held her tightly as she sobbed and her weight submitted to gravity, and asked "How?"

"Well we know drugs were involved but we 'aven't gor all t'details yet"

As my wife and I sat on the armchair together with the world spinning out of control and our lives ripped apart, the bearers of our catastrophic news looked at each other and a strange, uncomfortable look passed between them. Stan stood, avoiding my gaze "A'll call in an' see if I can ger any more news fo' ye"

They both disappeared from view as we remained in each other's clinging, trembling embrace, frozen in time, suppressing panic by avoiding thought, dying a little ourselves. What we said or did or for how long is now forgotten, except that we held onto each other until our muscles ached, to stop being swept away by the hurricane raging through our life.

The officers returned to tell us, whilst surveying their brightly polished boots, that our son had not been found lying in the street, he had died peacefully in his own room and that drugs may possibly have been involved, they were not sure. They gave us the number of a public telephone kiosk in Leeds and said that Jill was waiting for us to call her. Both policemen then left looking cleansed and relieved.

I made Dorothy a hot drink, tucked her trembling body beneath a blanket and called the number. Jill babbled incoherently but eventually asked me to go to Leeds for her. I changed and drove Dorothy to her mother's house. By the time we arrived she was pallid and shaking violently, her legs would not support her and I carried her limp, defeated body inside. Leaving her alone to share the burgeoning nightmare with her mother, I drove the seventy miles to Leeds.

It was after 1am when I arrived and the canted, Victorian streets of Headingley were dark and foreboding. I entered the house silently, reverently, and crept up the narrow, winding staircase to my son's room. Inside that empty place I sensed death but also something else, black and sinister, unexplained. Outside in the night air I leant against the car, mind and pulse racing, until I heard the clamour of urgent voices as a dark mass of people climbed the cobbled hill. Jill emitted a shrill cry as she detached from the group and ran to me. She flung her arms around my neck and we stood in the middle of Manor Drive, consoling each other as neighbours emerged from shadows, gathering about us, comforting, supporting, mourning my dead son.

On the return journey I noted that Jill was drunk and had a can of Superstrength lager in each side-pocket of the khaki parka she was wearing. One that Stefan had given her. She chattered nervously and perhaps excitedly all the way back to Kendal, mostly about herself and of course what had happened to Stefan. She informed me in detail of events leading to his death. She was an ex-nurse with in-depth knowledge of drugs and their effects she asserted, and her brother Tim was a qualified medical doctor. It was a longer journey incoming than outgoing, as is often the case.

I drove straight to Burneside where I found my wife in a worrying condition. Her white pallor was now tinted blue, she shook uncontrollably and her attempts at speech were incoherent. I picked her up bodily again, carried her to the car with Jill chirping away incessantly behind me, and drove to the car park I had built a few years earlier at the local hospital. She was given sedation by a sympathetic nurse whilst Jill, still visibly drunk, annoyed even Dorothy by attempting to instruct the nurse in her duties. This very same nurse, a pleasant and attractive local girl with whom I was briefly acquainted, also had the terrible misfortune to lose a son a few years later.

The following day Dorothy asked me to tell my father what had happened. I think an affinity had grown between them during our problematic years and she maintained a respect for his wisdom and life-experience. He and Mary came round to the house as did many other friends and relatives, offering any assistance and practical support they could. Dorothy again slipped into shock as well-meant words brought home to her the enormity of what had befallen us, and I called the doctor. During the wait for his arrival Mary forced copious amounts of tea and cigarettes into Dorothy's mouth and looked at me in bewilderment. The room was semi-full when the GP arrived and sat next to Dorothy on the sofa. He held one of her hands whilst Mary held firmly onto the other, and spoke to her softly. I kept myself busy slicing sandwiches and ensuring everybody's cups were full. Doctor Buckler, a nice if naïve young man, sat amongst us for quite some time, murmuring encouragement with sad, genuinely sympathetic eyes, when Mary piped up in her broad Glaswegian accent "Wheer's that piggin' doctor fer chrissake?"

Not even Dorothy could suppress a smile at that, particularly when I explained to Mary that the piggin' doctor was sitting on the sofa with her.

I answered dozens of telephone calls and opened scores of sympathetic cards and letters. I went shopping, tidied the house in continuous cyclic maintenance, nodded, murmured politely and shook my head gravely in perpetual discussion about Dorothy's condition, and eventually was grateful for the break imposed by returning Jill to Leeds. She had been speaking with my father and told him she was now virtually homeless and needed a proper home for his forthcoming great-grandchild. He replied that she was welcome to stay with him and Mary if she wished. I had not really appreciated or considered this dilemma over the past few days, but replied that it would be a good idea for her to relocate to Kendal and that if she preferred, she could live with Dorothy and I for however long she wanted, we would be more than happy to have her with us. She threw her arms around my neck again and thanked me enthusiastically.

Dorothy and I drifted automatically through the next week or so, with me constantly telephoning Millgarth police station in Leeds for more information about Stefan's death, and eventually being summoned to officially identify his body. Jill telephoned and I agreed to meet her at the chapel of rest. We met there on an oppressively dark and stormy evening. She had walked and was apparently sober, and I had first to fill in and sign a series of forms. The Coroner's constable looked at me as I entered the visitors' area of the chapel and declared that there was no doubt about the relationship between Stefan and I, because we looked so much alike. Jill added with a beaming smile "Oh God yes, that's the first thing I thought when

Robert and I met"

When the signing was done Jill and I sat silently for a while before being gently and tactfully ushered to the entrance of a long corridor, at the far end of which, outside an open doorway and at a 45 degree angle to it, stood a wheeled bed. I knew that the person lying on that deathbed was my son, and a wave of love and sorrow engulfed me, sapping the strength from my limbs. I began the long walk towards him but my eyes kept blurring and my right shoulder hit the wall. I wondered if it would be acceptable for me to sit down on the floor for a minute, and also why the obvious need for seating in this corridor had not been addressed. In the event, I leant my back against the wall, staring at the bed until Jill touched my arm, whereupon I resumed placing one foot in front of the other. An attendant wheeled the bed through the open door and we followed. On reaching it I gripped and held onto the metal frame, looking down through my tears at Stefan's ashen face. He looked peaceful, handsome, and very young. The undertakers had unnecessarily brushed his thick, black hair back from his face so that I could identify him more easily. I smoothed it back down over his brow. He was cold and smelled of clinical substance. I looked at him, reaching out and touching his perfect features whilst my brain struggled to cope with the need to override millions of years of evolutionary programming – and accept the visual fact of a living parent's dead offspring. I breathed deeply to keep calm and avoid breakdown, reminded my son that I loved him dearly, that I would be with him again one day, then bent and kissed his forehead.

"He would have liked that" whispered Jill.

I did not realize on that day that a further abomination had yet to be inflicted on his body, the horrific post-mortem examination, and had I realized would have protested violently to protect him. Incredibly, Jill requested a full written report of this gruesome operation and read it out to Dorothy. Thankfully, it stated clearly that no sign of long-term drug or alcohol abuse was found.

Many of his friends made the journey from Leeds and other parts of the country for the funeral, and the cars lined up outside the house stretched 500 yards up the street and out of sight. Burneside church was packed to the doors after my brothers and brother-in-law helped me carry him inside.

Stefan's adopted black and white cat, Sylvester, had continued to live at the flat, often on his own and hungry but snuggled into Stefan's thick motor-biking pullover. We took him with us on the day Jill moved to Kendal and cleared the flat of belongings. In a corner of the dark and dusty basement of the building stood a small wooden cupboard, the door of which had come loose from its rusting top hinge. Dampness had caused mould growth on its surfaces which were partly entwined in grey cobwebs. The cupboard was part of a small collection of furniture, the rest having by then disappeared, which had been stored by Stefan in preparation for family life in the future, at a different house. Upstairs, in the room where he died, all had changed. In the kitchen, the few things he left behind were also gone but in the basement, his little cupboard remained as an unseen monument to his life, his optimism and his indomitable spirit. I left it there.

The move had immediately beneficial effects on Dorothy, who brightened significantly given such a needy recipient of her attention. She cooked, fed, cleaned, pampered, advised, planned for and entertained in earnest. She had a mission in life once again and though her son was gone forever, her renewed vocation was unmistakably linked to him and his memory.

Jill gained healthy weight in addition to that imposed by pregnancy. Her eyes lost their jaundice, she looked healthier, more attractive and even taller as renewed confidence straightened her previous stoop. She now bathed regularly in hot water and said that with all things considered, she could not remember being as happy since childhood.

I hardly noticed the abrupt change in lifestyle. Jill was educated, well-spoken and pleasant company. She and Dorothy went everywhere together, walking, shopping, visiting, entertaining, more shopping. I was relieved to see them getting along so well and apparently happy considering the circumstances, and the whole situation at this point appeared to be far better than I could have hoped for. I had taken time off work but now felt able to return and also continue the Higher National Certificate course I had started to better my future prospects, at Carlisle College. I quickly fell back into a routine of always having something to do at home, especially at weekends, and now planned even more ambitious projects. Sometimes though, even this submersion in the mundane and thoughtless routines of life could not prevent me from lapsing into my own private and frightening thoughts.

Staring blankly out of the train window on a stark March morning en-route to the historic city of Carlisle, I remembered on hearing the call of "Tickets please" from down the carriage, that I did not have one. I probably did have time to purchase one, albeit with some inconvenience before boarding the train, but made a conscious decision not to do so. That the collector was now vigilantly approaching sent a little surge of rousing energy through me. He rumbled along the aisle declaring his mission in an Asian accent, thrusting a pink palm under my nose as I looked deep into his eyes until they averted.

"Tickets please" he continued along the corridor.

The world outside the window rushed past at ninety miles per hour. I absently watched a flat path that ran parallel to the rail line between it and the open fields beyond. I imagined myself hurtling along that deserted path on my racing cycle, revelling in the fitness needed and power exerted, the silent speed and freedom and lung-bursting gulps of cold, eye-stinging air. I pictured the low winter sunlight glinting off the alloy frame of the bike as its gearing purred and clicked with well-oiled efficiency to transport me as if in flight, through the green and pleasant countryside. Suddenly, with the violent intervention of a bullet moving faster than imagination, I was transported to the far-off viewing platform of another scene: It was Stefan as a young boy when he first asked me to remove the stabilizer wheels from his bike. After first refusing I relented at his insistence and took them off, keeping them nearby for what I expected to be a prompt refit. Stef went out onto the tarmac footpath in front of the house and fell off that bike more than a dozen times. I could see red scrapes on his little arms and knees but he kept his stubborn head down and picked himself up again and again. Just less than an hour after he started his personal quest he accomplished it, and looked up smiling to the bedroom window from where he knew I watched, as he and cycle glided smoothly down the middle of the street. My love for him and respect for his dogged determination were physically palpable. Before long he was entertaining me to virtuoso performances of his own cyclo-acrobatics, again on the road outside the house, some of which I captured on cine-film. On that strip of juddering celluloid, to the accompanying click-click-click of the projector, my little son turns his beautiful, smiling face towards me with his hair blowing in the breeze, and that jolting reminder of my staggering loss caused my head to jerk back against the railway carriage seat in shock. I gasped for air and my heart pounded.

Several years ago on an American television documentary, I witnessed a very similar reaction from a distraught middle-aged woman whose daughter, some time previously, had been abducted and murdered. A police officer took her at her own insistence to visit the deserted, scrubland shack where her daughter had been imprisoned for a time by her eventual killer. The woman asked questions of the officer, who had participated in the investigation of the case. She asked if there were any snakes in the vicinity because her daughter was afraid of snakes, and was there any drinking water in the shack because there did not appear to be?

In my opinion the policeman was too brutally honest despite his kind words, and should have tempered the harsh reality of his replies to take account of the fragility of the questioner. The woman's face was brought vividly alive by her newly-ignited imagination. Her once-hopeful eyes registered absolute horror as she struggled to come to terms with the reality of her daughter's ordeal. Her head jerked and hands fluttered defensively in front of her face as if to ward off an actual physical attack. Again and again her worst fears turned to reality and those harshly cruel facts shook her to the core of her very existence. Seeing the inescapable pain of that existence still haunts me and I can only hope that poor child's mother managed to find some peace in the years on earth left to her.

STEFAN ROBERT MACGOWAN
6th AUGUST 1970 – 2nd FEBRUARY 1993

Jessica with her grandad

Clockwise from top left: Gordon; Pamela; Robert; John

Twenty One

"Why does the lamb love Mary so?
The eager children cry.
Why, Mary loves the lamb,
You know.
The teacher did reply"

(Elizabeth Hale – 1830)

IN THE EVENINGS AND at weekends I busied myself constructing a loft conversion to facilitate all the needs my new granddaughter might require. It incorporated a two flight staircase with half-turn landing, newels and spindles in fan formation, built-in cupboards, bespoke wardrobe and two roof-lights.

The first inkling I had that things were not as I hoped on the family scene was when Jill started bringing cans of lager home and drinking them whilst sitting around in my dressing-gown. Dorothy disapproved of having alcohol in the house and used the fact that Jill was endangering her unborn child by drinking to excess, to mount a mini-crusade against it. Smoking was never attacked with such gusto, but then Dorothy also smoked. At this time I was un-aware that drinking during pregnancy was considered as poten-tially harmful as it was, and therefore undecided as to the wisdom of Dorothy's blunt and uncompromising approach. Jill said it relaxed her, she only drank in the evenings, albeit all of them, and as far as we knew that was her total consumption. We did though, take her out and about quite a lot and were often invited to parties or family functions where she always insisted on going for drinks. I became worried on noticing that when Jill was at the bar she always downed one or two quick ones before returning with the order. Most of the time I just kept quiet in my contentment at things going at least as smoothly as they were. Dorothy was not as complacent though and her growing hostility made Jill nervous and unsettled, but we managed to muddle through to the time of the birth, which was dif-ficult and during which Dorothy assisted with the actual delivery. Our granddaughter, Jessica Amber, was born to the world in the late afternoon of 9th September 1993, the same day and month as my brother John's birthday. She was kept in intensive care at Lancaster Infirmary after the birth and I assumed it was because of the problematic delivery. Only later was I told that because Jill had been a heroin-addict for thirteen years and it was not clear whether she was still using the drug, the baby was monitored to see if the same addiction had been transferred through her mother's bloodstream. Luckily – and only by luck, it had not.

On the other side of the ward in a plastic box like the one Jessica lay in, was a liver-coloured premature baby who did not receive visitors at any time. I asked a nurse why and was told that the single mother was very young and had abandoned the child, who was also quite ill. On each of my daily visits to Jessica I never failed to talk to that little being, often bringing a secret flower to place beside her as she lay there fighting silently for a life which would almost certainly be ultimately painful. I would have gladly picked that little baby up and carried her off to a life where she would at least be loved and wanted and cared for. One day the plastic box was empty and the nurse looked at me with tearful eyes that answered the question I dreaded to ask.

Our lives were picked over like dead carcasses by social workers to ascertain that Jessica was coming home to a healthy environment. We were interviewed at length and told that if Jill had been left to her own devices, Jessica would have been taken into protective care at birth. Evidently two children had already been removed from Jill's custody and placed with adoptive parents. It worried us that she had given up her children so easily without any provision for future contact or any apparent regret. She even volunteered to sign the adoption papers earlier than necessary.

Three days after Jessica was released from hospital Jill left her with us and went on a daytime drinking session. She came home drunk and took the baby to bed with her despite the fact that Jessica was not tired. Shortly afterwards we heard Jessica screaming and ran upstairs. She had caught her ankle under the headboard and was hanging upside down over the edge of the bed. Her mother lay obliviously asleep, snoring loudly, and never woke for several hours. Dorothy reprimanded her next morning and their relationship deteriorated further. Coming home drunk became a routine habit for Jill but worryingly she also took Jessica on her drinking sprees. The baby once arrived home with her hair chopped off raggedly in a 'style' which Jill described as a haircut but Dorothy did not. Jill had obviously wielded scissors around the baby's head whilst inebriated. Another crisis point arrived when Jill literally staggered into the house after drinking and smoking cannabis. She had been to a day-time party given by one of her new friends and swayed the quarter mile home hanging onto Jessica's buggy. The party's host later told us with a mixture of amusement and concern, that our granddaugh-ter's mother had acquired the nickname 'Two Cans Jill' alluding to the fact that she was never without a can of Superstrength in each coat pocket. The look of terror in Jessica's eyes on arriving home that day alarmed us and finally convinced Dorothy to involve Social Services. This opened another traumatic and disturbing chapter in our lives. The senior social worker responsible for Jessica's safety and wellbeing under the law, Joyce Hawthorne, responded to Dorothy's report by telling us that Jill had done the right thing on all of these occasions. She had brought her baby home to us so that we could protect her from negligence and harm. Jill's negligence and harm! Joyce informed us from her position of authority on childcare that we were providing a safeguard for Jessica and Jill was taking full advantage of that provision. She waved away as unimportant our queries as to how we were supposed to ensure her safety at times when the baby was out alone with Jill, and added that the only real way of testing Jill's competence as a mother would be to withdraw our protection. We said surely that would invite Social Services in-tervention which might result in Jessica's removal, and Joyce replied that yes it would, but that we would have a very good chance of acquiring custody of the child! We thought that sounded dubious and risky and in any case, we would never allow Jessica to suffer just to comply with Social Services requirements. Joyce stated there was no other action she was prepared to take at that point, we were protecting Jessica very efficiently and Jill could therefore do more or less as she pleased, unless we took the option of evicting her from our home, which would open up a whole new situation. We asked her opinion on Jill's drug-use whilst in charge of Jessica and Joyce declared with a guffaw that most social workers smoked cannabis themselves! We felt confused and that Joyce must be testing us in some cunning way. Perhaps she was gauging our reactions to stress or something, particularly as she had previously insisted we report everything about Jill's behaviour to her, especially concerning any drug use. We said that reporting Jill to Social Services was certain to sour relations with her even further, and there did not seem to be much point in reporting anything anyway given Joyce's currently lenient attitude. She however, instantly adopting a sterner approach, instructed that we must report absolutely everything and that if we did not we would not be co-operating with Social Services, which was certain to be bad for us in future dealings with them she confirmed gravely.

There now set in a deep, mutual distrust between Dorothy and Jill, who did manage to modify her reckless behaviour for a while. Jill did not want to leave our home, declaring that she was too well-fed and catered for, and that she was certainly unable to look after Jessica on her own, having failed so miserably in the past to care for her children and knowing that she had a current problem with alcohol. The situation was far from ideal and likely to get worse, but Jessica was thriving so we persevered. Jill soon stepped up her drinking however, and also began sitting around the house in flimsy nightwear when I was present. She spoke conspiratorially to me about Dorothy, urging that I should 'get rid of her' because she only worked part-time, wasted £20 per week on cigarettes and I deserved someone better. Did I realise that her own age was closer to mine than Stefan's? she asked in all seriousness. I laughed and made it clear I was not interested and never would be. She looked at me for a long moment with something sinister in her eyes. I did not mention the conversation to Dorothy, knowing it would cause further antagonism.

Continually seeking ways to improve the situation we all valiantly went on holiday to Spain together in the spring of 1994. The first few days went reasonably well. We took Jess to the pool each morning where she whizzed around on her plastic duck, and devised a meals system whereby Dorothy and I would eat together at the restaurant first, slightly earlier than normal, whilst Jill waited in the foyer with Jess. For some undisclosed reason she did not want to take her daughter into the restaurant nor allow us to. I ate quickly, never had dessert, and as soon as I finished went to take charge of the baby so Jill could join Dorothy (I learned to eat fast as a kid to claim my share whilst it remained available) On the fourth day I emerged from the restaurant and found Jill slumped at a smoke-filled bar just off the foyer, with Jessica parked in her pram next to the toilet door. Jill was obviously drunk so I took charge of Jessica whilst her mother slept it off, again. The following day she left Jess alone on the beach whilst she swam in the sea, and afterwards abandoned her as she remained drunk for four days. Back at the bar she picked up a stranger, took him to her room and disowned her daughter altogether when we knocked on the door the following morning. She did invite us in though, to see her conquest languishing in bed. He was an off-duty policeman she told us. On the day we left, hotel staff had to force their way into Jill's room because she was too drunk to open it from the inside. She attacked some teenage boys outside the hotel because they laughed at her drunken antics and continued drinking at the airport to the extent that she was initially refused permission to fly. We vouched for her behaviour to at least get her home intact and related the delights of our holiday to Joyce in compliance with her orders. We were not surprised by her response: Jill had done exactly the right thing when she needed to drink by handing Jessica over to us! We now considered Joyce to be almost as dangerous to Jessica's safety as Jill undoubtedly was.

Following the head injury that Stefan sustained, I helped him prepare a case for Criminal Injuries Compensation which he took to court on his own and won on principal, without legal assistance. Attempting to calm a volatile situation after a friend's party, he suffered a wound to the head which was actually witnessed by the police, who subsequently gave evidence supporting his claim. The court initially awarded him an advance payment of £2000 and advised him to seek legal representation as the final settlement could be a considerable sum, well over £100,000, in compensation for the chronic headaches, intermittent dizziness, blurred vision and loss of balance which, according to his consultant neuro-surgeon, would significantly reduce his earning potential for the rest of his life. The bottle hurled at the police officer from thirty yards away hit Stefan on the right temple, permanently indenting his skull. The injury, in the professional opinion of his new lawyer, was ill-treated to the point of medical negligence at the hospital he attended, and this factor could increase the amount of compensation dramatically. The prescribed medication he took to ease the resultant pain proved insufficiently effective. At first we assumed that when Stefan died his claim became void, but were advised that it could continue in the name of his daughter. It was a major relief for me, knowing what I had recently learned about her mother including the fact that she intended to live off state benefits for the rest of her life, that there might be some independent provision for Jessica's future. One of the most important aspects in my opinion was that although Stefan would never be able to help, advise or support his daughter personally, he could bequeath her this life-enhancing legacy. We discussed these factors and agreed that all monies received should be secured in Jessica's name until she reached a responsible age. Dorothy however, after initially agreeing, suddenly declared her opposition to the plan, her reason being that when Stefan compiled his claim he asserted that the injury had adversely affected his confidence and ability to form relationships, but he had done so with Jill. Despite our arguments that it was Jill who approached him, thus requiring little initiative on his part and that a relationship in its true sense is hardly necessary to create a baby anyway, Dorothy remained adamant that revelation of Stefan's fatherhood would ruin his reputation as a truthful person. She dismissed all future discussion of the matter and there ended the prospect of one act whereby Stefan could have significantly helped, even in death, his only child. It was also in effect, a denial of that child.

Jill remained silent to Dorothy's decrees, apparently in agreement with them, but there now emerged further evidence of her own, separate agenda. Evidently Jill assumed the claim documents had already been lodged by me and she was therefore sitting pretty in a home where she was well taken care of, with a baby almost wholly looked after by others, all expenses paid from either my earnings or the benefits she and Dorothy claimed, and a large amount of money within her grasp. All she needed to do was sit tight for a while. She calculated that together, Dorothy and I were strong but divided we might collapse and allow her to live as she pleased. Having failed to dislodge Dorothy she now switched her attack in my direction. She provoked arguments before using Jessica as her trump card and declaring that the atmosphere was not good for the child. In an amazingly audacious move she threatened that if Dorothy did not get me out of the house she would take Jessica to live in a London squat! Dorothy co-operated and accompanied Jill to discuss the situation with Joyce Hawthorne, who despite other failings easily perceived the true nature of the visit as she listened incredulously to Jill's intricate plan. A meeting ensued where we were each allocated a so-cial-worker and mine, Jan, said we could all apply independently for custody of Jessica and that I would be applying from a very strong position; possibly the strongest of the three. Jan was removed from the case by Joyce a few days later.

Jill's transformation from subdued victim of circumstance to aggressive tactician continued, empowered by recent events and her relationship with Joyce. She was articulate, could be charming and knew all the survival tactics of the desperate, long-term drug addict. She employed her talents to attain power over those controlling her lifestyle and was now on the verge of winning all. It had worked like a dream for her, I was to be thrust out, maligned and banished from my home but even at this point I did not see only malice in Jill, I saw someone damaged by life and desperate to survive it, and I think she actually felt sorry for me as her sacrificial lamb.

Throughout the whole of this period I continued to care and provide for Jessica. I took her out in her buggy or sling or simply carried her in my arms. I fed her, bathed her, changed nappies, a skill at which I became quite expert, comforted her when she cried and kissed her often. I took her everywhere with me and she became the main focus of my life. I was Jessica's Grandad.

Twenty Two

"...Those golden yesterdays
Was there ever a sound like child laughter
Was there ever such talk as theirs"

(Spike Milligan – Circa 1980)

MY SISTER PAMELA AND her husband David had for years wanted an extension to their home as the spatial needs of their two boys, Robert and Stuart, expanded. The architect living next door had declared problems related to the unusual shape of the 2-block's twin-peaked roof and in connecting an extension to it. He had alternatively suggested a single-storey appendage, but this would not satisfy the family's requirements nor exploit available space to the maximum. Dave's brother-in-law, Mick, the owner of a building company, had echoed the architect's opinion and consequently the extension had never even reached planning stage. After a few drinks at a party given by Pam and Dave one summer's evening, she and I strolled into the rear garden to see what I thought the roof problems actually were. The two peaks rose from eaves to ridge level on both front and rear elevations, in addition to the one gable peak (the house being semi-detached) The structure comprised random, mortar-pointed limestone with massive, rough-hewn quoins rising at each corner.

"Yes" I said looking over the top of my glass "I can see what they mean"

"Mmm" Pam replied "Looks like we'll never get our extension"

Jessica, a toddler now, came running out into the fading sunshine and hugged my leg with sticky fingers.

"Mind you" I said, picking her up and whirling her in a circle "I can see a way round it"

Pam stopped in mid baby-talk sentence to Jessica "Can you?" she asked in surprise.

"Think so. I'll have to check the floor to ceiling levels from inside but I think you could simply drop the extension ridge below that of the rear peak, follow the same eaves line but just below it so the two roofs don't actually meet, and bring the outer wall in a couple of feet so the quoins are still visible from the outside, but don't present such an uneven line to connect the extension wall to. That'll also avoid an unsightly vertical joint between the two structures on the gable wall, as they'll meet at an internal corner and not on a flat plane"

Pam continued to gaze, trance-like, at the rear of her house as Jess sat down on my foot and wondered what we were looking at "Chuck-chuck" she exclaimed, pointing to birds in the sky (Jess that is, not Pam).

"It wouldn't be quite as big as if you took it right to the existing corner" I advised "But will be a lot simpler and cheaper to build, and will give a better appearance"

Pam stared at me and said "Come on then"

"Where?"

"Let's check the ceilings and stuff"

"Now?" I said, gazing forlornly at my almost-empty glass.

Jess assisted by pulling the tape measure and giggling as I took a quick check on the relevant floor and ceiling heights in relation to the existing ridge.

"Looks okay" I said as Pam's face slowly creased into a smile "The left side of the extension rooms will have a little slope where the walls meet the ceilings, but nothing too obtrusive"

"Don't mind slopes" interjected Pam quickly.

"Tell you what then" I said with an increasing thirst "I'll do a little sketch and if you like it we'll go from there"

"Come on then"

"Where?"

"Little sketch!"

"Now?"

"Yep, come on Jess, let's take Grandad for another walk"

Within a few weeks I designed the extension and produced scaled drawings which were accepted by the planning office, then priced and built it making a healthy profit from a quotation which Pam and Dave were more than happy with. Les, my training partner and I, with whom I was now half-squatting over 400lbs, carried out all the drainage, foundations and joinery, but I contracted the other trades to contacts within the industry who were also friends I had known for years. Further enquiries about my new, one-stop service followed and I thereby became fully self-employed, which allowed me more time to spend with Jessica. There grew between us a very strong bond as I carried on unobtrusively with my life, being pleasantly polite, and waiting.

Twenty Three

"Suffer little children, the bible says
But they've suffered enough
In so many ways"

(Author – 2007)

I DID NOT HAVE to wait long. Jill's newly revealed confidence led to increased boldness in her actions, which in turn led us all into a watershed situation. She took Jessica out one Saturday and we received a telephone call from Dorothy's niece Lorraine, at about 7.30pm. Lorraine was out on the town with friends and had seen Jill slumped in a telephone kiosk outside the New Inn. Lorraine asked where Jessica was and Jill replied barely coherently that she could not remember. We eventually found Jess at the Waterside home of a convicted drug-dealer, whose girlfriend told us that Jill had dumped her daughter there around lunchtime and not been seen since. She also told us that Jill was still using various drugs. Hours later with Jessica safely in bed, Jill staggered through the door and started screaming at Dorothy. I got between them and she turned viciously on me. Bloodshot eyes wide she screamed so close to my face that her spittle landed on my skin "I'm going to pat you in facking prison you interfering borstard"

"What?" I asked.

"If you don't get the fack out of my house I'll ring the police and tell them you assaulted me"

"Your house?" said Dorothy in surprise.

"This facking house!"

"Just go to bed Jill and sleep it off" said Dorothy, turning towards Jessica's room as we heard her cries.

"GET OUT OF THIS HOUSE" Jill screamed at my back as she followed me halfway up the stairs.

"Go to bed" I said calmly over my shoulder.

"Right" she said with determination, clumping back down the stairs in her high-leg paratrooper boots. She picked up the hall telephone and as Dorothy and I watched incredulously, imitated a panic-stricken voice which was obviously well-rehearsed, telling the police that she was being assaulted at that very moment and they must "GET HERE NOW, NOW, NOW!"

Walking out onto the landing in response to a male voice from the hallway, I looked down on a young policeman trying to peer through the frosted glass of the lounge door. He moved cautiously and did not attempt to enter the room as he said "Hello in there"

I replied with my own "Hello" and he started, his already drawn truncheon held in front of him defensively.

"Robert MacGowan?" he asked.

"Yes" I replied "What's the problem?"

He came slowly up the stairs as Dorothy came out of the bedroom holding Jessica, who had still not calmed down sufficiently to resume sleep after the trauma of the evening. We quietly explained the situation to him and after apologizing for the intrusion he left the house. Jill was staggering about in the road outside and when she realized that the officer was leaving alone, she screamed at him "You're facking useless"

He told her to get away from the house and come back in the morning when she had sobered up. She continued shouting until the officer threatened that if she continued he would lock her up for the night. She mumbled off into the darkness, tripping over the kerb as she went.

After this incident Dorothy realized her mistake and decided that Jill, not I, had to find alternative accommodation, even though I had not even attempted to exercise my legal rights in that direction. I allowed her to make these decisions with little comment even though the house was secured in joint names and I paid the mortgage, and had spent thousands of pounds from my own pocket improving the property to her taste, but her betrayal and lies about me had registered in my memory. We informed Social Services that we were still willing to look after Jessica and provide a long-term home for her, but that Jill was too disruptive. A series of meetings followed and we were eventually asked to participate in an experimental procedure, whereby both Jill and Jessica would be taken into foster care so that the mother's ability to look after her daughter unassisted, could be assessed professionally. Both they and Jill acknowledged our value in Jessica's life and neither party wished our involvement to cease or even diminish. Despite having doubts about Jessica's safety and disagreeing that she should be used as a testing-ground for her mother, we were assured that the foster carer was a true professional and our granddaughter would be more than safe under her supervision. We were keen to co-ordinate with the authorities so reticently agreed to this plan. Mother and daughter were moved to a foster home at Grayrigg, a small village in the countryside to the north of Kendal, which was to be the scene of a major train derailment disaster in February 2007. Village facilities did not include a pub so we reasoned that was at least one promising factor. Unfortunately however, it lay on a direct bus route into town.

Despite the problems of living together, it was a sad and tearful farewell when they left. As Jess was carried out of our home looking uncomprehendingly back at us, it felt to me like a second bereavement and I knew that I must do all within my power to protect her. I could not rely on strangers to carry out that task efficiently, particularly not Social Services. The night before they left Jill said to me with tears in her eyes "Oh well, back to survival mode"

She realized that her plan had been thwarted and she would not after all become mistress of her domain. Not yet at least. We now had the opportunity to watch from a distance and saw clearly as she made full use of her manipulative powers of survival. The 'true professional' foster carer turned out to be a woman called Annette Clement, who used to run a fish & chip shop on Kirkbarrow and 'took people as she found them' Her husband plucked chickens in the kitchen and according to Jill 'kept dead things in buckets around the house'

The household was a jumble of up to eight foster children coming and going constantly, one of which was Annette's own granddaughter. These were added to by visitors, relatives, social workers, live and dead animals, and apparently anyone else who happened by. This was a distasteful situation for Jill to find herself in, but also one which she could easily manipulate to her full advantage. She did not fool everyone with her cloying appeals for sympathy but was certainly successful 90% of the time. Jill said one night after a few drinks that Joyce also had an illegitimate child and was therefore 'easy to get to' that she had a weight problem, was married to 'a weasel' and was herself, very unhappy. I actually recited this assessment to Joyce who, although leaking signs of extreme irritation at my audacity, claimed to be in full command of the situation.

The fact is that neither she nor the whole Social Services' child protection department could be in full command of Jessica's or any other child's safety, if for no other reason than that they only work from 9am to 5pm, Monday to Friday. At times when the vulnerable are most at risk, evenings, nights and weekends, the children are effectively abandoned. Social Services' Child Protection Team protects only when it is paid to. These work hours were used as an excuse for various failings by Joyce and when I asked the obvious question 'Why don't you work shifts?' she said they would not be able to recruit the right kind of staff if they had to work shifts. I replied that if they were not prepared to work shifts to protect children then her whole department was staffed by totally the wrong people anyway. Joyce lamely assured that there existed a 24 hour emergency telephone number, but in the case of anyone in need of out-of-hours protection in Kendal, help lay forty miles away at Carlisle. On trying the number I discovered that a person in need of emergency help had first to fritter away vital minutes on trivial details and then be directed, often in a state of panic, to the local police station. Getting through to most police stations during busy periods is an achievement in itself, and vulnerable families traditionally avoid contact with the police and Social Services anyway, rendering the system virtually useless. There have been and continue to be, regular cases of horrific abuse and murders of children under Social Services' protection. We were worried to say the least.

When we first visited Jill and Jessica at their foster placing there was a barrel full of what appeared to be butchered hens standing in the kitchen with blood trickling from it and Jill burst into tears as we greeted her, saying "Please get me out of this bloody slaughterhouse"

She described the foster-carers as 'the tightest bastards on earth' referring to their penny pinching mentality regarding the supply of food, and that they were so stupid she had to 'talk to the farm animals for intelligent conversation'

Social Services were not above grovelling when they saw fit, and pleaded with us to maintain contact with Jill and Jessica, even though their pleadings were not needed in Jessica's case. They described us sycophantically as 'the solid rock in Jill's life' – it seemed things were not going as well as they had planned. Jill concurred

and constantly repeated her need of us. We decided not to desert
her but help in every way we could, in the hope that she would
become the mother that Jessica deserved. We visited thrice weekly
and were available at zero notice. Nothing on earth was or would be,
too much trouble for us. We called at the foster home often and at
different times of the day as opportunity and Jill's requests dictated.
General daily activities were usually under way: cooking, cleaning, ironing, washing and hanging clothes, but Jill never seemed
to be around at these times. Jessica was usually downstairs, lost in
the throng of troubled humanity but Jill was always 'resting in her
room' though from what she rested, nobody knew.

On returning from days out Jess would become upset as we
drove up the rocky access lane, and Jill said she would cry for up to
half an hour after we left. This became too traumatic for me and I
tried waiting in the car but Jess would point at me from across the
yard and wail out her unhappiness. Then we arranged that I would
collect her and Dorothy would take her back. The feeling of help-
lessness was a tangible pain I could not cope with and I seriously
considered more than once, putting Jess back in the car and driving
to some far-off place where she could be happy all the time. On re-
flection this may not have been such a bad idea.

One bright spring morning when I arrived to collect her at Jill's
request I found her in the kitchen with Annette's granddaughter,
aged 8 or 9 at the time. Jessica appeared to be asleep with her head
on the girl's shoulder, but when she turned around Jess's head fell
back and I could see the whites of her eyes roll in their sockets. I
was instantly alarmed though the girl said the baby was just tired.
No-one else was around and the house was unusually quiet. She
said Jill was asleep and Annette had gone to pick someone up at
Manchester Airport. There was no sign of Annette's husband. I took
Jess and walked quickly to the car after confirming that Mr Clement
was out in the fields somewhere and the girl was not home alone. I
had learned repeatedly not to rely on Jill's presence as a safety measure; just the opposite in fact. Jess's head flopped from side to side
and her eyes continued to roll and I knew her condition was not due
to tiredness. I strapped her in the child-seat and set off for home,
but had to stop to take off my pullover and prop her head to avoid
it colliding with the window pane. She was a rag doll. I drove the
few miles as fast as I dared with her on board and rushed her inside.

Dorothy knew by my face that something was wrong, took one look at Jessica and told me to put her back in the car – we were going to the hospital. Before I had strapped her in Dorothy was feeding her water from a bottle, which Jess gulped down. She was still drinking on arrival at the Westmorland General but, although she was more hydrated than she had been, the examining doctor became aggressively angry towards us. He assumed that we were Jessica's parents and actually shouted at us that she was dangerously dehydrated, and could easily die if she did not receive immediate attention. Only when he learned the true situation did he calm down sufficiently to say that he had been very close to calling the police there and then, and would in any case make a full report. He attempted to improve Jessica's condition but was still very unhappy with her responses and ordered her to be sent to the Baby Care Unit at Lancaster for intensive treatment. She was whisked away in an ambulance with Dorothy in attendance. I followed in the car. At Lancaster Jess recovered but was still detained for observation and further re-hydration by drip-feed. Dorothy called the foster home and had to wait over ten minutes until Jill came to the phone. She was told that her daughter was in intensive care and replied "So everything's under control then?"

"Yes but she's not out of the woods yet" Dorothy answered.

"Well as long as you're there I'll leave it until she comes home, I'm so tired"

Only later did she call back to say that Annette had advised her to attend the hospital as it would 'look better' Social Services provided a taxi.

Dorothy and I always doubted the value to either Jill or Jessica of living in foster-care, and were now acutely aware of the dangers it posed.

As the Kendal hospital report was unavailable to us we asked Joyce to obtain a copy but she said the doctor in question had now left and it could not be found. However, I asked a nurse that I knew to check, and she told me that the report was on file and not difficult to locate, it had taken her less than three minutes. I was now fairly sure that Joyce was a liar in addition to negligent, and discussed this with an uninvolved social worker. She told me that they are not officially bound by the truth, and will lie if they think it is in the best interests of the child they are protecting. She was dumbfounded though when I explained the situation to her and asked how this particular lie could possibly be in Jessica's best interests.

Jess was soon well again and saw a re-run of the Sooty show which was on tv when I was a kid, and was enthralled. I tried in all the likely shops to buy her a toy Sooty but failed because he had been out of production for years. There was a Sooty-shaped charity collection box on the bar in the Black Swan and I asked Ruth, the landlady, if I could buy it. She promised to ask the collector whether it could be sold next time he called, and word was now out on the street that I was looking for Sooty. Pretty soon I received a report that he was alive and well and living at Alton Towers amusement park, over a hundred miles to the south. Apparently the park was leading a mini Sooty & Sweep revival and character glove puppets were on sale there, so we set off in that direction post-haste. We found the Sooty emporium, sat through three live shows, then bought a puppet and took it for a walk round the rides and attractions. Jess found a ride she liked, one with giant cups and saucers spinning in their own individual orbits on top of a large revolving deck. It looked safe enough, was officially suitable for her age group, and she climbed aboard whilst Sooty and I looked on from the perimeter. After the ride she dutifully vacated her cup and as she approached I said "You can have another go you know" (There was no limit once the entrance fee was paid) Her little face lit up with surprise and pleasure and she raced back to her seat. After that ride she smiled across at Sooty, returned his two-handed wave and stayed in her seat, as she did the next time and the time after that, and the time after that. I eventually beckoned her over and said the little fella was hungry and she alighted from her saucer, took a few steps towards us but then with a giggle ran off and jumped aboard a different cup. I moved in to the edge of the deck, hoping to grab her when it came to a standstill but when it did she happened to be across the other side, giggling even louder. I moved to a different position but when the next ride stopped and I was closer to her, she jumped straight out and ran across the platform, from where she smiled triumphantly at me. I realised that stealth was required so waved to her as the ride started up again, and as the cup spun her round Sooty and I ducked low so she lost sight of us. We stayed hidden but kept her in view, and when the ride began to slow I judged about where she would stop, got into position and ambushed her before she could run. Sooty grabbed her by the sleeve and I hoisted her onto my shoulder, where she shrieked with laughter as I carried her off. Most of the other spectators laughed too. On the way home I put the puppet on my hand and pretended Sooty was driving and waving at passing cars as I said 'hello' in a puppety voice. Jess loved the unscheduled performance and we laughed all the way home.

The next time I visited, Sooty had been relegated in favour of a far more intense interest "Come on gwangwad I've got a surprise" she announced excitedly as I got out of the car.

"Have you darlin' what is it?"

"Come on, sit down quick. Look"

"Oh it's a kitten"

She placed a black kitten on my lap whilst giggling, then brought another, ginger and white one from a box behind the sofa "Look"

"Another one" I exclaimed as she kissed them both "Are they yours?"

"This one's mine" she confirmed proudly, indicating the ginger one "An' that's mum's"

"What're they called?"

"Star, this one"

"That's a nice name, why Star?"

"Cos he looks like a star, silly"

"Yes he does, is he a boy kitten?"

"No, a girl"

"Oh"

"He's lovely isn't he?"

"He is"

"He's a little darwin, come on little darwin" she coaxed, carrying Star round the room like a baby, hugging her tightly.

"What's the other one called?"

"Lunar"

"Oh, did you think of that name?"

"No, mum. Lunar's her's an' Star's mine"

"Where did you get them?"

"Wew, they come from a farm a long way, then a amial hopsital at Gwaywigg (the Wainwright Sanctuary) then we got 'em"

"Did you go to the animal hospital for 'em?"

"Yeah, in Stephen's car"

"At the weekend or yesterday"
"Not yesterday, at weekend"
"Oh, and then what?"
"Then we bringed 'em home an' fed 'em"
"What do they eat?"
"Just had some milk 'cos weren't vewy hungwy"
"They're lovely aren't they"
"Yeah, little darwins an' Lunar's a little sweetie"
"She is"
"Lunar's a boy"
"Oh, well, what's that mark on her, sorry his, leg?"
"That's where he had a 'jection"
"Did he?"
"Yeah, at hopsital"
"Like you did, remember?"
"Yeah, but I didn't have any fur cut off did I?"
"No, you just got a lolly afterwards didn't you?"
"Yeah, a red one, but it wasn't the amial hopsital"
"No, it was the people hopsital"
"Yeah, I love them kittens don't you?"
"Course I do, and I love you too"
"I love you too, should we get another lolly?"

Twenty Four

"A dog in hand is worth two in the ginnel"
(Author – 2007)

MY COURT APPEARANCES AND preparation for them plus my contractual duties for various construction companies, left me with a measure of legal knowledge, the basic tenets of which could be usefully applied to many situations. Personally preparing a case which successfully defended me against the police themselves as opposed to civilian witnesses, also earned me some notoriety. That the facts of my defence convinced a crown-court judge and jury that the police were lying, had secretly beaten me up and should pay compensation for their actions, brought many people to my door for free advice. They sought tips on divorce, finances, injuries and criminal proceedings.

When Owen Thirkle was caught at the wheel whilst banned, after previously being jailed for repeated drink-driving, he was working for me as a labourer at Silloth. His solicitor told him that he was almost certain to be incarcerated again, but Owen was desperate to maintain his job and family life. He convinced me that he had made a genuine though stupid mistake, not unusually, and asked if I could help him in any way. I wrote him a letter to take to court. His family, including Irish father-in-law Mick Healey who was also a good friend of my father and I, attended the hearing in support, all sitting in a neat row as Owen pleaded guilty to the charge and threw himself upon the mercy of the magistrates – often an unwise decision. After an outline of the crime his antecedents were read out to the grim-faced magistracy who remained ominously silent. Pens danced with finality across pads before the defence was asked for any extenuating circumstances they wished the court to consider. Owen's lawyer stood wearily and spoke about his client's courageous efforts to lead a trouble-free life, his loyal family and the fact that he now had a permanent job. The three magistrates maintained their expressionless composure and stared, unmoved and unimpressed at the struggling solicitor as he pleaded for leniency. Finally he paused, cleared his throat as he picked up a crumpled paper from the desk, and asked politely if he might read out a letter from the defendant's employer. A look of irritation crossed the supercilious face of the senior magistrate but silence fell as the solicitor held up the letter before him. It compellingly described Owen's semi-heroic efforts to work in harsh conditions, the long, grinding hours spent toiling on the rugged Solway Coast and his selfless devotion to duty. Owen later recalled that the whole court including the magistrates, listened in absolute silence to the testament and as it progressed he turned to his wife sitting next to him, with an expression which conveyed the first sign of hope that he might remain free. She returned his glance and he saw that she was crying, and as he turned back to look at the softening countenances behind the magistrates' bench, he realized that even he, knowing full well that what he was listening to was 95% bullshit, also had tears in his eyes.

At the end of the oratory silence continued in inertia until the magistrates turned to each other and agreed it was time to retire and consider their decision. They asked whether the employer or his agent was present in court but of course, I was not. Twenty minutes later they re-entered the courtroom to inform Owen that, owing to the regard in which he was held by his employer, the court felt that his best chance of rehabilitation lay in retaining his present job. He would receive a suspended sentence but keep his immediate freedom.

Kevin Swanton was a business colleague who owned a roofing company, but also a friend and neighbour whom I had advised several times on legal matters. He participated in the sport of hound-trailing, which involves racing trained dogs over natural terrain following an aniseed-scent trail. The distance covered by the dogs, which are bred from foxhounds but not used for hunting, can be several miles and the sport is rarely seen outside the English Lake District and parts of Ireland.

Kevin told me a story one day about an incident which involved him:

One sultry August day he and his wife Penny took a young and promising hound 'Lunesdale Icon' to race at a meeting in the Ulverston area, near Barrow-in-Furness. This particular venue had given them cause for concern in the past. An owners' syndicate comprising a group of gambling men whom Kevin regarded as none too fussy about rules and regulations, raced in the locality. This worried him sufficiently that immediately after the race including Icon commenced, he strode swiftly to the crest of a lofty knoll looking over the Torver fells, from where to monitor progress. Through his binoculars he watched the flitting white specks moving through the verdant landscape until the leading dog turned for home about a hundred yards in front of its nearest rival. The trail led the pack directly towards the base of the knoll upon which Kevin stood, which is why he picked that vantage point, and into the surrounding foothills. As the leader neared, Kevin saw that it was in fact his hound, followed by that of the syndicate. They raced through ravines and hillocks towards a short mountain pass which is accessed through a narrow passage (or ginnel) between flanking rocky outcrops. Kevin's dog slowed to negotiate the narrow entrance and as it did a dark-clad human figure popped up from behind a boulder with a plastic bucket in hand. He waved the container in front of the dog, which stopped and sniffed at whatever lay inside and the figure, who Kevin now recognized as a syndicate man named Saunders, immediately grabbed the dog and pulled it to one side. Kevin stared in amazement as the second-placed hound ran past his own, straight into the ginnel and the lead. Struggling to contain his wrath, Kevin began to clamber down the rock face to rescue his dog and mete out some rough justice to its hobbler, just as the captured animal was released. He turned and headed speedily back to the finish line to confront the cheats but having time to calm down and reassess his intended actions on the return trek, he went instead to a race official and reported what he had seen. The incredulous steward took copious notes with appropriate gravity.

Following advice from the event organizers and governing body, the Hound Trailing Association (HTA), Kevin lodged an official complaint against Saunders who was suspended from membership of the HTA and any participation in its affairs, pending inquiry. He refuted the allegations and an official hearing was arranged to take place at the Thirlspot Hotel, just off the A591 near Keswick. Kevin asked if I would prepare a written statement of his version of events for submission to the hearing and I duly did so, but just prior to the appointed date he persuaded me with the promise of a pint and a bar meal, to accompany him in general support. Whilst sipping lager and chatting to old friends in the hotel foyer, a woman came along the corridor calling out "Mr Swanton's solicitor please?"

I turned to Penny with a puzzled look "Didn't know he had one"

"I think that's you Bob" she smiled.

"Me?" I asked in horror.

She nodded and I looked around in desperation for Kevin, who had conveniently disappeared.

"Ah, that's you I'm told" said the woman, clasping sheafs of paper to her ample bosom "Would you come with me please"

I rose stiffly like a faulty robot and followed her tightly-clad bottom to an ante-room, where a seated occupant also rose and held out his hand "John Batty QC" he announced as we shook "Representing Mr Saunders"

"Rob MacGowan" I answered, resisting the urge to add any humorous lettering of my own.

"Now, I just need to run through the basic rules of engagement" twittered the woman with a smile after introducing herself as the mediating solicitor acting on behalf of the HTA.

In a break during her description of how and when questions should be asked in accordance with Law Society guidelines, Mr Batty leaned in my direction and enquired pointedly "Could I ask what your legal background is Mr MacGowan?"

For the briefest of moments I considered telling him that I was a persistent offender but instead said lamely "I don't have one, I'm just here as Mr Swanton's friend"

"Ah" he replied with a flourish "Thought I hadn't come across the name before. Just so I don't take unfair advantage you understand?" he added with a smirk.

"Oh don't worry about that, nobody else does" I parried, wondering what the hell Kevin had let me in for.

The 'courtroom' was an impressively oak-panelled guests' lounge incorporating a long table positioned parallel to an end wall. Behind the table was seated an old sparring partner, Roy Laidler, with two assistants.

The Laidler family was prominent in trailing and local bookmaking, and Roy's intelligent fair-mindedness had led him to an elevated position in the HTA. He rightly took his duties seriously, knowing his decisions affected the pockets of working men, and I expected no favours from him. I nodded respectfully. The rest of the court was made up of senior HTA officials, through the throng of which Mr Batty and I were directed to our opposing seats. Kevin had re-appeared and sat to my immediate right. The allegations were read out and Kevin confirmed as the accuser whereupon the hobbler, sitting close to his barrister, was asked to reply. Mr Batty immediately launched into a speech about the absurdity of the charges which he declared should not possibly proceed against his client. The main reason cited was that he personally, had been to the relevant knoll and found it absolutely impossible to see the ginnel from that particular point. He thereby effectively declared Kevin to be an outright liar "Isn't it true Mr Swanton?" he pressed his attack "That you have had past dealings with my client and the syndicate of which he is a member, which resulted in an unsatisfactory conclusion for you and that you are here tonight, simply to exact your own vindictive form of revenge for that embarrassment?"

After a brief pause Kevin whispered "What the fuck's he talkin' about?" as the room hushed in expectation.

This surprise suggestion of an ulterior, completely selfish and vengeful motive for Kevin's accusations immediately threw a different light on proceedings, and Mr Batty resumed his seat smiling smugly to himself.

Kevin and I wallowed in abject confusion for several long seconds following this unexpected tactic. Batty was obviously bolstered by our apparent incompetence and I could practically see doubts growing in the collective mind of the court. I gathered my thoughts and gambled on a quick reposte in an attempt to regain some composure and credibility, or at least time to think.

"The only other dealings Mr Swanton has had with Mr Batty's clients" I addressed the bench "Were on another occasion when he suspected them of cheating but on that occasion he had no proof of his suspicions, so did not proceed further. This time he has the required proof but you are right in one respect Mr Batty, it was those previous dealings which led Mr Swanton to the vantage point from where he could view the fairness or otherwise, of the race in question"

Batty sprang to his feet and nodded at the bench "We have already declared without reservation that it is impossible to see the hounds in the ginnel from the place indicated by Mr Swanton. We have actually carried out a reconstruction of the race at that point and when the dogs enter the ginnel they cannot be seen"

I fumbled with some papers, giving me time to evaluate.

"So you claim that once the dogs enter the ginnel they disappear from view from the knoll?" I retorted.

"Most definitely"

"And you have been there yourself and personally witnessed this?"

"Yes"

"But before they enter they can be seen clearly?"

He hesitated "Er, yes"

"Then we do not differ in our assessment of the situation"

"Pardon me?"

"Mr Batty, you said just a few minutes ago that you personally, had witnessed the fact that not even the ginnel itself could be seen from the knoll. But to know when the dogs enter the ginnel it seems plainly obvious that you must first be able to see it, or at least its entrance. Were you lying then or are you lying now?"

A clamour erupted at my audacity in calling the lawyer a liar, and wooden chairs creaked dryly in the silence that followed after Roy re-established control.

"I am certainly not a liar sir" affirmed Batty "And I do not re-member saying that, no, I did not say that"

"OH YES YOU DID" chanted the observers like a pantomime chorus line.

"Oh yes you did" I echoed softly after the rumble had subsided.

The hearing continued for some time but I had managed to sug-gest that the lawyer had lied to the court, or had taken their hearing so lightly and with such indifference that he had not bothered to prepare adequately. They found in Kevin's favour and Saunders was banned from the HTA for life. We had beaten a qualified barrister in a legally-binding court hearing. I have yet to collect my bar meal.

I stood in the Rainbow one evening listening absent-mindedly to a song on the over-loud juke-box which took me back in time, with a companion who does not wish to be named and whom I will refer to as Lou. He mouthed something at me and I leant closer to listen "Look at that bastard" he said with venom in his usually-placid voice, nodding at a group of males huddled in a corner.

I looked and shook my head in confusion.

"Fuckin' drug-dealer" he spat.

I looked again "How d'ye know?" I asked.

"A've bin watchin' the twat fer twenny minutes. E's gorra wad in 'is pocket big enough to choke a fuckin' donkey"

Drug-dealers were not my favourite animals "Think I should go over and smack 'im?"

"E'd just be back again tomorrer. The bastard wants lockin' up. They're round the fuckin' schoolyards now y'know, an' I've got kids growin' up in this shit!"

"So ring the cops an' get the ass'ole locked up"

Lou thought for a moment "Think I should?"

"Well personally I'd rather cave 'is fuckin' skull in"

Lou laughed "Watch me pint" he said, and disappeared.

The police hauled the guy in and he was fined a few quid before crawling back out onto the streets. A lady officer from Kendal Drugs Squad, who lived at Barrow, later offered us money to help them break the drugs supply line from Liverpool. But that's a different story.

Twenty Five

"This thought is as a death,
which cannot choose
But weep to have that,
Which it fears to lose"

(Shakespeare – Sonnet 64)

MARY TOAL TELEPHONED ONE day to say that she and her daughter Katherine had just seen Jill, who was very drunk, on Blackhall Road. I asked what Jill was doing there and it seems she was staggering around the bus station. I asked if Jess was with her but she was not, so I telephoned the foster home to make sure she wasn't lost again and drove to the terminal with the intention of getting Jill home safely. She was nowhere to be seen, obviously having already left. At a later Social Services case conference I asked Annette to comment on the fact that she had not reported Jill's behaviour on this occasion, and she shouted across the room, obviously agitated, that Jill was not drunk that day. I asked how she knew that as when I had telephoned her she had no idea where Jill was, except that she was not caring for her daughter at that particular time, Jessica being with Annette. She grumbled but did not attempt an explanation, and I suggested that she was either mistaken or lying on Jill's behalf. She again shouted across the room and was reprimanded by the conference chairman. This brought a flood of tears from Annette, who apologized to Dorothy and I at a private meeting in the chairman's office, where he agreed that the present arrangement was not suitable for Jessica's safety. Although Joyce had recommended that Jessica's name be removed from the 'At Risk' register, I protested and the chairman ensured that she would remain on it, and even added the risk of 'emotional harm' to the already existing 'physical harm or neglect' Joyce's obvious dislike of me intensified.

Our vigilance had made it clear to all that Joyce's idea of the foster placement had been a bad one, was not providing even minimal protection or benefit, and was actually harmful to our already tenuous relationship with Jill. The law decreed that mother and child could not be parted without overwhelming evidence of danger to the child, evidence that Social Services claimed was not yet in place because of our interventions. As Joyce put it 'For drug abuse to be a factor in the removal of a child from its carer even temporarily, the carer has to be virtually caught sitting with the child on his or her lap whilst shooting up' The only alternative plan according to the chairman was for Jill and Jessica to live as an independent unit and continue to rely heavily on us for 24-hour support, adding that if we had not been continually there for Jill to fall back on, our granddaughter would probably already have been taken into care. The chairman assured us that as long as we maintained our protection Jessica's removal would not become likely, and if it did we would almost certainly be asked, as closest blood relations who had already proved their reliability, to house and care for her "So" he said, looking up from his desk "Social Services as a department has to abide by the letter of the law at all times, even if we do not always agree with the law. If you and your wife feel unable to agree to Jessica living alone with her mother, which certainly does carry risks" he added, indicating Jill's three-inch thick file on his desk "You have only one other course of action – simply remove your support long enough for her mother to flounder" He looked down at the gold-topped pen between his manicured fingers.

"You know we can't do that" I answered.

"I know" he said sympathetically, rising from the desk and holding out his hand "Best of luck to you both"

Jill and Jessica went to live at a shabby, cramped and damp two bed-roomed house owned conveniently by Annette, midway along Anne Street. They were charged an amount for rent exactly equal to the maximum payable by the benefits system – working for a living was a subject Jill would not even discuss. She immediately threw herself into a frenzy of drink, drugs, parties and long periods when she was simply 'asleep' The police were called to the house on numerous occasions to restore order or investigate neighbours' complaints. After an MMR injection Jessica screamed so loudly for 'six hours' that Jill 'had to apologize to the neighbours next day' The baby's left eye turned permanently inwards during a febrile convulsion that awful night, though her mother did not even notice until I pointed it out the following morning. Jess underwent repeated corrective surgery and has had to wear glasses ever since. Jill admitted later that she did not summon us because she was still under the influence of drugs and alcohol, and also to letting Jessica suffer rather than risk losing her newly re-gained lifestyle.

We visited constantly and thankfully Jess stayed at our home more often than she did with her mother. Jill did however, always make certain that Jessica was with her for any visit from Social Services. On the rare occasion of an unannounced visit, she would simply not answer the door and pretend she wasn't at home. Social Services never enquired further. Previous to our contribution Jessica failed to thrive and lost weight. These facts were recorded by health visitors but no official action was ever taken to protect the child. I became more convinced that Joyce's hatred of me was causing her to act in an unprofessional manner with regard to Jessica's safety, and told her so. She listed her qualifications and admonished me for calling into question her professional judgement!

One of the neighbours at Anne Street, Roland Lim, told me that Jill only fed Jessica bits of cheese and broken biscuits, and that she often sat around with him and other teenagers at the multi-occupancy house next door, drinking Superstrengths and smoking cannabis whilst her daughter was left at home alone. I asked her about this and she said "Well, yes but it's ok 'cos I've got a baby-monitor"

After visiting the house but failing to waken Jill despite hearing Jessica crying from inside on several occasions, we eventually took the advice of the police and consulted a solicitor. He was an eminent member of the Child Protection Panel he told us, and after hearing some of the evidence advised us strongly to take the matter to court and apply for a residence order. We considered his advice, satisfied ourselves that we were acting in what we believed was Jessica's best interests, then began collecting evidence to indicate that her mother was incapable of caring for her.

Joy Cavanagh appeared to be a sensible girl. She had moved to Kendal to boost her job prospects, the town being in a popular location benefitting from its close proximity to the Lake District. She acquired a room in Anne Street at a shared house which happened to be next door to number 24, Jill and Jessica's home. I made her acquaintance when Annette, who owned both houses, asked me to fit locks to internal doors in segregation of her growing number of tenants. Joy, not knowing of any connection between her neighbour and myself, told me that when they first met, Jill made lesbian suggestions to her – half jokingly but seriously enough to worry Joy. Jill offered drink and drugs but Joy repeatedly refused. Some weeks later as we got to know each other better, Joy told me something which she had previously been afraid to tell anybody: Jill had bragged that she and her husband 'killed Stefan and got clean away with it'

I had only known Joy for several months and this revelation was so stunning that I hardly knew whether or not to believe it, but wondered whether she would really dream up something so dramatic. I thought that even if Jill had said such a thing to Joy, it was possible that she was merely attempting to impress and excite the younger girl, to whom I did believe she was sexually attracted. Jill had hinted to me before that she may have bi-sexual tendencies though at the time I presumed she merely wished to portray an exotic image of herself. I considered this information at length before telling Dorothy. We discussed the implications further and decided to stay calm, not disclose any information generally at that moment, and concentrate on preparing for the upcoming court case.

Jill's best friend and confidant at the time was Paula Middleton, nicknamed Crazy Paula by some who thought they knew her. On 6th June 1995 I visited her at home on Kirkbarrow and she answered the door in a grubby nightgown. She was officially single at the time and though I could hear someone shifting in bed upstairs, she asked me in. Apparently, her twins were still living at the Clements' foster-home where she and Jill first met. I told her I was worried about Jessica and that Dorothy and I were going to apply for custody. She said that was definitely the best thing that could happen because Jill was 'not safe' I asked what she meant by that and she said that Jill did things that were weird. The thing that worried her most was that Jill locked Jessica in an upstairs room on her own for hours at a time, often going out or to sleep whilst Jessica was left with 'a bag of toys' to amuse herself. Paula broached this subject several times with Jill and also the fact that Jessica was not fed properly, but Jill stressed that Paula must never say anything to anyone about how she cared for her daughter 'especially not Social Services or Jessica's grandparents' Paula said that Jill relied totally on our support and bragged about how she so easily conned us into providing it after making sure that Dorothy and I bonded as soon as possible with Jess. Paula became tearful and I asked if she was alright. She answered that she was certainly not the best mother in the world but at least she tried whereas Jill just coasted along using everyone she met, including her social worker "Mine watches me like a bloody hawk but not Jill, she gets away with murder" Paula sobbed.

"So how come she's your friend?" I asked, pondering her last word.

"Oh I'm so alone at the moment, and depressed about maybe losing the twins. I know she uses me and manipulates me into doing anything she wants but I just don't have anybody else to talk to"

"Do you think she's a competent mother?"

She thought for a moment and sniffed back a tear "No, in all honesty, I can kind of relax when I'm with her and have a laugh, you know, but deep down inside she is some kinda weird"

She fell silent and I told her quietly and without embellishment, what Joy had told me. She let out an agonized wail. I said that I knew it was upsetting but she sniffed and shook her head, wiping away tears on her soiled sleeve "It's not that" she squeaked.

"What is it?" I asked gently.

"She told me the same thing"

We sat motionless, staring at each other, keeping the horror of the revelation in the air between us. A little drop of moisture hung precariously from the end of her nose "I even told my priest about it"

"What did Jill tell you?" I queried, wanting to know if her story corroborated Joy's.

"That Stef's headaches were really bad and his normal tablets weren't doing any good"

I nodded.

"So Jill's husband gave him some different tabs, DF118s I think and some of her Valium as well. A cocktail she called it. She said they got away with it and weren't even questioned by the police, nobody was"

Jill has never denied making this statement.

Dorothy and I took this apparent indication of our son's murder seriously, and pieced together all the information we had so far about Jill, most of it from Jill herself and the rest from Social Services:

She moved to a Leeds rehabilitation clinic after thirteen years heroin addiction, which started at art college in London. She knew

Jamie Blandford, infamously jailed for international drug trafficking, and financed her own addiction by supplying other users. She supplemented these earnings by working in Soho sex clubs, if not openly as a prostitute then as an 'escort' She was quite frank about this and bragged about how good she looked in a leather miniskirt. She had other jobs for short periods including motorcycle dispatch rider, auxiliary nurse and concert administration assistant. She claimed to know Mick Jagger and Michael Jackson and had photographs of herself in their company, and had evidently been on tour in Germany with Eric Burdon of The Animals, after writing to him directly. Her father was a wealthy commercial artist living near Roger Daltrey of The Who, in Sussex. Her mother died shortly after Jill came to Kendal. At the rehab clinic she met her second husband, David Clarke who was also a patient, originally from the North East and several years younger than Jill. She had a baby born in 1991 from a previous relationship and gave birth to her second child in 1992. Although Jill came off drugs at the clinic she turned immediately to alcohol and according to her own statement 'was drunk for most of the time she lived in Leeds' She admitted abandoning her first child to go off with Clarke, and that her second child was taken into care after being consistently undernourished and repeatedly bruised. She was rejected by her father during this period and banned from his home. He eventually blamed Jill for causing her mother's death – the cancer which killed her being apparently exacerbated by stress. She was not allowed to visit her mother's deathbed, even though I offered to drive Jill to the London hospital where she spent her last days. These experiences were obviously traumatic for Jill, but it was frightening to imagine what behaviour had prompted such actions by once-loving parents. Both children were adopted and Jill has had no contact with them since. One child was infected by her with Hepatitis, contracted through her shared use of contaminated needles, and all her contacts in Kendal had to be screened for the disease. Purely by chance Jessica escaped infection but it is disturbing to know that Jill conceived her in full awareness of the dangers. She continued to drink heavily, abuse Valium, cannabis and other drugs, was convicted of theft and sectioned under the Mental Health Act several times. At rock-bottom she was penniless, effectively homeless on the streets of Leeds, and desperate.

Stefan was born in Kendal on 6th August 1970 and lived his tragically short life free from major trouble or trauma, though he dabbled with drink and drugs at various times. He was unfortunate enough to leave school in 1986 when Margaret Thatcher's domestic policies had all but frozen British industry. Unable to secure the electrical engineering job he wanted he drifted into landscape gardening and construction, but his heart was always elsewhere. He became frustrated with his prospects and eventually left for a different life in Leeds, where he and Jill eventually met when she landed on his doorstep the very day after he received an initial compensation payment for his head injury. Stefan firmly believed, because Jill impressed the notion upon him, that she had trained as a nurse and was expert in the use of drugs and medication. She told me proudly that he relied on her knowledge and always asked her advice. As I probed her on this subject, she let slip that on the night he died, Stefan asked if the drugs her husband had given him were safe. Whether she believed they were, which seems very unlikely, or whether after a few Superstrengths she got her lies and truths muddled is not known, but she confirmed to me that she told Stefan the drugs were 'weak' and he could 'take as many as he wanted' She stated categorically that Stefan was very careful about his medication. During the fateful evening after taking the drugs Stefan went to the downstairs toilet. Several minutes later according to Jill, he shouted upstairs for her to come down, telling her that he could not urinate. She turned on taps and told him to jump up and down to encourage normal operation, but never once did she tell him that the malfunction was probably the result of his body closing down in response to the drugs she had given him. She must have known because she described this shutting-down response in detail to me during a later discussion. The house where the Clarkes had lived together was stoned and set alight the day after Stefan died. David left the area alone that day and evidently returned to his native Tyneside. The very same day, Jill hitch-hiked to the North East but was unable to locate her husband, so returned to Leeds. The situation at that point was that Stefan, who had a legitimate claim to a large sum of money, was now dead and Jill carried within her the sole heir to that money. She had official witnesses in the form of a Housing Officer, Social Worker and Health Visitor, all of whom had recorded, at Jill's insistence, that the baby she carried was Stefan's.

On revelation of what we suspected, CID officers arrived from Leeds and lodged themselves in Kendal for a week. They carried out preliminary murder inquiries with Jill as the suspect, and David Clarke was apprehended at a hostel for the homeless. At Joyce Hawthorne's instruction, but for no legitimate reason other than her apparent wish to influence the investigation in Jill's favour, we were not allowed to see Jessica for over six weeks and decided that her safety was of prime importance whereas matters regarding Stefan could be postponed to a later date. On the understanding that we would be reunited with our granddaughter and could re-instate our protection of her, we disassociated ourselves from the murder inquiry and custody case, both of which then floundered without being heard in court. Jill was relieved and happy to re-enlist our assistance in caring for Jessica. Joyce could barely conceal the pleasure she derived from being able to wield such power over us, and insisted that we had to suffer the additional indignity of meeting our granddaughter on supervised visits at a Social Services location. The attendant social worker said "This must be Joyce bloody Hawthorne's doing is it? It's bloody ridiculous" and went outside for a smoke, though I think she used normal tobacco only.

Twenty Six

"Trying, trying to do what's right
Working hard day and night
Struggling to be, the person you should be
Hoping to live, the life that could be
But alas, perhaps one needs to
Find the happiness that freedom leads to"

(Author – 2007)

OUR SON'S DEATH AND the fight to keep his daughter safe brought Dorothy and I closer together than for quite a while. But the screaming outrage in our heads eventually quieted to a rumbling murmur and normality relentlessly returned to nullify our shock. Implacable time resumed its march to an inevitable future and just as surely, old problems re-surfaced.

Her moods began to fluctuate again as she fell back into depression. She sought medical help but became more and more unhappy. At least this time she did not sneak off with the month's housekeeping money while I was out at work, but told me calmly that she was leaving, and as I listened to her words I knew that this time was and had to be, different. We had reached a major turning point in our life together and events had changed me considerably. I had been faithful, supporting and loving, and now as she packed to go once more, I knew instinctively that it was time to move on with my own life. I always suspected that the damage done by me earlier to our marriage could never be repaired and I was prepared to accept the consequences. But it was more than that – her repeated desertion at times when I needed her most had finally broken the chain of guilt that shackled me to her.

As I watched my wife's well-practised actions I fell into the strange calmness that I had come to know at challenging times in my life. I felt great sadness and loss almost but not quite, like bereavement, and as she walked across the road and away from the house we had tried so hard to make a home, looking back at me with pity in her eyes, I felt more than anything, relief. Something between us that should have been beautiful was dying forever and I knew that life would never be the same.

My mind now became free and open to the outside world, which I welcomed wholeheartedly in to the reality of my existence. I had virtually paid for the house that I had put so much work and hard-earned money into over the years but I no longer wanted to live there nor have anything to do with it. I walked out one day with a couple of hastily-packed bin-liners over my shoulder and left it all to Dorothy. That's all she really wanted at that point anyway, and despite her lies and deceit I did want her to be happy after her obvious and un-deserved suffering.

The depressed economic climate of the time had caused construction work to dry up for many, interest rates had soared and small companies folded with chilling regularity. I was contacted by a company to whom I had been recommended by Haygarth, who had also fallen prey to bankruptcy, and spent six months alongside Alan Wharton, who I took with me, installing domestic drainage at a development in Sandside, on the shore of Morecambe Bay and in sight of the viaduct we climbed as kids. Knowing this work would soon come to an end and that alternatives were scarce, I enrolled on a Higher National Certificate course in Building Studies at Carlisle College, hoping that this qualification would equip me for more secure future employment. The course was accelerated, cramming two years' work into one, but I passed with numerous credits and merits. I also passed an exam and 'Professional Interview' to join the prestigious Chartered Institute Of Building, based at Ascot, without the usual specialised preparation.

After completing the course I got a job on the highways' surveying team for Cumbria County Council. The actual surveying was uncomfortable because it was always done in winter and did not involve sufficient physical activity to keep warm, but I enjoyed the computer-work and documentation. This involved plotting node numbers for previously unrecorded roads throughout the county, and transmitting the data to the Ministry Of Transport archives in London. However, one icy morning after working on survey reports for the M6 motorway, I was involved in an accident which injured my lower back and kept me off work for several months. The forced inactivity weighed heavily on me both physically and mentally and for a period I worked for the Citizens Advice Bureaux as an office volunteer, in an attempt to prepare myself for a return to site. Once up and about I re-commenced light training with Les Mitchell to regain my health and strength and it became habit afterwards to call into Bumbles Restaurant in the town's shopping centre, for coffee. Les asked me one morning if I would write him a letter to a woman he had met through a dating agency, the details of which had been supplied by another gym member. I did so and rolled around on the floor laughing as he stuttered his way through the first telephone contact with her "Are you available?" he asked!

Seeing how much fun this was I also met several attractive ladies, who assisted the process of separation and prepared me for future choices I would have to make. Every one of these women had been hurt and damaged in some way by men, sometimes successively, thereby losing confidence and most unfortunately trust, in the process. They were stranded in a lost, limboid world and for a time I was lost with them but nevertheless, and perhaps because of their experiences, they were always good company. Meeting them provided some valuable lessons about relationships and kept my focus on the future.

During one visit to the restaurant we were discussing a joinery contract I had been offered by Katherine Toal, when I looked up to see a lovely, dark haired girl looking straight at me from the other side of a glass screen. Our eyes locked but I said nothing, and smiled at her as we left. A few days later I asked her out on what was to be the start of a three year relationship. Julie was a qualified secondary school teacher from Lincolnshire with an A-grade, A-level in maths and an Honours Degree in English. She had a fun-loving, effervescent nature with virtually unlimited energy. Throughout the summers of 1997 and 1998 and despite pain from my back injury, we hiked up a series of Lakeland fells and mountains to venture onto such precipitous promontories as the climbers' traverse to Pillar Rock, Striding Edge, Sharp Edge, the eye of Nape's Needle and of course Scafell Pike. Our trips always ended with a meal and generous amounts of lager, and I always brought back a small rock from each trip. I painted the date and location on each before laying them at Stefan's graveside in an act of homage to him. No mountain on earth is too high for me to climb and my constant lumbar pain added more meaning for me – it was penance. They remain there to this day apart from a few which have been sadly stolen, wording intact, at the little riverside cemetery across from Cropper's paper mill at Burneside, just outside Kendal. I continue to add to the collection periodically.

Julie drove me to Glasgow airport for a flight to Canada after my mother was injured in a car crash. On arrival at Calgary I was met by her and Alex. She was bruised but otherwise fine, and eventually we headed west in Alex's lorry-sized camper van from the town of Olds into the foothills of the Rocky Mountains, then up towards the glacier at Saskatchewan Crossing. I'd been on holiday to Florida a couple of times, once witnessing a space-shuttle launch, but this was something different. Turning south we drove down the spine of the Rockies, camping at night, before descending into British Columbia where we parked up outside Alex's nephew's house at Creston. From there we drove back into the mountains a few days later looking for bears, and later in the week across the US border into a Montana indian reservation near the Badlands, before heading back to the flat prairies of Alberta. Bears were scarce but I did see the black hills of Dakota which were sung about in the 1950s by Doris Day, often accompanied unofficially by my aunty Doris and me, and sometimes her dog, Lassie.

Julie and I wined, dined and discussed many topics. She taught me the correct usage of the oft-troublesome apostrophe and I convinced her with the help of the Oxford Dictionary, that 'agreeance' is not a generally-recognized word, which is strange as I now use several such unconventional expressions myself, in addition to a liberated view of punctuation. She encouraged me to seek sources of income other than that earned in the building industry, which she correctly deduced was not good for my health, and to further my education towards that end. As a result I enrolled on a series of part-time adult education courses. On occasion we argued and she would react by telling me to leave her house, which by then I had all but moved into at her invitation. I would do so but she would then always find me, apologize, and we would resume where we had left off. This habit of hers did though, bring back the old feelings of insecurity cultivated for so long by Dorothy and I asked her to desist. She did, but never for long enough and one evening after we had drunk some wine she issued the threat again. I walked out that night and never went back. She sought reconciliation but I had

moved on swiftly and with certainty. When we met she was rent-
ing a cramped terrace below the old Kendal Green Hospital where
my mother injured her back working as a skivvy. We moved to a
large detached house with an enormous, landscaped garden and
eventually, when I had convinced her that she could afford to buy,
to a three bed-roomed home in a good location just prior to the
start of the dramatic house-price escalation in 1999, which quickly
trebled the value of her new home.

Gillian was a petite, blue-eyed blonde with an hour-glass figure and
cut-glass accent honed to perfection in Hampshire's private schools.
She was manager of the K Village retail outlet-centre housed in
the refurbished K Shoes factory, where I went to buy new walking-
boots. She was stylish with a sporty car and a little house just off
Windermere Road. We went out a few times and despite still having certain feelings for Julie, a relationship rapidly developed. We
had been together just a matter of weeks when she contacted me in
a mild but tearful panic. She had been offered an excellent financial deal by her employer Metropolitan Estates Property Company,
based at Wigmore Street in the City of London, to manage a sister
outlet owned by the same company. Her terms, conditions and facilities were to be greatly enhanced and her brief was to bring back
into profitability, an outlet which was losing money.
   "So why the tears?" I asked.
   "It means gewing to live in the North East" she said, dabbing her
smudged mascara with a motifed handkerchief "And you're here
and we've just met and everything was gewing sew wonderfully"
she sobbed.
   "The North East?"
   "Yes" she replied, doe-eyed and mournful.
   "See whatya mean"
   "Exactly" she said with a renewed whimper.
   "Whereabouts?"
   "North Shields"
   "Shiiit!"
   "Ew God" she wept.
   She began commuting between the two centres as a build-up to
eventual management change-over, and I drove across to spend a
weekend with her at a hotel in Whitley Bay. Most North Easterners

seemed blissfully unaware that the rest of the country still regarded their area as an impoverished, downtrodden industrial wasteland, inhabited by uneducated ex-miners with flat hats, whippets and loud-mouthed women who drank too much and fought half-naked on Saturday nights. Apart from driving through to the European ferry-terminal a year or so previously, I had never set foot in the North East since I was ten years old when we visited aunty Florrie in Hebburn. The prospect of actually living there was not initially attractive but one weekend was sufficient to dispel my fears and replace them with an open-mind, which eventually turned into true affection for the area and its people. I arrived at the onset of a major regeneration period which dragged Tyneside out of its long-endured doldrums. I had never seen such a massive conglomeration of major construction companies, many based in or around Newcastle, with building projects buzzing on every corner and over every hill. The convergence of trades and personnel was unprecedented, new homes rose from the ground apparently overnight like well-fed mushrooms, commercial-build shot up on any spare plot of ground rendered vacant by slum-clearance and new money from a financially united Europe pulsated through the local economy with investment-fuelled energy.

A leisurely drive up the east Northumberland coast to Bamburgh and Lindisfarne convinced me that I might not miss the open, lofty spaces of my Lake District homeland as much as I thought. Driving along the A1058 Coast Road from Newcastle to Tynemouth I marvelled at the sheer size of the moon that illuminated the road as would daylight, its every detail clear in air swept clean by the sea breeze, and the panoramic landscape unobscured by undulation in the flat Tyne estuary. The space was enormous, bereft of hillock-induced claustrophobia and felt ideally suited to my newly-unobstructed outlook on life. I suddenly realized just how desperate I was to get away from the place of my birth, but although Jessica was by now five years old and hopefully out of immediate danger, I knew I would miss not seeing her every day. Consoling myself in the knowledge that she was only two hours away at most, I told Gill that if she wanted me to, I would go with her. She did, and we moved to a new flat in Union Street, North Shields, just across from the Magnesia Bank pub, on 1st April 1999. I returned to Kendal constantly to see Jessica and brought her over the Pennines regularly for long weekends, at Easter, Christmas and summer holidays. North Shields became a second home to her.

My intention had originally been to transfer the embryonic design and build service that I had kept ticking over in the Lakes, even whilst working for the council, and develop its potential in the North East. I commuted for a few months during the relocation period but soon realized that with so many construction jobs available in my new home area, offering significantly higher salaries than Kendal's rural rates, I would be better off taking advantage of that situation at least for a settling-in period. Within a week I had taken up employment as Site Agent for Barratt Homes, running a site at Forest Hall, Newcastle. I adjusted quickly and smoothly to the faster-paced city life and began to enjoy again the big-company buzz that I had left behind at Taylor Woodrow.

Gill's was a high-profile job and I had to accompany her to many official functions. Venues included Newcastle and Sunderland football club corporate suites and in particular, Kingston Park, home of the Newcastle Falcons rugby team, where we were served five-course dinners after being chauffeured there in security-company boss Derrick Halliwell's Mercedes. At these functions we invariably met and were often photographed with, a host of international sportsmen.

We bought a new house in a regeneration area close to the Royal Quays, where Gill's retail centre was sited, and watched it increase rapidly by over 300% in value. Gill's Kendal house was sold for a 60% profit as prices soared nationally, and we became thankful at not declining the eastward move to this fishermens' town on the North Sea shore.

Reading up on the area at the library in Northumberland Square, I discovered that the North Shields' fishing industry originated in the thirteenth century to serve the Priory at Tynemouth, once taken over as a garrison by Henry VIII, but financial conflict with Newcastle, eight miles to the west, prevented full development of a true fleet until the mid 1800s. Until then, local netsmen sailed out from their rudimentary huts or 'shiels' (from where the town derives its name) in small boats and coracles. As trawling developed, so did industries supporting it and processing its produce. Workers' cottages proliferated on the quayside until a small township had grown up around the port, which also welcomed international shipping to its deep-water berthing facilities. The North Shields' economy was built upon sea fishing, which was the very life-blood of the town. When their way of life was taken from them by politicians, many of its people became lost.

The decline of the British fishing industry decimated many communities and cast many workers onto the employment scrapheap. North Shields was one of the areas worst-affected. Dissatisfaction and frustration compounded into feelings of isolation and second-class citizenship under Margaret Thatcher's tightening of the financial screws during the late 1980s. By 1990 a virtual ghetto of unemployment and neglect was strangling the town and the resultant unease and heavy-handed policing eventually exploded into riots in the Meadowell area. Intense social unrest festered throughout the summer of 1991 and expressed itself in a growing wave of crime including burglary, assault, robbery and car theft. Tension between local youths and police strained to breaking-point and open hostility on the streets. Police employed ever more stringent methods in maintaining civic order and the young Meadowellians responded with their own vehement opposition. Most were unemployed with no qualifications and little hope of change, as had been their families for two or three generations before them. The social stigma clung to local teenagers like the smell of their over-applied cheap aftershave and the ever-present, luridly-branded sports clothing. A brash, uncaring attitude to life's conformities evolved as an alternative to complete social disintegration and provided a new stratum of interaction, shaped by their own rules. Lack of identity was salved by a printed polyester uniform, crass language and lifestyle, and petty crime which supplemented their various state benefits.

On a balmy evening in the second week of September 1991, Dale Robson and Colin Atkins, described as 'joyriders' by the police but with pride as 'professional car thieves' by friends and family, were pursued by patrol cars until the stolen vehicle occupied by the pair crashed into a lamppost. The impact killed them both. A rumour immediately circulated that the death car had been rammed by a police pursuit-vehicle and the Meadowell erupted into a frenzy of revenge, frustration and hate-fuelled crime against the society that valued their lives so cheaply. Anger and property burned and the police retreated. The following day, Tuesday, was quieted by re-organized mass policing but by Wednesday copycat riots broke surface in Newcastle's similarly downtrodden West End. Properties were firebombed in Elswick and Scotswood. Sections of previously docile communities turned into vicious mobs which snarled their anger loudly and vociferously and police officers fled the streets. The authorities, fearing significant proletarian revolt in an area listed high in the top 1% of most deprived localities in Europe, finally heeded their citizenry's complaints and planned strategies to quell and mollify the rebellion. This appeasement of the populace was a major factor leading to the massive regeneration programme which swept the North East region at the pre-dawn of the new millennium, and to which I came in the early spring of 1999.

The shock of the Meadowell riots left a fear in and also of North Shields, which dissuaded industrial investment and prolonged widespread unemployment. This kept property prices low but those choosing to buy at regeneration area prices moved into the locality with a mixture of enthusiasm and trepidation, after discussions with the local police, the council and existing residents, regarding predicted crime rates, property values, infrastructure plans, and general lifestyle expectations. As home-buyers moving into a risky area we shared with neighbours a distinct pioneering air, but with a determination to succeed and protect our investments.

The Crescent had been well-designed to create a small, residential enclave close to amenities, routes and services, and once the properties began to sell they all went quickly and values rose immediately. The initial rises increased our confidence and the Crescent began to mature into a relatively sought-after location for those seeking to purchase profitably within a certain price range. Buyers took pride in their new homes and Gill liaised with the police and residents to set up a Neighbourhood Watch scheme. One house stood empty and we discovered that it had been bought by a teacher from Basingstoke relocating to a job in Wallsend. After he had completed the purchase though, his southern wife decided that she did not wish to venture into the barren wastelands of the frozen North, so he rented the house to a tall, slim and fairly attractive girl who moved in with her baby. She seemed to be a pleasant enough person who lived a relatively normal lifestyle and went about her business quietly and politely. Her arrival hardly caused a ripple on the tranquil surface of our newly-created community. After a few months though, it became evident that some of her associates were not quite so pleasant. A bloke in his twenties who always wore a dark blue baseball cap pulled down over his eyes and drove a matching blue car, moved in with her and life on the Crescent suddenly became livelier. Soon there was up to half a dozen vehicles parked outside the house at one time, music played loud and visitors called all day and most of the night. One of the neighbours, Ronnie, discovered that the blue-hatted guy was a local drug dealer and that he had virtually turned the house into a brothel. The residents banded valiantly together and some took immediate action, devising a surveillance system which noted every visiting vehicle's details and relayed them to the police. When these efforts produced no visible results a hard-core action group employed their own measures. Airgun pellets pinged off the blue car and even thudded into the blue hat from concealed sniping positions during daylight hours. Blue-hat would crouch low out of the car like a cop in a television show and run for cover in the house. I took no active part, considering myself above such activities, but dispensed certain tactical advice. After dark the car's tyres were regularly punctured by the swift tap of a joiner's mallet on the head of a grindstone-sharpened six inch nail, making sure the holes were in the sidewall where repairs were difficult. The blue paintwork was scratched deeply and mirror stems snapped as a matter of course. The grande-finale ensued after an attack by the drug gang or its customers, on one of the innocent neighbours: The blonde girl had the baby taken from her by Social Services and slithered further down the slope to abject misery, but was falsely told that the two gay men living next door had reported her to social workers. The two gays were happy and harmless, but soft targets. Verbal confrontations ensued across the garden fence and were followed by minor damage to the gays' property. Thefts from the garden led to a break-in to their house through the patio doors, which then needed expensive repair, and the theft of a TV and audio equipment. This open violation of the neighbourhood enraged the radical residents, who gathered again for a council of war.

A few days after the house-break one of the gays, Paul, knocked on our door and asked directly for help. He knew that Gill ran the Neighbourhood Watch but hinted to me that more direct measures may be necessary. I maintained my approach of non-committed, passive advice and he ended up in tears on the sofa. I genuinely felt sorry for him and his non-deserved plight but could not become directly involved in the situation. I had trodden a risk-laden path through life but was now older, less agile, and needed to preserve my own priorities and those of my loved ones first. We sympathized though, reassured where possible, and although I did not mention the intention to Paul, began taking after-dinner strolls around the Crescent.

The neighbours' action-group waited until blue-hat was home one evening before launching an all-out attack. Lead bounced off the front windows of the house and rocks thudded into the war-torn car, but this was merely a cunning diversion. A separate detachment climbed onto the railway embankment to the rear of the house and opened up on the windows with powerful catapults. The marksmen had been practising for weeks. Screams, clatter, thudding up and downstairs and desperate female shouts including "Holy Jesus they're puttin' me windis in" were heard from the besieged semi, as the upstairs windows followed by the patio doors shattered under a sustained hail of fire. Once these main targets were taken out silence fell, except for the mournful cries and wails from inside. The hit-squad scurried back to observation posts, their excitement at a crescendo. Blue-hat made one of his jinking, low-slung runs for the car, and drove away speedily on four flat tyres. The metallic scraping of wheel-rims on asphalt could be heard long after the vanquished enemy had disappeared from view. Troops from both units of the neighbourhood watch now retired to their individual bases for cups of hot cocoa and at least the second half of Coronation Street. They felt elated and satisfied but slightly nervous about what consequences might befall them, following their uncharacteristically cavalier actions.

The immediate and somewhat disappointing effect was that blue-hat moved out of the house but still visited regularly with a burly, shaven-headed accomplice. He obviously retained control of the girl and therefore the house and any action therein. The frequency of his visits quickly increased as did renewed visits from her guests. The girl was still seen trudging alone to and from the shops or nearby metro station, but her eyes were glazed and focused only upon her feet, her movements robotic and un-coordinated. She was thin, gaunt, her hair lank and clothes unkempt. She never smiled now.

I continued my evening walks after tea, enjoying the cool air

and finding the moderate exercise quite efficient in speeding diges-
tion. The light, bright, action-filled evenings were receding with the
summer, and autumnal darkness threatened early intervention. I
turned my collar up to a frosty chill in the dank air as I left home
at about 6.30pm one Wednesday evening, and headed left around
the Crescent. I walked more quickly now, exercise not vigilance my
main objective, and hardly noticed the blue car until almost upon
it. I instinctively looked towards Paul's house but my attention was
distracted by a shrill scream from the adjacent one. Inquisitiveness
slowed me as I came abreast the lounge window of the blonde girl's
abode, and actually stopped me in my tracks as I looked in through
the open curtains. The lights were on to counter the gathering
gloom and I could see figures moving about at the rear of the house,
in the kitchen area. My jaw tightened as I watched blue-hat pursue
the girl across the open-plan interior and knock her to the ground
with a swinging right-hand punch. He then kicked her in the ribs
and stood over her with clenched fists, snarling as she screamed in
terror. She wiped blood from her once-pretty face before attempting to rise, and I watched in horror as his right arm raised again to
swing down at her.

"What the fuck's your problem pal?"

The bodyguard had been sitting in the car waiting for his boss
to complete business in the house and now stood right in front of
me. I was not confident and fearless as in earlier years, and turned
my gaze towards him as if in a trance. I looked deep into his bulging eyes in search of what lay behind them, before turning slowly
back to the window. This time he shouted into my right ear "I SAID
WHAT'S THE PROBLEM ASSHOLE?"

I waited a second before turning towards him again and holding
his contorted stare "Pardon?" I asked softly.

A quizzical, confused look spread slowly across his broad coun-
tenance as his large head tilted ever so slightly to one side. I shifted
my right foot into leverage position, about half a yard behind the
left. His forehead now smoothed as his brain prepared his body
for violence, and his meaty hands emerged from the pockets of his
black, woollen overcoat. Mine reached up to grab the lapels of the
coat and jerk his head forward to increase impact velocity, as the
upper ridge of my forehead crashed onto the bridge of his bulbous
nose. He fell in a heap on the pavement and I glanced down at his

bloodied face for a moment as I passed and turned down the garden path. As I reached the door another staccato scream rang out which stopped me at the step. I quietly opened the unlocked door and stepped inside to evaluate the scene:

The girl was on the floor with her back against the sink unit doors. Blood, tears, mascara and mucus ran down her face and dripped off her chin onto breasts half-exposed above the ripped halter-neck. She stared up at blue-hat who loomed menacingly over her, through wide, unblinking eyes. He stood with bloodied, clenched fists, feet wide apart, hat pushed back on his head. Her gaze withered past him to me, and he noticed. She looked at me with an expression that first questioned then pleaded to be rescued, freed, begged me to be her saviour. He turned slowly round and tried to comprehend what my standing there indicated for him. He had probably seen me on the Crescent and knew I was a neighbour, but we had never spoken one word to each other. He was taller and stockier than he looked from a distance, with a not too unpleasant face now it was partly out from under the ever-present hat. He reached back and slid the largest kitchen knife from its central slot in the canted, pine-effect block next to the bread bin. Outside on the frosty ground, the black coat stirred. I walked forward until within range of a long punch and then stopped and looked into his eyes. Beads of sweat from the exertion of beating the girl stood on his forehead and upper lip. He made a small, quick, threatening movement with the knife and I once more, after a long absence, felt that involuntary nervous twitch of an embryonic smile at the left corner of my mouth. I noted how he moved the knife and responded with a little feint of my own. The blade moved in exactly the same arc and I easily caught his wrist in my left hand as I shot a right cross into his face. Teeth gave way to knuckles. He stumbled back against the sink as the knife dropped to the floor, blood dripping from his mouth. I stood back as he straightened up, gathered myself into the classic attack stance, slid my left foot forward eighteen inches and unleashed possibly the hardest punch I have ever delivered. His head snapped back violently sending the hat, dislodged at last, into the dirty grey sink water. His hands dropped to his sides as cognitive links between brain and limbs were severed, his knees buckled and he slumped to the floor in vertical descent. As he fell the back of his skull hit the edge of the stainless-steel sink, leaving in it a bloody, crescent-shaped dent.

The girl gawped open-mouthed at her fallen tormentor and then back to me. As she did I noticed a flicker of movement behind me, reflected in the kitchen window above the sink. Tensing as I realized the bodyguard was upon me I stepped between blue-hat and the girl, grabbed a large saucepan from the cooker hob and swung it round like a baseball bat. Spaghetti Bolognese filled the air as the heavy steel pan clanged into the minder's left temple, knocking him sideways. But his heavily-muscled shoulder bounced easily off the light, plasterboard partition wall, dislodging a picture of bread, cheese and wine from its panel-pin hanging. He lunged at me with outstretched hands and a strand of pasta hanging from his left ear, and we both fell back against the sink. His powerful fingers closed around my throat as he bent me backwards over the sink top and I watched blood trickling from the half-inch gash in his nose, resulting from our earlier confrontation. I scrambled up on top of prostrate blue-hat in an effort to gain height and keep myself upright, and threw a few punches at my opponent's ear. With no leverage the punches had little effect and I was desperately thinking of an alternative strategy when a metallic thud rang out, and a further small serving of spaghetti splattered onto the window behind my head. The girl, now up on her feet, had panned him from behind. The blow did not bother him too much but he was slightly annoyed when she grabbed his nose and burrowed a red-painted finger nail into his eye socket. He let go of me with one hand to shrug her off and I smashed a half-full cup of cold coffee into his face, an action which seriously disrupted his attack. He reeled away wiping spurting blood and dripping caffeine from his cheek, and looked back in time to see one of the matching, pine-coloured bar stools hurtling down upon his skull. Catching my breath I surveyed the wreckage of kitchen and drug dealers, whilst the girl repeatedly banged the still inanimate blue-hat across his limply recoiling head with the sharp edge of the now empty spaghetti pan. I left for home and a nice hot shower.

The house was raided and sealed shut by the police a few weeks later and the dealers were never seen on the Crescent again. The girl, whose name I never knew, disappeared but re-emerged on the Crescent two years later. She had a new boyfriend but no baby. At the time of the spaghetti fight I was fifty one years old.

Twenty Seven

"But now he's gone without a trace
This world is surely a lesser place"

(Author 2007)

NEWCASTLE IS NOW A lively, revitalized city with a wealth of un-modernized or otherwise-spoiled Georgian and Victorian buildings. Coated for decades with black industrial grime they were re-gener-ated along with the rest of the city and North East region in general, to reveal some of the finest classical architecture in Britain. Coming from a predominantly rural area and also from a building back-ground, I was fascinated by these stone-built structures, many of them listed as of national and even international importance, and began to take an interest in the actual procedures and methodolo-gies employed in their construction.

Leaving for work early one June morning a leaflet dropped through the letter box along with the usual post. It listed courses available at local colleges and universities and I noticed one entitled Architectural and Urban Conservation, being run at Northumbria University, Newcastle. I left it in the hall by the telephone and glanced at it over the next few weeks, remembering how I had en-joyed the HNC and Access courses, wondering if I was capable of achieving a university degree and relishing the prospective chal-lenge. Still troubled by my back injury and looking to the future I eventually telephoned to ask for general information and was invited along for an informal chat with the course's main tutor, Craig Wilson. He was very positive about the course and the need throughout the world for the skills it would provide, in caring com-petently for our architectural heritage. He sold the subject well and I was hooked on the idea of being an active authority in the conser-vation of Listed Buildings. I enrolled but decided to continue earn-ing whilst studying. I left Barratt and became self-employed once again, taking on the maintenance operation for Yetholm Properties, based in St Mary's Place, Newcastle city centre. I was responsible for structural and internal inspections, preventative and reactive repairs, garden control and administration. Yetholm both owned and managed for other owners, about fifty large Victorian houses in and around the city which provided temporary homes for some of the fifty thousand students thronging the streets during term times. I had targeted this operation specifically because the care of these old houses tied in nicely with the aims of the course upon which I had enrolled.

The combination of my building experience and determination to succeed during the course, allowed me to cope with the academic work whilst still working virtually full time. The student lifestyle did not sit well with me though and I found the often arrogant attitude of some tutors towards their younger students, difficult. I was promised by Craig Wilson that the course was well subscribed and would comprise at least 50% adults, but this did not turn out to be the case and I felt somewhat out-of-place and betrayed by him. I did though, enjoy the physical activity, fresh air and fast results of the maintenance work. There was plenty to do and I had to employ help during the very busy student holiday periods, when most of the major works were carried out. Jessica often accompanied me on these summer operations when she came on holiday, and loved throwing junk out of upstairs windows – watch out below! I paid her £2 per hour plus all the sweets she could eat.

Students in general, I discovered, are not the cleanest living section of the community and my positive perception of the cleanliness of the far-eastern races, gained during my stay at the Aux Trois Bonheures restaurant in Lausanne, was terminally shattered. One of my worst experiences however, concerned a youth from Kent. I was trying to track down a rent-debtor who had disappeared from our system, and eventually revisited the previously inaccessible property in question, to force an entry. As usual the door, in Arthur's Hill, Fenham, did not open to knocking but did to use of a crow-bar, and I knew something was amiss even as I entered. It was a hot afternoon at the end of August but the heating system had obviously been left on. I gently opened the vestibule door and ducked a bee-sized bluebottle which swooped towards the daylight like a stooping peregrine. It was one of many filling the air space as I bobbed and weaved through the house, expecting at any moment to trip over a dead and rotting student. I reached the closed door to the kitchen and could actually hear the intense buzz of insect life from the other side. A tentative entry unleashed a dense cloud of black flies against which my fists automatically lifted in defence. The place was crawling with infestation due to the waste food that had been left slopped and scattered around. The intense heat had perfected incubation facilities and I crouched low to open every window in the house before turning off the heat and escaping to the outside to gulp fresh air once more. Thankfully however, there was no evidence of student death.

I took a clearance team in before the contract cleaners would even enter the house, and they had to clean throughout three times before it could be re-let. We never located this particular debtor nor recovered his debts, but I did uncover the story of his downfall from neighbours and the university:

On arrival he had been a relatively fine lad with a zest for life who made friends easily. He spent his first year reasonably productively in class and healthily enough in the halls of residence. The second year however, took him into the dark and dangerous world of private accommodation as he moved with five others to the West End. He was evidently an inwardly timid boy who had been bullied early in life and as a consequence craved the acceptance of his peers. His resultant jovial persona and affected confidence often thrust him into the central limelight of his social circle, and the large five bed-roomed house, although a hike from the bright city lights, became a popular venue for parties, casual sex, crashing down and shooting up. As the seedier side of life enveloped him, his more sensibly ambitious associates deserted and left him to the mercy of those with more immediate needs. His desire to co-operate led quickly to a drug problem of his own, which eventually curtailed his studies and meaningful contact with anybody whose aim was not to fleece him. His housemates left one by one and the inner core of his life collapsed. Perhaps if he had been closer to home and family he might have survived in better condition, and not fallen prey to the petty criminals who now occupied his house and very existence. He fell heavily into debt and eventually disappeared from the Yetholm tracking system. The police raided the house several times to clear it of undesirables and after disinfecting, redecoration and re-furnishing it was restored to a rentable residence. I have no idea what became of the unfortunate student but he never showed up at class again and proved untraceable. Hopefully he is still alive and his parents have not had to face the nightmare of his death, in addition to their other disappointments.

Every moment of my spare time was spent studying and staying ahead of demanding schedules both at university and work, and this took an inevitable toll on my home life. Doing the course had been partly Gillian's idea, reasoning that my degree would free her from having to work ever again, but I don't think she realized the level of commitment required even without working concurrently. We did far less together as a couple, my focus and concentration were always somewhere else and I think it is true to say that I began to lose interest in her sexually. She became frustrated and insecure and we gradually drifted apart, though I was not unfaithful to her despite opportunities, until certain that the relationship was over. I finished the course, achieved a Bachelor of Science Degree with Honours and also won first prize in a building design competition.

In the early hours of 19th February 2003, a few months before the end of the course, I received a call from my brother-in-law, Dave, saying that my father, then aged 79, was very ill in Kendal hospital and relatives had been advised to attend. I left immediately and drove far too quickly to Kendal but unfortunately he died before my arrival. I was bitterly disappointed but he was still on the ward and I was able to spend some time alone with him. Gill accompanied me to his funeral and to my surprise so did Dorothy, but with a friend whose behaviour would be atrocious at any time and particularly at my father's wake. I nodded an acknowledgement to my ex-wife but we did not speak directly. I saw the old, connective look in her sad eyes and perhaps a lingering trace of the love we once shared. Memories of our past life together came flooding into my mind as we glanced at each other for a brief moment, but that life was over and we could never again be the people we once were.

My father 'the old fella' was a lifelong heavy drinker, smoker of untipped cigarettes, habitual gambler and never regretted one second of the time he spent on those activities. Though a very intelligent man, he was also a grafter and worked for several years on Billy McDade's Irish gang of heavy hand-diggers, laying gas pipes. One of the gang, Billy Frizzell, once received an emergency call from back home on 'the auld sod' and had to return there at short notice. My father left himself short to loan Billy money for the fare and that, along with other acts of generosity that he was well known for, were never forgotten. At the funeral, both Billys plus many other of his former friends and workmates, personally shook my hand with real sadness in their eyes. They included Bob Brolly from Coleraine, a lifelong friend who was for a time married to my mother's youngest sister, Gladys. My father came out of retirement to work with Bob and his son Robert Jnr, clambering around in factory roof spaces and living away from home when well into his seventies, installing fire-extinguishing sprinkler systems.

The attendees were probably cheered up during the cremation service when we played 'The Wild Rover' dad's favourite song, to see him off.

"Jesus Christ" I said to my brother John on the way out "I thought the paddys were gonna start singin' along there for a minute, there was definitely some feet tappin"

"Yeah" he replied with relief "I thought we'd made a bad choice there for a second or two but hey, it's done now and it woulda suited the old-fella"

We had the wake at the Sawyers'Arms, where the most dedicated drank and reminisced for a solid 12 hours. Frizzell said it was the best send-off he'd been to and old Gordon would have been proud of us.

After the cremation I took my father's ashes home with me to Tyneside, where they rested for four years until my departure from there was imminent. I then carried them back to the town he loved and scattered them by the viewing point on Helsfell Nab, overlooking Kendal and not far from the Black Swan, where I had spent many hours talking with him and his beloved brother Duncan; may they both rest in peace. He was never the best father or husband that I could imagine and neither was I, but he was an honourable man and I would have entrusted him with my life.

Twenty Eight

"So long as men can breathe or eyes can see,
So long lives this and this gives life to thee"

(Shakespeare – Sonnet 18)

"This is your testament
Your footprint in the sand
Here is your monument
The legacy of your hand
Though now, we are torn apart
Every hour of every day
You touch my heart"

(Author 2007)

I RENEWED SOME OLD contacts at the cremation and began receiving telephone calls from previous customers requiring building services. I took the work on through friendship and politeness more than necessity but also with a return to Kendal in mind. I resumed the long commute back and forth at weekends and it became a regular routine which continued into the winter months. The gruelling workload both in the Lakes and the North East eventually told and I began to go out socially at either end of my weekly journey, to rest and relax. I met people from both my past and future and at first was unsure which way life would now take me – forward or back, east or west?

I became acquainted with a girl from Shields called Bev Riach who worked at the DEFRA office on the Fish Quay, across the road from the long and extremely steep Ropery Stairs which I tramped up and down for leg and fitness training. We got on well but were not destined to have a lasting relationship. We kept in touch though as my life with Gill dissolved and she increasingly made the journey back to her roots in the South. I was actually becoming quite serious about a girl from Prudhoe called Kiran, when I received a telephone call from Bev one day at work. She said she realized we were not going to become a couple and she had actually started a relation-

Robert MacGowan

ship with someone else, but was I seeing anybody at the moment? I answered that I was but not yet in an exclusively serious way, why? She replied that one of her friends had just bought a house on the corner of the street where I lived. I said I hadn't noticed and she told me that her friend, also called Beverley, was a lovely girl and didn't I think it would be a good idea for us to meet up, being neighbours. I ummed and erred a bit and Bev said she had already mentioned me to Beverley, who had agreed to a meeting – us being neighbours.

"Well I always try to be neighbourly, what's she like?"

"She's the same age as me, we were at school together, quite tall, very slim and a brunette, with straight glossy hair in a mid-length bob"

"You've rehearsed that haven't you?"

"Yes"

"But is she attractive?"

"She's very attractive"

I got her number.

As Beverley lived on the corner of the Crescent as it joined the main street I passed her house every day en-route to and from work, but only managed to glimpse her silhouetted through the window, ironing clothes, on one occasion. I liked Kiran very much and we had discussed a joint future together, but I was becoming intrigued by the new neighbour that I had not yet met. I was however, aware that the mystery element may be the kernel of my interest and might evaporate upon our first meeting. Kiran remained a priority but although she was a tall, extrovertly attractive woman who turned heads everywhere, some essential ingredient was missing for me. I still sought that extra little piece of chemical attraction and knew my future did not lie in Prudhoe, looking out over the green countryside south of the Tyne. I was though, reticent to hurt such a lovely, warm person whom I had grown to admire and respect and who gave me strength to face the future as opposed to dwelling in the past.

I passed Beverley's house one day just as she was pulling out in her blue Fiat Punto. We looked at each other for a moment though she was hidden in shadow, and I knew I had to find out more about the woman who flashed a defiantly proud look at me from behind her chic sunglasses. She was now a challenge, definitely slim and stylish and I dropped a note through her door that

251

day, mentioning Bev Riach. I telephoned that evening and she sounded bright, bubbly and intelligent and we arranged to meet at the weekend, at Fitzpatrick's in Tynemouth – a blind(ish) date!

I got there early and sat across from the pub in the car. I waited but she did not show and I began to think she had probably changed her mind. At one point a car with two women aboard pulled up and I thought one of them might be her, but a girl of about twenty five alighted and went into the pub, obviously meeting someone inside. She did look lovely though and I thought about following her in, but only for a reckless moment reminiscent of my past. I waited until twenty minutes after we were supposed to meet before deciding to ring her mobile, which is when I discovered that I had left mine at home. I drove back and phoned her from there. She answered, had now arrived at Fitzpatrick's and said "If you're not here in five minutes neither will I be"

I screeched back to the pub but she was not outside. Fearing that she had already left I ventured in to make certain she was not there. I glanced around whilst automatically making for the bar but could not identify anyone I thought might be her. Feeling a bit despondent I ordered a drink and surveyed the clientele again from a more advantageous viewpoint. Still no likely candidates but I did notice the girl who had entered earlier standing near the door, apparently on her own. She held a bottle of fizzy blue stuff with a straw in it and appeared to be looking in my direction, though I realized the toilets were also in her line of vision and that her companion was probably paying a visit. She kept glancing over though and I attempted to return her look with a winning smile, being as careful as possible not to give the impression of some sad and lonely pervert. She was tall with straight, light brown hair, very slim with long legs clad in skin-tight jeans and pointy, high-heeled boots. She had a tantalizing strip of toned midriff showing below a short black jacket, and I felt sure that she was now looking straight at me with a semi-amused, possibly irritated expression. I felt guilty and looked away, hoping her gaze was directed at someone behind me, but it was not and her companion was taking an unusually long time even for a woman, in the toilets. I decided to venture forth, conjured up a mental picture of myself as James Bond on an off-day, and attempted to appear nonchalant as I sauntered in her direction. She lifted her head and looked down her nose at me

Clockwise from top left: Alex & Edith on boat in Pacific; Gordon & Mary at table in Rainbow; Stefan with his 21ˢᵗ birthday present; Stefan with bottle of Jack Daniels

Clockwise from top left: Jessica wearing riding-helmet; Jessica; Jess & Rob with bikes in North Shields; Beverley with big blue scarf

as I approached, and my courage wavered. I reached the last possible point at which I could be merely passing by casually, looked directly into her pale blue eyes and said "Hello"

"You took your time didn't you?" she replied confidently.

"Excuse me?"

"You took your time, coming over, thought you'd changed your mind. And by the way, you're forty minutes late"

"Christ, Beverley?"

"Yes and you're lucky I'm still here, when this drink was gone so was I"

"Sorry, I forgot my phone and went back for it"

"Yeah right"

"Honestly, I was actually here early and saw you come in but didn't recognize you, though it was from a distance"

She smiled tolerantly, as at a naughty child "Can I have another drink please?" she said, holding out her empty bottle, red-striped straw still protruding from the neck.

We visited a few other pubs around the town square and in one of them, whilst she was talking, I leaned over and kissed her cheek. In the last pub I touched the taut, smooth skin above the waistband of her jeans, and we ended up kissing passionately amongst the throng of noisy customers, our bodies pressed tightly together. I made a mistake though when she took me home for coffee, by trying to make love to her on the sofa. She threw me out and would not see me for weeks. When I persuaded her to meet me again I behaved a lot better and discovered that she was a very strong-willed person, who turned me on sexually more than any woman had in a long time.

At this point I was still actually living in the same house as Gill, though our relationship was over, but now the general atmosphere deteriorated dramatically to the point where we reached a financial agreement and I left. She had already decided to move back to the South and we both knew we would never see each other again. When we met she was lonely despite her high-profile job and good looks, and was in quite serious debt to the point where she was refused a mortgage. When we parted she had come to terms with herself and her past, was much more confident, debt-free and had made substantial profits on the property market after I carried out free refurbishments for her. I wish her well and hope she can overcome the insecurities evidently created during a privileged but stifled childhood. I completed my work in Kendal, moved in with Beverley and regained a zest for life that I had forgotten existed.

Despite and throughout my turbulent upheavals I strove to keep one thing constant: my relationship with Jessica. She continued to visit regularly and I always managed to find new adventures for her to ensure that she always enjoyed a wonderful time when with me. We walked, cycled, swam, toured, visited friends, built sandcastles on Tynemouth Beach and made 'fun-stations' from cardboard boxes for her cats. We had garden parties to which she invited all her new friends from the Crescent, indoor parties at home and restaurants, went to the cinema, the Theatre Royal and the Newcastle Arena, and horse-riding along the shore at South Shields. We shopped till we dropped and laughed till we cried. One hot and sunny afternoon as Jess played in the sand at Tynemouth after splashing in the sea with Stuart (Pam's youngest son) she seemed to be staring into space and I asked if she was alright. She continued to gaze out across the tranquil water and said quietly "I love this place" We named it Jessica's Beach after that.

I realized that my change of partners might be unsettling for her but she seemed to take it all in her stride, and everyone she met loved her sweet, gentle nature. Her mother though, as Jess grew older and required less supervision, became less grateful for my contributions to her care. She had maintained a relationship with a new partner, Steve, whom I respected as a stabilizing influence on her and whose mother Muriel also spent time with Jessica. Jill's Hepatitis curtailed her drinking habit when she was told the drugs that were keeping her alive would not be effective if mixed with alcohol. Not long after however, the police raided her (and Jessica's) home because they had detected that she was receiving drugs through the post, and discovered that she was also growing cannabis in the loft! Jill's father, also with a new partner, was belatedly attempting to make inroads into his granddaughter's life and Jill manipulated this development with her eye on a chance to inherit some of his wealth. Dorothy was still on 24-hour callout and I had become far less useful in that respect after my move to the North East. I had outlived my usefulness.

Jess got along well with Beverley, who could discuss latest fashions and current pop music without sounding ridiculous, but their growing fondness for each other was cut dramatically short. She and I drove to Kendal one Friday afternoon for a snatched visit as our commitments presented the opportunity at short notice. We went to meet Jess out of school as I had often done previously over several years, and often been asked to by her mother. Jill did not normally bother to meet her daughter but for some reason she turned up on this particular afternoon. She had not met Beverley before but came straight over to where we waited in the car. After a brief exchange she peered in through the window and said frostily "You must be ...?"

"I'm Beverley"

"Umm" responded Jill turning away with a toss of the head.

She left but later telephoned my mobile to say that she had been speaking to friends and was not happy about our meeting Jess without her permission. As most of the things Jess and I did together were without her mother's knowledge because she never expressed any interest in them, I did not take her pseudo-indignant speech seriously and in any case, would not be dictated to by her on any subject I could think of, least of all my private life or the care of the child she had neglected from birth. She continued her attack and I refused to give way on any significant points. It later became clear that she then proceeded to contaminate the precious relationship that Jess and I had with strict orders not to even speak to me. Unaware of this I turned up outside school a few weeks later and sat in the car where many others were parked along the roadside. Jess came out with her neighbour Ashleigh and another friend, both of whom had visited Shields with her, and saw the car. Jill was not there to meet her but I could tell instantly that something was wrong. When Jess saw me she looked around cautiously – obviously checking that her mother was not about, before walking slowly in my direction. There was a muffled conversation taking place between the three girls, Jess was hesitant whilst her friends pulled her towards the car. I rolled the drivers window down and said cheerfully "Hello girls"

"Hi" they answered in unison.

"How was school?"

"Mmm ok, boring as usual"

"Does mum know you're here?" Jess asked nervously.

"I'm not sure why?"

"Cos er, I don't think you're supposed to be here"

"Oh aren't I? Why not?"

"I don't know it's just what mum said, you know what she's like..."

"Yeah we know" giggled Ashleigh "She's an alien, ha ha ha"

"Well I'm sure it'll be ok, do you want a lift home?"

"Yees we do, don't we Jess?"

"Not sure" she answered, fidgeting with her satchel.

"Come on Jess" encouraged Ashleigh.

Jessica was still nervous and glanced over her shoulder towards a group of chattering mothers with an obvious fear that can only have been induced by quite serious threats.

"Do you remember the picture of the horse I said I would draw for you?" I asked reassuringly.

"Ohh, yes"

"And the stirrups and bit I said you could have?"

"Yes"

"Well I've brought them over and you won't be able to carry them with all your school stuff as well"

"Yes, yes we want a lift" chanted Ashleigh, opening the back door.

Jess remained nervous and fearful as she scanned the area furtively before climbing into the back of the car with her friends.

"Buckle up" I said.

That meeting with Jessica was one of the saddest I have ever experienced, and I knew that serious, irreparable damage had been done to the relationship between my granddaughter and I. Damage that I stupidly thought even Jill was incapable of. Shortly after this I was told by her that Jessica did not want to see me again and there ended the 12-year, loving and protective relationship between us. The initial realization of what Jill had done was devastating but then a strange thing happened – the memory of my son, Jessica's father, came to my rescue. The crushing, protracted pain that I expected and that Jill intended to follow this parting, was deflected in an unexpected way. When I had not seen nor even heard from Jessica for some months I did not miss her in the agonizing way that I had when her absence from my life was imposed by conniving Joyce Hawthorne. Twelve years after his death I began to miss my son even more than ever. Jessica's arrival had eased the pain of

Stefan's death and now the memory of him was easing the pain of her absence. Memory though, did play one last cruel trick. When Stefan died he was a robust 22-year old who had some experience of life, but I remembered him not only as he was then. Visions of him as an innocent, vulnerable child whom it was my duty to protect crowded my mind. I remembered his little hands holding onto me tightly on the back of my motor-bike, coming home from school and showing his mother and I how he had learnt to skip, and us struggling to keep straight faces at his un-coordinated movements. I recalled his beautiful face lighting up at the sight of his birthday and Christmas presents, his night-time kisses and morning yawns and a thousand little things that are parents' treasured memories of their children. At least the finality of his death had allowed closure of my journey through life with him. There can be no such termination with his daughter until I die and although I have written and sent messages, and drive past the end of her street at least twice on every visit I make to Kendal, I have never seen her since. I think about them both every day.

Once again I carried on as best I could. The losses in my life weighed heavily at this time but Beverley helped me to cope. She is younger than I and maintains an even more youthful attitude to life. She kept me busy and refused to let me isolate myself in sorrow. I was accepted into her large circle of family and friends where life was pleasantly normal and where I was made welcome, and could again shelter from the storm. The considerable force of Beverley's spirited and indomitable character met with the oft-immovable rock of my own personality with an occasionally volatile, energy-producing reaction which ultimately formed a well-balanced relationship, with enough strength to withstand the rigorous tests of time.

My university degree turned out to be less valuable than I had hoped and opportunities for conservation officers proved rare.

I had tried to escape site-based construction to a more civilized work environment, as advised by my doctors and the aching in my joints, by joining firstly a firm which repaired damaged properties for insurance companies, and then a supplier of kitchens to the commercial housing sector. Both positions were luxuriously office-based but I could not settle to them or to the reduced remuneration, and returned to the harsh world of construction as a Site Manager for N B Clark of Morpeth, Northumberland.

Duncan Clark was a big, burly, down-to-earth ex-rugby player and I liked him immediately. I also liked the way that he and his brother Jeffrey, ran their company. They were country people and their philosophy of rewarding ability, effort and application and allowing their managers to manage with autonomy, appealed to me as it had when I worked for the Haygarth brothers, 13 years earlier.

My first project was the demolition of flats and a community-centre on Union Hall Road, Lemington, Newcastle, and building of social housing units in their places. I controlled the site through to successful completion but was also physically active when management duties allowed. I spent many hours concreting foundations and driving a variety of earth-moving equipment, and one afternoon at the end of October 2005, when joiners were scarce on site, I fixed a few staircases into position. Due to a fault in the alignment of the stairwell wall to the trimmer beam in one plot, work carried out by a sub-contractor, the stair stringer snapped whilst I stood on the top tread. I fell 2 metres onto the concrete ground-floor, the impact of which broke my left arm at the elbow. I was patched up at Rake Lane Hospital, North Shields, and returned to work the following day, restricting myself to supervisory duties. This mishap coincided with a very rainy period which confined me to the site office much of the time. A discussion with a colleague about this injury and previous ones led to mutual reminiscing about life in general, at the end of which he said I should write a book. I thought about the prospect for a while as marble-sized raindrops hammered against the already-cracked window pane, before fishing out a pen from my battered desk and beginning this story in a blue, pocket-sized notepad supplied by timber merchant, J T Dove of Orchard Street, Newcastle. I carried the pen and pad and subsequent replacements around in the thigh pocket of my khaki cargo pants, and they consumed many of my spare moments over the coming months.

On completing the Lemington Job I transferred straight to the assistance of a colleague, Neil Redpath, who was under pressure and in difficulties building another housing project at Montrose Gardens, Morpeth, where I took over the main build including timber-frame structures and brick cladding. Over the next ten months all went reasonably well with us hitting handover targets even though two months were lopped off the overall completion programme. In January 2007 internal finishes were nearing completion on the middle section of units and as a result we looked like being temporarily overloaded with joiners. Neil declared his intention to sack three of them who were from Newcastle. All the other joiners came from Northumberland as did Neil, and benefited from his unprofessional favouritism. I reasoned that a better plan was to build bases for the next construction phase and drop the joiners onto timber-frame erecting to keep the site rolling. Up to that point we had used specialist sub-contractors to install the timber-frames but they had proved unsatisfactory. However, Neil said "No I'd rather sack the townie bastards. They can't put kits up anyway"

"I'll work with them to make sure they're ok" I countered.

"No fuck 'em, I want rid of 'em"

I had a word with Duncan and although the Newcastle joiners had no experience at all in timber-frame construction, we kept them on after I guaranteed that no mistakes would be made, the work would be of good quality, cost-effective and completed to programme. Wry smiles broke out on site as we were expected to fail miserably. My reputation was now on the line along with the joiners' jobs.

Like a retired gun-slinger returning for one last shoot-out I retrieved my tool-belt from its place of storage and strapped it on the following day after slackening off a couple of notches. I had planned and mentally rehearsed every part of the coming operation and we strode out into the morning, long shadows cast on dusty ground by the low winter sun, like the Earp brothers en-route to the OK Corral. Hammers hung at sides like Colt 45s, spirit-levels across shoulders like Winchester rifles, grisly chins set and our steely gaze on the stacks of timber components before us. One of the gang even had a cheroot hanging from the corner of his mouth.

The plan held and on the 11th day we nailed the last roof-truss into place. Final checks confirmed that the building was true in every dimension, and the city boys had proved a point. They could now class themselves as timber-frame erectors which would open up a whole new field of work for them, and I was humorously dubbed the Patron Saint of Joiners for saving their jobs, even if only temporarily.

A strong west wind blew up the following morning and I looked out of the site-office window to reassure myself that our newly erected structure stood firm. It did. At the south-west corner of the site an empty black bin-liner was whipped out of a rubbish skip by the wind and unfurled as it floated a few metres off the ground. Nearing the gable wall of a new block of flats the updraft swept the bag high in vertical ascent until it cleared the gable-peak and levelled out on a gentler breeze. It relaxed into an almost perfect horizontal plane and drifted eastwards like a low-profiled stealth-bomber. I watched as it approached trees at the south boundary of the site, wondering whether it might catch in the branches as racing-balloons often do, but it glided in a faultless arc up and over the leafless, grasping limbs. Beneath its shadow a flock of wood-pigeons erupted in a flapping panic, dispersing right and left away from the hovering object. Three or four herring-gulls winging in from the east, suddenly banked steeply from its flight path and I realized that the bag had been mistaken for a hunting bird of prey. It glided ominously over the roofs of houses to the east site-boundary and a cacophony of rasping squawks heralded a squadron of crows which had hastily scrambled to the attack. The mob gained altitude and performed a few inelegant swoops on the unheeding alien as it drifted nonchalantly past. The crows, assuming they had chased off a predator, re-grouped and returned to base. How easily I thought, can something or somebody that is completely harmless be mistaken for something that is not, and vice-versa.

I had often given passing thought to the possibility of spending more time abroad in a fairer climate, far away from any building site for health reasons if for no other, but never proceeded much further than general discussion. Beverley and I were chatting about this one day after watching 'A Place In The Sun' on television when she, with her usual direct approach said "So are you just going to sit around talking about it until you're too old, or are you going to do something about it?"

Suddenly the subject of idle dreams and chatter took on more substance as I looked at her and knew she meant business.

"What do you think I should do about it?"

"Well at least find out if it's possible"

"If it is are you up for it, would you go with me?"

"Of course I would silly, we're a couple and in love aren't we?"

"Course we are but what about your career and friends and family – your life?"

"I will always love my family and friends but my life is with you now, and I want to be where you are"

I went out to Tesco that very day and bought some current magazines on properties abroad to rent or buy, and within weeks we were looking at flats on Spain's Costa Blanca. This area is rated by the World Health Organisation as one of the best places on earth regarding climate, diet, lifestyle, sporting opportunities, and an excellent health service. An additional, important factor for us was that it is very accessible from the UK. Served by the large airport at El Altet, just outside Alicante City, it represents the shortest flight time to the sun from the chill winds of home and can also be easily reached by train, boat, car or even pedal cycle, as Stuart Clegg and I had proved 34 years previously.

We were shown a range of accommodation and at the end of our last day viewed a sea-front apartment for rent on Guardamar Beach. Whilst eating pizza later in a nearby restaurant Beverley suddenly said "Do you know something?"

"What?" I asked between pepperoni mouthfuls.

"I don't want to be this close to the sea"

"Really, why not?"

"Because it's bloody cold compared to a few miles inland"

"S'pose it might be a bit chilly in winter"

"Anyway, we fly back home this afternoon" ended Beverley with circumspect finality.

Just then my mobile rang and I answered a call from James, an English agent based in Alicante.

"Hi James, how's things?"

"Hello Rob" answered the young rep in his public-school accent "You remember the village apartment you asked to see the other day but we couldn't view because the street-market was on?"

"Er, oh yes, the penthouse as you called it?"

"Yes, yes that's the one, well I've just spoken to the owners and we can have a look this afternoon if you like?"

"Oh, we fly back today you know James?"

"Yes I know, Phil's picking you up at five but I can get you in for a quick look at three if that's convenient?"

"Just a minute James" I said, placing my hand over the phone and turning to Beverley with a roll of the eyes "James wants us to have a look at that top-floor apartment we couldn't get into"

"Oh, well we did want to see it but have we got time?"

"No, not really, I'll tell him no"

"How long would it take?"

"Not long, it's about fifteen minutes from the hotel but we haven't packed yet"

"Oh, let's go if only to be polite, packing's a lot quicker for the journey home"

We had seen the apartment from a distance and liked the look of it. Described as having a roomy lounge/dining area that opened onto a balcony, fitted kitchen and bathroom plus two good-sized bedrooms, it was fully furnished with every possible amenity. The feature that made the upper apartments in this small, 2-storey block so attractive, was the large roof solarium commanding 360 degree, elevated views of the surrounding countryside including the craggy and lofty edifice of nearby Monte Callosa. On entering the flat we liked its open-plan spaciousness, which easily accommodated an 8-seater dining table, 3-piece suite and 'American style' kitchen, after viewing so many which felt cramped. The finish, incorporating tiled floors, solid pine woodwork and polished-granite worktops, was excellent and the sunroof was enormous, stretching the full length and width of the apartment. The roof was serviced with outdoor lights, a cold tap to water plants and shower in the heat of the day, and electric sockets to power a drinks fridge, radio, laptop etc, for complete outdoor living in the sunshine. We were definitely interested and went outside to assess the orientation of the block regarding sunlight. The apartment was on the south west corner but James said the Spanish preferred to face east or north away from the punishing heat of the summer sun. However, Beverley interjected immediately that sun from the west in the late morning and afternoon, would add natural light and warmth to the interior in winter. I tended to agree, the flat had air-conditioning anyway to dispel unwanted heat, and noticed that there was an attractive, open aspect to the south west after checking my compass.

The apartment lies in a sleepy, working village to the south of Alicante Province, not far from the historic city of Orihuela. The powdery white sand of seven-mile-long Guardamar Beach, so popular with Spanish holidaymakers from Madrid and regarded as one of the best in Spain, is fifteen minutes drive south east and a further ten minutes to the airport. It is therefore well situated for peace and quiet as opposed to a holiday home on the coast, but still relatively close to the sea. The streets are wide and empty, small children play safely in them and old ladies sit out in the evening shade where they often converse with surprisingly polite teenagers and those nice Ingleses from the new apartamentos. There is a large village swimming pool, kept scrupulously clean by attendant lifeguards and paid for by El Consejo Municipal (the council) a smaller, private pool and a large bar/restaurant at the end of the street, manned efficiently by the affable Jose and Miguel.

So here I slump atop our penthouse roof, a few potted plants already in place, on my very comfortable sun-lounger which is conveniently coloured in the broad black and white stripes of Newcastle United, completing the first draft of a story which I began writing on a rain-sodden building site in that far off city. My body is turning brown and recovering from its injuries. The bones broken long ago in my foot, knee, ribs, elbow, both hands and nose, are not as painful as they were in the cold British winters, and my worn joints move more freely of late. A large striped awning protects me from the fierce overhead sun and if I put my head above the enclosing walls of the terrace, a cooling breeze blows gently and constantly across the rooftops, sometimes carrying tiny particles of red sand over the sea from the Sahara Desert. Beverley's deeply tanned body casts a slim shadow across the circular glass table in front of me as she places an iced gin & tonic on its shiny surface. She moves, her athletic limbs glistening with cream, to a matching lounger out in the open sunlight. I take a cool sip and close my eyes, practising again the necessary adjustments to leisure in a world where haste is superfluous. Later but at no specific time, Beverley and I will walk, slowly for now because my damaged feet are still troublesome, around the edge of the village to collect fruit from where it hangs by the roadside. Yesterday we took a light picnic into the cool air of the Sierra de Crevillente mountains and afterwards, drove south to enjoy shepherds' pie and champagne with my cousin Carol and her husband, Kenny, at their home in Torrevieja. Tomorrow we are dining out with our neighbours, Alan and Tina Fletcher, at one of the many pleasant restaurants dotted around the countryside.

The virtual silence and total tranquility induces torpor as my mind wanders, unrestrained by necessities, to the life, its labours and torments that I have left behind. The village church clock chimes to inform me quietly and unnecessarily of the time of day, as I drift into half-sleep and see in my mind's eye, a figure sitting opposite me across the glass table. It is a young man who looks familiar. He smiles at something out of my line of vision and I turn to see a young girl, also familiar, sitting on the edge of a third lounger, next to Beverley. The girl is laughing and talking to the man as he packs towels into a patterned cloth bag lying open at his feet. Beverley seems unaware of their presence. The girl rises as the man stands and stretches his muscles, the bag slung over his shoulder, and as he turns towards me I recognize my lost son – my memory and imagination have brought them together at last – the living daughter and her dead father. They silently say goodbye to me and walk down the tiled steps to the street, but before leaving Stefan turns to look back and raises his hand in farewell, just as he did the last time I saw him at Christmas in 1992. I raise my hand in response – I can see it stretched out in front of me, but it does not wave goodbye – it reaches out with fingers spread wide as if to catch something fleeting. I try to speak but cannot because my throat is constricted, and feel an overwhelming urge to follow him – to somewhere as yet unknown to me.

Beverley kisses me tenderly and strokes my head as she looks into my eyes at the inner sadness she knows to abide there. I know that my son will not return and can never again sit with me – except in my dreams and memories. And with that thought comes again the thudding shock of reality that I first felt many years ago, on a train bound for Carlisle – he is gone – forever, but love for my lost son has not diminished and nor has the pain of remembrance. These things will always survive, as I wish them to. I miss him dearly. Life has taken much from me, but to lose those things I must also have had them to begin with, and I am eternally thankful for the time I was allowed to share with Stefan and Jessica. They enriched my life and I would not have missed one second of the hours I spent with them. I keep my memories forever safe in the part of my mind that treasures those things which are valued most of all, and which never fade. Until we meet again, fly free.

In Memoriam

Stefan Robert MacGowan
William Gordon MacGowan
Duncan MacGowan Jnr
Duncan MacGowan Snr
Margaret MacGowan Snr (nee Lockhart)
Mary Ellen Davison (nee Pomphrey)
Jack Davison Snr
Jack Davison Jnr
Nora Mitchell (nee Davison)
Pauline MacGowan
Alexander Jay Lucas
Walter Wagner
Stuart Clegg
Michael Gallagher
Mark Postlethwaite
Jeremy Nattrass
Glen Rose
Alan Nicholson
Alan Wharton
David Thexton
Derek Ward
Patrick Gallagher
Malcolm McLeod
Archie Boardley
Desi Warren
Shorty Garnett
Shirley
Martin Luther King Jnr

The Author:

Robert MacGowan was born in the South Lakeland market-town of Kendal, Westmorland (now incorporated into Cumbria) in January 1952. He grew up on a council-estate with his parents, sister and two brothers, and attended Dean Gibson Roman Catholic School before qualifying for Kendal Grammar. After a difficult childhood he left school at age 15 with no qualifications and followed his father's footsteps into the building industry and amateur boxing. He became a father at 17 and over the ensuing years fell foul of the law on several occasions after bar-room brawls, but gradually progressed into site-management. Along the way he earned extra income to support his family as a bouncer, bodyguard and bare-knuckle street-fighter, but also as a portrait-painter. After an industrial accident in 1994 he enrolled at a local college to improve his future employment prospects and attained several 'O' and 'A' Level qualifications, followed by a Higher National Certificate. Moving later to the North East he won a building design award and achieved a Bachelor of Science Degree with Honours, from Newcastle's Northumbria University, and eventually emerged as a self-taught professional artist, architect, poet, author and legal-advocate.

His life was blighted by several tragedies including the death of his son, Stefan, the collapse of his 20-year marriage and forced estrangement from his beloved granddaughter, Jessica.

He now writes and travels with his partner, Beverley. Contact him at:

macgowan5599@googlemail.com

ISBN 142514984-7

9 781425 149840